COLONIAL
NEW JERSEY

A HISTORY

A HISTORY OF THE AMERICAN COLONIES
IN THIRTEEN VOLUMES

GENERAL EDITORS:
MILTON M. KLEIN & JACOB E. COOKE

JOHN E. POMFRET

COLONIAL NEW JERSEY

A HISTORY

CHARLES SCRIBNER'S SONS, NEW YORK

FOR SARA

CONTENTS

ILLUSTRATIONS

EDITORS' INTRODUCTION

The American colonies have not lacked their Boswells. Almost from the time of their founding, the English settlements in the New World became the subjects of historical narratives by promoters, politicians, and clergymen. Some, like John Smith's *General History of Virginia*, sought to stir interest in New World colonization. Others, such as Cotton Mather's *Magnalia Christi Americana*, used New England's past as an object lesson to guide its next generation. And others still, like William Smith's *History of the Province of New-York*, aimed at enhancing the colony's reputation in England by explaining its failures and emphasizing its accomplishments. All of these early chroniclers had their shortcomings but no more so than every generation of historians which essayed the same task thereafter. For it is both the strength and the challenge of the historical guild that in each age its practitioners should readdress themselves to the same subjects of inquiry as their predecessors. If the past is prologue, it must be constantly reenacted. The human drama is unchanging, but the audience is always new: its expectations of the past are different, its mood uniquely its own.

The tercentenary of John Smith's history is almost coterminous with the bicentenary of the end of the American colonial era. It is more than appropriate that the two occasions should be observed by a fresh retelling of the story of the colonization of English America not, as in the case of the earliest histories, in self-justification, national exaltation, or moral purgation but as a plain effort to reexamine the past through the lenses of the present.

Apart from the national observance of the bicentennial of American independence, there is ample justification in the era of the 1970s for a modern history of each of the original thirteen colonies. For many of them, there exists no single-volume narrative published in the present century and, for some, none written since those undertaken by contemporaries in the eighteenth century. The standard multivolume histories of the colonial period—those of Herbert L. Osgood, Charles M. Andrews, and Lawrence H. Gipson—are too comprehensive to provide adequate treatment of individual colonies, too political and institutional in emphasis to deal adequately with social, economic, and cultural developments, and too intercolonial and Anglo-American in focus to permit intensive examination of a single colony's distinctive evolution. The most recent of these comprehensive accounts, that of Gipson, was begun as far back as 1936; since then a considerable body of new scholarship has been produced.

The present series, *A History of the American Colonies*, of which Dr. Pomfret's volume is part, seeks to synthesize the new research, to treat social, economic, and cultural as well as political developments, and to delineate the broad outlines of each colony's history during the years before independence. No uniformity of organization has been imposed on the authors, although each volume attempts to give some attention to every aspect of the colony's historical development. Each author is a specialist in his own field and has shaped his material to the configuration of the colony about which he writes. While the Revolutionary Era is the terminal point of each volume, the authors have not read the history of the colony backward, as mere preludes to the inevitable movement toward independence and statehood.

Despite their local orientation, the individual volumes, taken together, will provide a collective account that should help us understand the broad foundation on which the future history of the colonies in the new nation was to rest and, at the same time, help clarify that still not completely explained melodrama of 1776 which saw, in John Adams's words, thirteen clocks somewhat amazingly strike as one. In larger perspective, *A History of the American Colonies* seeks to remind today's generation of Americans of its earliest heritage as a contribution to an understanding of its contemporary purpose. The link between past and present is as certain as it is at times indiscernible, for as Michael Kammen has so aptly observed: "The historian is the memory of civilization. A civilization without memory ceases to be civilized. A civilization without history ceases to have identity. Without identity there is no purpose; without purpose civilization will wither." *

As a small colony, New Jersey has attracted less attention from historians than its more prominent neighbors. In the present volume Dr. Pomfret has integrated the research that has been done into a comprehensive narrative, selective rather than encyclopedic in its coverage, and interpretive as much as factual in its design. In his bibliographical essay, he has also illuminated the extent and the limitations of the scholarship already produced on the subject. His history of colonial New Jersey, suggesting as it does the unexpectedness of that colony's action in 1776, broadens our understanding of the coming of the American Revolution. Prosperous economically; socially diverse but without the marked tensions of class, race, religion, or ethnicity; without pronounced ideological antipathies to Parliament or the crown; and with a wide degree of local "democracy," New Jersey had few deep-seated reasons for separating from the mother country. In 1776 it paid the price, although not entirely unwillingly, for being "a cask tapped at both ends," impelled to revolution by the actions of its more militant neighbors in Pennsylvania and New York. To appreciate the hesitancy of the "garden colony" no less than the precipitancy of Massachusetts and the doubts and indecisions of thousands of good Americans in other colonies is to begin to comprehend the mystery of the

---

* Michael Kammen, *People of Paradox* (New York, 1972), p. 13.

events of 1776. New Jersey's colonial history, viewed in conjunction with the histories of the other twelve colonies, clarifies the meaning of a revolution whose inception, however fortuitous, produced consequences so momentous that they live with us still.

MILTON M. KLEIN
JACOB E. COOKE

PREFACE

Two centuries ago the Reverend Andrew Burnaby described New Jersey as "the garden of North America" and added that it had "some trifling manufactures" but could not succeed in commerce. Still titled "The Garden State," New Jersey's official seal exhibits the goddess Ceres together with three plows, symbol of her time-honored preoccupation with husbandry. Today small New Jersey, the most densely populated state, is a leader in manufacturing. Though her economy is augmented by substantial agricultural and seafood production, only 10 percent of her population is rural.

The New Jersey "natives," called "Jerseymen" by themselves and "Jerseyites" by scoffing neighbors, are a rapidly disappearing segment. Residing in ancient villages, north and south, these folk constituted for decades the balance wheel of the body politic, the inheritors of the strong moral codes of Quaker and Presbyterian and of John Witherspoon's "philosophy of common sense." Modern New Jersey has been overwhelmed by industrial armies and by "amphibians" from New York City and Philadelphia. Known facetiously as "the bedroom of New York City and Philadelphia" and dismissed by the late critic Edmund Wilson as "the slave of two cities," such observations are far from original. In 1846 Bishop George Washington Doane, himself a Jerseyman, lamented, "We have been too willing to become but little more than the appendage to two chief cities that lie upon us, to the right and the left."

More to the point the bishop asserted further, "We have well nigh forgotten that we have a history. We have almost lost our sense of identity." Fortunately historians throughout the past half-century have to a degree corrected this deficiency. This work attempts to recount the history of New Jersey from her origins through the American Revolution. Without sacrificing the narrative approach, an effort has been made to unravel her complex beginnings and to convey throughout an understanding of a colonial heritage made up of a variety of economic, social, and cultural components.

In many respects the development of colonial New Jersey is not dissimilar to that of other colonies. Part of this parallelism lies in the sharing of a century-old English heritage and part in the similarity of adjustments made everywhere to the American wilderness. But the experience of New Jersey was, to a degree, unique. Even before the English conquest of 1664, Dutch and Swedes fostered settlements within her bounds, and long before the Puritan towns appeared in the north, New Haven Colony made endeavors to gain a foothold on the lower Delaware.

That New Jersey, under English auspices, began as a private or proprietary colony was not atypical, but a divided proprietorship was unusual. Unlike Maryland and Virginia, where the proprietorship was vested in a single family, the New Jersey proprietorships passed through many hands. When the "right of government" was denied her proprietors, the ownership of the soil assumed paramount importance. And since her complicated and cumbersome system of land distribution was based upon the title to proprietary-shares and fractions thereof, not only did factionalism arise among the proprietary claimants, but a hatred of the land monopolies was engendered among large segments of the population. In 1702 the proprietary system broke down. Unfortunately, the proprietors' land monopoly was not disturbed, thus provoking intermittent social disturbances that lasted until the War of Independence.

Noteworthy, too, in New Jersey's early history were the "Concessions" made by the proprietors of both East and West Jersey in order to attract settlers. Both these seventeenth-century "constitutions" offered liberal inducements, and both guaranteed a modicum of self-government and liberties to the individual. Through all the factionalism and turmoil of the hundred years following their promulgation, the guarantees of these early Concessions were fiercely invoked by the inhabitants.

New Jersey shared with Pennsylvania and New York a willingness to welcome settlers of all nationalities and all denominations. She was hospitable to the persecuted of all lands—England, Scotland, Ireland, and, later, Germany, Switzerland, and Ulster. In this respect New Jersey was a pioneer in the process of Americanization.

New Jersey's early history presents a galaxy of great names, some illustrious, others of dubious reputation. Her annals could not be written without reference to William Penn, George Keith, and Robert Barclay, Quakers all; or to James, Duke of York and later king of England, and his Scottish henchmen, the Earl of Perth and Viscount Melfort. Many of New Jersey's colonial governors made a lasting impress upon her early history—the sagacious Richard Nicolls; the martinet, Sir Edmund Andros; the notorious Lord Cornbury; the able Robert Hunter; the eccentric Lewis Morris; the pious trimmer, Jonathan Belcher; and the ill-starred William Franklin. Her religious leaders from George Keith to the noble John Woolman add variety and color to her heritage.

Lacking commerce, manufactures, or notable cultural achievements, colonial New Jersey was a rural, middle-class society. As governor after governor proclaimed, the colony afforded a comfortable living for those who respected law and order and who were willing to work. Few colonies in America were as tolerant of newcomers whose ways and customs differed so widely from their own.

As elsewhere, men had disagreements on public policy. In New Jersey's early history one encounters controversy over taxes and currency, over the conflicting claims of creditor and debtor, and over land distribution and absentee ownership. At times acrimony rose to a high pitch, but there was little bloodshed. Even in perilous times jail-breaking was the most violent manifestation of political and social disorder.

New Jersey's period as a royal colony began in 1702 and terminated with the War of Independence. Until 1747, when Governor Jonathan Belcher arrived, the assembly had made notable advances in self-government. Many came about because the lower house of the assembly was determined not to yield to the arbitrary acts of venal or self-seeking governors. Following the period of "salutary neglect," and especially after 1763, evasion and procrastination became more difficult as the crown and (for the first time) Parliament tightened the rule of the mother country. In a number of instances the assembly had to struggle to maintain certain of its earlier gains.

In 1775 this self-contained community of "plowmen," which hated taxes as much as involvement in imperial wars and adventures, was confronted with the series of events that led to her signing of the Declaration of Independence. Ill-prepared, as were many colonies, New Jersey was plunged into doubt and confusion. Rather than a united body marching inexorably toward independence, hers was a divided people, many of whom, if they had been free to choose, would have remained within the Empire rather than risk their lives and fortunes in a struggle for independence. New Jersey was not alone in this dilemma.

John Adams argued that the Revolution was in the minds of the colonists fifteen years before blood was shed at Lexington. But the uniting of so many different colonies in 1776, he added, "was perhaps a singular example in the history of mankind"—almost a miracle. Unprepared for such a momentous decision, New Jersey threaded her way haltingly toward independence. New Jersey's progress, fortuitously, was not marked by violence. No provincial parties developed pro and con to stir up the populace to fever heat. Few patriot factions were as determined or as radical as the famous "Essex Junto." Rather, independence was finally embraced because of the dedication of small groups of concerned citizens working unceasingly to convince their neighbors of the righteousness of the patriot cause. Throughout there was the strong determination on the part of the provincial patriot leaders to consult the voter at every step and the equally strong determination never to forsake the common cause that was uniting all the colonies.

New Jersey paid a high price for independence—economic disruption, public bankruptcy, and civil strife. Seeking the redress of grievances and the preservation of traditional rights and liberties, New Jersey's goals were not revolutionary. Her Constitution of 1776 was a highly conservative document. New Jersey produced neither a Sam Adams nor a Tom Paine. But of her adherence to the cause of the colonies—to the need of acting in concert with them—there was little doubt. Though she did not cope brilliantly with the rapidly changing course of events— what colony did?—and proved in some instances inadequate to the tasks of readjustment, New Jersey never turned back. On balance, the years 1775 to 1783 were her finest.

The writer has attempted to present the colonial history of New Jersey in its economic, social, and cultural aspects as well as the political narrative. Many of his findings and conclusions reflect those of a number of writers who, during more than a half-century, have contributed countless general and specialized studies, as well as those of his own excursions into facets of the story. The Selected Bibliography is intended as a guide to these studies and to further reading. To avoid repetition, the place and date of publication of a number of reference works have been omitted in the footnotes, and in the interest of brevity the short forms "East Jersey" and "West Jersey" have been used instead of the more formal "East New Jersey" and "West New Jersey."

I wish to acknowledge the unfailing assistance of the editors of this series, Milton M. Klein and Jacob E. Cooke. Larry R. Gerlach, himself a scholar of New Jersey history, has made many helpful suggestions. I am indebted to Miss Janet Hawkins of the Huntington Library, San Marino, for checking certain documents, and to the staff of the Harrison Memorial Library, Carmel, especially Mrs. Sheila Baldridge, for the use I have made of the interlibrary loan service. My wife, Sara Wise Pomfret, has been of inestimable assistance in writing this volume.

Carmel, California, 1973   JOHN E. POMFRET

COLONIAL
NEW JERSEY

A HISTORY

1

THE GENESIS OF NEW JERSEY

New Jersey was a Restoration colony, that is, it came into being with the accession of Charles II to the throne in 1660. Between 1664 and 1682, six new American colonies were founded: New York, New Jersey, Pennsylvania, Delaware, and North and South Carolina. The establishment of six colonies in less than a score of years reveals a renewal of English interest in American colonization. Already in the South, Virginia (1607) and Maryland (1632) were permanently settled; while in the North, Plymouth, Massachusetts, Rhode Island, Connecticut, and New Haven had been planted by 1638. The Restoration rounded out the occupation of the eastern seaboard. Two great thrusts are manifest; the conquest of territory between the Connecticut River and the Chesapeake and the extension of Virginia into Carolina.

The southern colonies were rural, with few towns. In Virginia, a royal colony since 1624, and in Maryland, the proprietary of Lord Baltimore, tobacco was the money crop. The plantation was the focus of economic and social life. Here resided the owner, his family, his servants, and his slaves. Supplies were brought in and the tobacco crop shipped out by water. The southern colonies were divided into counties and the counties into parishes. Both played a part in government. As in the New England town, local leaders emerged who found their way, as elected representatives, to the general assembly.

The New England colonies were planted by Puritans and other Dissenters who left England to live, in accordance with their religious tenets, free from the restrictions of the established episcopacy. They founded innumerable towns and enjoyed a large measure of self-government. Their local taxes supported their officials, their ministers, and their common schools. The meetinghouse served as church and town meeting. The towns elected representatives to the colonial assemblies.

By 1660 the colonies of this first period of English settlement were well rooted. In far from accurate figures one glimpses useful comparisons. Conservatively the population of Virginia was approaching 30,000, while that of Maryland was about 6,000. New England had a population of about 30,000. Massachusetts, including Plymouth Colony, totaled 16,500, and Rhode Island and the outliers made up the remainder.

The restoration of Charles II presaged new leaders and new policies. In making their adjustments to the new regime each colony strove to gain some advantage. The Restoration government, surprisingly, took no punitive measures against anti-Stuart New England for her disloyalty. New Haven Colony was absorbed by Connecticut through the influence of her Governor John Winthrop. Where Winthrop succeeded, Sir William Berkeley of Virginia failed. Loyal in exile and recommissioned by Charles II, Governor Berkeley sought concessions for Virginia in vain. Actually, the Navigation Act, far from being eased, was strengthened as England continued her commercial struggle with Holland. Because the latter was supreme in the Baltic and the Mediterranean, in Africa, and in the Spice Islands, the British merchant received strong support both at court and in Parliament. Charles II's principal minister, Edward Hyde (Lord Clarendon), and his colleagues set up special councils on trade and plantations, with merchant representatives, to support the imperial interest.

The navigation code, rounded out in 1663, not only limited goods shipped to and from the colonies to English vessels but specified that certain colonial products could be exported only to England, Ireland, and the British colonies. Most of the enumerated articles were West India products, but an important one, tobacco, was the money crop of Virginia and Maryland. The English merchant would benefit through the re-export trade; the

Dutch would be deprived of it; and the English treasury would gain through increased revenues.

Despite the shoring up of the navigation system and the formation of trade councils, there was as yet no well-defined colonial policy. The new councils functioned irregularly, and their decisions were advisory. The power to act rested in the king, the Privy Council, Parliament, and men of influence at court. During the early Restoration years the Earl of Clarendon heeded the advice of those who had shared long years of exile in the Stuart cause. A higher value was placed upon colonial enterprise, and the colonies were regarded for the contribution they could make to England's prosperity. The American colonies were presumed to be self-supporting. As a kind of *quid pro quo* they were allowed a modicum of self-government, and as a consequence they escaped much of the Restoration's religious persecution. Because of this seeming indifference they made large gains in self-government and religious toleration.

From his high position as lord high admiral, the king's brother, James, Duke of York, was influential in overseas activities. Clarendon himself, who had properties in Jamaica and who shortly became a proprietor of Carolina, was no less interested. The grant of Carolina to eight proprietors in March 1663 involved the small but powerful group of courtiers who were responsible for the second period of American colonization. They included Sir John Colleton and Sir Anthony Ashley Cooper, later Earl of Shaftesbury, who had already invested in Barbados properties; the Duke of Albemarle, kinsman of Colleton and Cromwell's former General Monck; the powerful Earl of Craven; Lord John Berkeley, brother of Virginia's governor; and Sir George Carteret. The latter two, close friends of the duke, were soon vested with the proprietorship of New Jersey. Five of this coterie served on the trade and plantation councils; three were principals in organizing the Company of Royal Adventurers Trading to Africa (after 1672, the Royal African Company); and two took part in planning the conquest of New Netherland. These eight, with the addition of Prince Rupert, a cousin of the duke, and William Penn, virtually complete the list of Restoration colonizers.

The Duke of York was a tower of strength to the anti-Dutch faction in London. He put the English fleet in first-class condition, eliminating waste and personally overseeing the navy contracts. Associated with him in the navy office were such notables as Berkeley; Carteret; Admiral Sir William Penn, father of the colonizer; and, incidentally, Samuel Pepys, the famous diarist. The duke also gathered around him a powerful group of merchants, traders, statesmen, and members of Parliament, all of whom were eager to challenge the Dutch. Among them were two colonials, Sir George Downing and John Winthrop, Jr., both reared in Massachusetts. Too bellicose for Charles II and Clarendon, these men received encouragement from the duke. James proceeded on many fronts. His Royal African and Morocco Companies possessed charters bestowing upon them monopolies of trade in Negro slaves, ivory, hides, redwood, and other commodities valuable to the English economy, and their expeditions harassed the Dutch. The Dutch, too, were aggressive, supplying Barbados and England's other West Indies settlements with cheap wares and with slaves and paying good prices for the islands' tobacco and sugar. The king, though sympathetic to the pleas of the merchants, did not wish to risk a war.

The starting point of New Jersey's history was the English conquest of New Netherland in September 1664. There a great wedge of land controlling the Hudson and the Delaware was certain to come to the notice of the anti-Dutch faction. The Dutch by 1655 had firmed their hold on this region by conquering New Sweden on the Delaware. New England, too, was unhappy with being blocked by the Dutch from the Indian trade on the upper Hudson. Downing and his American colleague, Samuel Maverick, were critical of Massachusetts for refusing to take the initiative. They and the wily freebooter John Scott, who had designs on Long Island, alleged that the Bay Colony had no regard whatever for the interests of the mother country.

Lord John Berkeley, Sir George Carteret, and Sir William Coventry, appointed as a special committee to look into the American situation, in January 1664 recommended to the Council for Foreign Plantations (of which Lord John was president) that New Netherland could be taken with three ships of the fleet, 300 soldiers, and 1,300 New England colonials. It was a remarkably accurate estimate. Two decisions were taken: to dispatch an expedition to seize New Netherland and to send a royal commission to investigate the alleged disloyalty of Massachusetts. The members of the commission were Colonel Richard Nicolls, commander-designate of the expedition; Sir Robert Carr, his second in command; and the Puritan-hating Samuel Maverick. On April 21, when the House of Commons resolved that "it would support the king with life and fortune against all opposition," the king, the duke, Parliament, and the merchants were of one accord. New Netherland would be reduced on the ground that the Dutch were interlopers, a far-fetched claim based on the right of discovery by John Cabot, who had skirted the coast in 1497. Winthrop, who was in close touch with Colonel Nicolls, guaranteed to furnish the colonial militia, and even Massachusetts promised 200 men, who were neither sent nor needed. Though the number of colonial troops mustered is not known, Director Peter Stuyvesant of New Netherland was persuaded that there were 2,000, too many for him to cope with.

Nicolls's expedition sailed toward New Netherland in May 1664. Learning in Boston that Long Island was in English hands, he dropped anchor in Gravesend Bay on August 18, then blockaded New Amsterdam's harbor. In all New Netherland there were hardly 7,000 Dutch, widely scattered. Those on Manhattan and elsewhere sent only excuses. In New Amsterdam itself there were only 150 soldiers and fewer than 300 men capable of bearing arms. On August 29 Stuyvesant gave up without firing a shot, and the terms of surrender were signed on September 8. Shortly afterwards Colonel George Cartwright took Fort Orange on the Hudson, and Captain Robert Carr captured Fort Casimir (Newcastle) on the Delaware. New Amsterdam was renamed New York; Long Island, Yorkshire; Fort Orange, Albany; and what became New Jersey, Albania. Before the conquest James had named Nicolls as his deputy governor; thus Nicolls remained in New York to carry out his assignment.

Just before the conquest Charles II, in the shortest and most hastily executed colonial charter on record, conveyed to his brother James the lands lying between the Connecticut and the Delaware; in addition, oddly enough, Nantucket, Martha's Vineyard, and a large part of Maine were included. Thus all of what was later to form New Jersey came under the duke's jurisdiction. The west bank of the Delaware was not included, but was placed under Nicolls by right of conquest.

The duke's patent, or—as it is commonly called—the New York Charter, was unique in that it was the only one issued to a member of the royal family. Like the Maryland grant, it gave the proprietor, the duke, full proprietary rights. There was no provision for an elected assembly. The inhabitants were called upon to swear allegiance to the king, and writs would run in the king's name. Thus when James himself ascended the throne in 1685, the transition of New York from proprietary to royal colony required a minimum of adjustment.

Richard Nicolls was one of the few competent governors ever to grace the middle colonies. A military man with a command during the Civil War and later service under the duke in France, he returned to London as a member of the duke's household. At the time of the conquest he was forty-four years of age. Naturally the duke was hopeful that his plantation would flourish. Despite the large powers conferred upon him, he ordered that the inhabitants be treated "with all humanity and gentleness consistent with safety and honor." Few Dutchmen left conquered New Netherland, and even Peter Stuyvesant resided in New York until his death. The duke himself at first directed policy; later he turned its direction over to an advisory council of his ablest aides. Through the years he was in close touch with his deputy governors—Nicolls, Lovelace, Andros, and Dongan.

The center of Nicolls's jurisdiction was Manhattan and Westchester County, an area that contained three-fourths of the inhabitants of New Netherland. Nicolls formed a poor opinion of Long Island, with its Dutch subsistence farmers in the west and its struggling English fishermen and farmers in the east. Nor did he take a brighter view of Staten Island or even of Albany with its inhospitable winters. He gave the Swedes and Dutch on the Delaware only scant attention, and he dismissed Nantucket, Martha's Vineyard, and Maine as useless appendages. He concentrated upon encouraging settlers from New England to migrate to the fertile lands of northeastern New Jersey.

On March 1, 1665 Nicolls issued a comprehensive code of governance—the Duke's Laws. Applicable at first only to York County, which embraced most of the English about New York, it was extended eventually throughout the proprietary. Borrowed chiefly from the Massachusetts code and thus based upon American experience, one may regard the Duke's Laws, in part, as Nicolls's effort to woo settlers from New England. Lacking provision for an assembly, freedom was given in local government, and the English towns on Long Island were permitted to retain their town meetings. Happily most of the local Dutch offices had their equivalents in the English system, so the transition from Dutch to English rule was easily accomplished. The Duke's Laws also provided a broad religious toleration for Protestants. No one could be molested, fined, or imprisoned for a difference in religious opinion. Each town was required to support a church of its own faith and could choose its own minister. Nicolls believed that only the most hide-bound New Englander could take exception, especially in the light of the religious persecutions then taking place in England.

Unknown to Governor Nicolls, for he did not learn of it until November 1664, the duke on June 4, by a deed of lease and release, granted two trusted friends, Lord John Berkeley and Sir George Carteret, a substantial portion of his propriety. New Jersey, named for the birthplace of Sir George, the isle of Jersey in the English Channel, embraced all the territory east of the Delaware and south of a line connecting 41°40′ on the Delaware with 41°N on the Hudson. New Jersey was a relatively small province of 7,500 square miles (4.8 million acres).

Sir George had followed the Stuart cause throughout his career, and Charles II freely acknowledged his indebtedness to him. Carteret also had served the duke during his exile, raising funds for him in a time of dire need. With the Restoration he was appointed vice chamberlain and treasurer of the navy. Like the hot-tempered Carteret, Berkeley was a royal favorite, though not as highly esteemed. He was vain, selfish, lacking in tact, and a place-seeker. After years of service in the army and in exile, he was appointed a privy councilor. Both men, as mentioned, took part in planning the conquest of New Netherland. Despite conjecture, the grant of New Jersey was a personal reward for loyalty, ever highly valued by the Stuarts. Certainly, if the duke's sole interest in his proprietary had been financial, he would never have made a gift of New Jersey to Berkeley and Carteret.

Governor Nicolls was dismayed when he learned of the Berkeley-Carteret grant. At the time he was engaged in the disposal of large grants of land to interested entrepreneurs. The Kill van Kull (Elizabethtown) patent was issued in December 1664, and the Navesink (Monmouth) patent of April 1665 was all but consummated. Indeed Nicolls was so discouraged that he asked to be relieved of his office. He protested to the duke that he was giving away the "most improveable" part of his grant. Not only were New Jersey's lands large in extent, he argued, but the soil in many places was rich. With several large tracts already sold he believed that the lands west of the Hudson would be rapidly peopled. He urged the duke to withdraw his grant on the ground that neither Berkeley nor Carteret knew its real value. Later he suggested that the grantees be given lands on the west side of the Delaware in exchange. There were others who shared Nicolls's views, among them Samuel Maverick, who was then residing in New York. Maverick contended that when the duke made the grant he was probably not aware that he had constricted his domain to within sixteen miles of the Hudson River. All these appeals, direct and indirect, failed. James did nothing beyond restoring Staten Island to New York.

The newly created province of New Jersey afforded a variety of geographic and physiographical features suitable for settlement. There were four topographic zones running diagonally from northeast to southwest toward the Delaware River. The Appalachian and Highland zones of the extreme northwest were about twenty miles in breadth. The former included Sussex and half of Warren County and was practically uninhabited in colonial times.* The Highlands to the east, a limestone area

---

* The southern border of the Appalachian zone touched the Delaware at Phillipsburg; that of the Highlands at Frenchtown and that of the Piedmont at Trenton.

interlaced with fertile valleys, were relatively inaccessible because of the many rifts of the Delaware. Some economic activity
developed as timber found its way to New York City and the iron
ore deposits stimulated the establishment of forges and furnaces.
Bog iron was plentiful throughout New Jersey; witness the works
at Tinton in Monmouth County, founded by Lewis Morris, Sr.
late in the seventeenth century, and the emergence of the
industry in the south in the eighteenth century. Moreover, in the
Piedmont zone east of the Highlands there were deposits of
copper ore, and New Jersey copper was shipped to England in
the eighteenth century. The most extensive copper mining was
carried on by the Schuyler family near Newark from 1720 to
1775.*

Agriculture and stock raising, the chief occupations by far of
colonial New Jersey, were carried on in the Piedmont, with
intrusions into the Highlands to the west and the Great Coastal
Plain to the east. The Piedmont, also a zone twenty miles in
breadth, extended from Bergen County diagonally to the Delaware at Trenton and accounted for a fifth of the province. It
contained arable soil, heightened in value by innumerable
alluvial deposits. Its farms became the richest in the province and
its concentration of population the greatest. The earliest settlers,
entering New York and Raritan Bays, quickly penetrated the
rich valleys of the Hackensack, the Passaic, and the Raritan.
Through the years they pushed westward toward Morris County
and south up the Millstone, the principal branch of the Raritan.

The Great Coastal Plain, with its three large subdivisions—
sandy coastal plain, pine barren, and Delaware River land—occupied the southern half of New Jersey. The coast, though
providing inlets for fishermen, was uninviting to settlers. In
earliest times whalers and fishermen from Elizabethtown, Long
Island, and New Haven established bases at Cape May and
Tuckerton, and those who remained for the winter found patches
of fertile land on the Cape May Peninsula and about Little Egg
Harbor where they engaged in pasturing and farming. Behind

---

* The Dutch operated a mine at Paaquarry in the Kittatinny Mountains
and built a 100-mile road to the Hudson at Esopus (Kingston).

the sandy shores and marshlands lay the impenetrable pine barren whose timber and bog iron were exploited in the eighteenth century.

A secondary center of population developed along the Delaware below the fall line (Trenton). This hospitable part of the Great Plain contained countless pockets of alluvial soil drained by innumerable creeks from the Assinpink in the north to the Cohansey River in the south.* With ample rainfall and loamy soils, this area was well suited to agriculture. Since tidal influences were strong and the river navigable below Trenton, the Delaware was destined to become a great highway of transportation.

The New Jersey climate was inviting to settlers, though both Dutch and English commented that the winters were colder and the summers warmer than in Europe. Both delighted in the large stands of timber and the profusion of berries, nuts, and fruit. Melons, pumpkins, maize, beans, and even a coarse type of tobacco were cultivated by the Indians. The settlers also made good use of the natives' medicinal herbs. As early as 1625 the Dutch were cultivating wheat, oats, hemp, and flax, and soon beasts of burden were introduced, along with milch cows, sheep, and hogs. The food supply was augmented by game, poultry, and fish. Geese, wild turkeys, deer, rabbits, and squirrels were everywhere, while the oceans, bays, and rivers teemed with fish. Cod, haddock, plaice, flounder, and herring were familiar to the settler, but the striped bass was new to him. Oysters, crabs, lobsters, and other shellfish were abundant. Oyster shells, converted to lime, yielded mortar, which together with the native timber satisfied all building needs.

When Berkeley and Carteret received their patent in 1664, the Lenni-Lenape (Delaware) Indians† and a small number of

---

* These historic creeks from north to south were the Assinpink, Crosswicks, Assiscunck, Rancocas, Pennsauken, Cooper's, Newton, Timber, Mantua Raccoon, Oldman's, Salem, Alloways, Stowe, and Cohansey. The Maurice River, further east, flows into Delaware Bay.

† Reputedly the only Indian tribe bearing an English name, that of the rive named for Lord Delaware.

Dutch and Swedes resided in New Jersey. The Lenni-Lenape were the most important tribe of the large Algonquin linguistic family of the northeastern part of North America. They occupied lands in New York, New Jersey, and Delaware from the headwaters of the Delaware to the Bay and eastward to the Atlantic. The Lenni-Lenape tribe embraced three principal subtribes: the Munsee in the north, the Unami in the center, and the Unalachtigo in the south. Of an estimated total of 8,000, probably from 2,000 to 3,000 lived in New Jersey. They rarely warred with one another. All were dominated by the Iroquois confederacy of central New York under a chainlike system of suzerainty which, in fact, extended south and west to the Ohio. Culturally the Iroquois were highly sophisticated, with a mature political and social system. The Lenni-Lenape, by contrast, were relatively primitive—a marginal folk subsisting by hunting, fishing, and a simple form of agriculture based upon the maize-beans-squash "complex" typical of all the northeastern woodland tribes.

The Lenni-Lenape rarely attacked the tribes west of the Delaware; thus they were disturbed only when bands from the west under pressure from their neighbors invaded their lands. The New Jersey Indians lived in small villages along stream banks but moved about from time to time in search of better sites. Many bands spent the summer and fall along the coast, where they lived on fish and shellfish. A number of groups dried fish against the winter.

Relations with the natives—as elsewhere in the colonies—were never entirely satisfactory. The gap between the Indian and the European was too great. When they were brought into contact through barter, the Indian, resistant to change, did not profit; he was devastated by the white man's diseases and was susceptible to his strong drink. The white trader, dependent upon the Indian for his peltry, gave him in exchange trinkets, cloth, and tools, then firearms and liquor. The laws prohibiting trade in the latter were never very effective. The white man also wished to purchase the Indians' lands, a process the natives never fully understood. To them land meant hunting territory. Moreover, because of the distribution of authority within the Indian band, the settler frequently found that the purchase he made from one chief was challenged by another. To the European this was a source of major irritation. Unhappily the white man's pattern of working for pay never made much sense to the native.

The Dutch were less successful in their dealings with the Indians than the English who followed them in New Jersey. The Dutch regarded the Indian with a suspicion that developed into contempt and hatred. The series of Indian wars about Manhattan, discussed later in this chapter, brought ruin to the sparse Dutch settlements in northern New Jersey. In the end the Dutch were convinced that the Indians were cruel, vindictive, slovenly, and indolent. The English were more patient and understanding, with the result that there were neither Indian wars nor massacres until the frontier troubles of the mid-eighteenth century. Governor Nicolls insisted that transfers of land must be preceded by Indian purchase, and this policy was adhered to. Later, when the Quakers settled on the Delaware, they too were deeply concerned about their Indian relations. In time the Indians were to recede to the west, so that by the end of the colonial period only a small remnant was left. Today a few names on the map, loan words in the dictionary, and, for the more sophisticated, the borrowing of a number of material traits are the principal reminders of the Indian presence.

In 1664, with the English conquest, about 200 Dutch were residing on the west bank of the Hudson in what is now Bergen County, a spillover from Manhattan. Likewise on the east bank of the Delaware, a hundred Swedes, Finns, and Dutch had drifted over from the western side. Both movements were resumed to a degree in the eighteenth century. In time Dutch migrants to the valleys of the Hackensack and the Raritan would render parts of New Jersey more Dutch than Manhattan; while small Swedish settlements such as Raccoon (Swedesboro), New Stockholm, and Repaupo would flourish long after those on the west bank had been absorbed by the English. The presence of the Dutch, Swedes, and New Englanders in New Jersey before the English takeover furnishes a prelude to the English settlement.

In 1609 Henry Hudson, a seasoned English navigator employed by the Dutch, crossed the Atlantic in search of a northwest passage. Although he failed, he did penetrate the Delaware and Hudson basins, and his reports prompted several enterprising Dutch merchant traders to probe further. Captain Hendrick Christiansen set up small trading posts at Kingston and Albany, while other ship's captains, among them Adriaen Block and Cornelis May, reconnoitered New York Bay, Delaware Bay, and the two great rivers. In 1621 when hostilities were resumed between Holland and Spain the Dutch founded the Dutch West India Company. Though primarily interested in trade, the company was given leave to establish colonies. The English, alarmed by the appearance of Dutch ships on the Delaware and the Hudson, warned that by right of occupation the English had already made good their title to all lands between 41° and 45°N.

In 1623 the States General formally constituted New Netherland a colony, and a year later small groups of families were transported to Fort Orange (Albany), to Fort Nassau, opposite Philadelphia, and to the Fort of Good Hope (Hartford). Manhattan was not settled until 1626. What appeared to be an auspicious beginning was soon dissipated by the company's poor management and incompetent governors. Its directors and stockholders were more interested in a return on their investment than in the welfare of settlers. The quest for furs was never-ending, and in the process the farmer was overlooked. The company was slow to realize that settlers were essential in defending the colony against Indians and in slowing the ever-expanding English in Connecticut.

In 1629, in an effort to divest itself of responsibility for settlement, the company had created a system of patroonships, vesting an owner with certain manorial rights. Five such grants were made: one in New York, three in New Jersey, and a fifth on the south bank of Delaware Bay. Only that of Kiliaen Van Rensselaer, the Amsterdam jeweler, located near Albany was successful. Michael Pauw, an estate owner, was granted lands on the west bank of the Hudson and became the first landowner in New Jersey. His purchases included Hoboken-Hackingh, Horsimus (Ashimus), and Paulus Hook. Soon called Pavonia, this district was the site of the first white settlements in New Jersey.

When Michael Paulusen, Pauw's agent, appeared, he built dwellings at Horsimus and at nearby Communipauw. Pauw's patroonship did not last long, since his and the others, with the exception of Rensselaerswyck, were canceled. Pavonia was a failure because too few settlers were sent, and henceforth the fate of this district depended on the fortunes of the company.

When William Kieft became director-general of New Netherland in 1638, he was instructed to shore up the weak government and to bring new life to the colony. The results were unfortunate. The hostility of the Indians was stirred up in 1639 when Kieft threatened to impose a tax on them payable in furs. In 1641 trouble loomed again because of an Indian's revenge murder in New Amsterdam. A committee of twelve "select men" warned the director against retaliation. The unrest was augmented when the Mahicans, a strong tribe to the north, sought to exact tribute from the tribes about Pavonia. In the foray seventeen white settlers were killed, women and children were seized, and the remnant fled to Manhattan. By February 1643 no Dutch settlers resided north of Hoboken, and in all Pavonia only ten whites remained.

Despite the admonitions of the Committee of Twelve, the warlike Kieft determined to attack the Indians. Eighty of them were slaughtered near Communipauw. Retaliation was swift; Indian bands joined together and laid waste farms from Pavonia to the Connecticut River, and not until 1645 was a peace agreed upon. Disappointed with their presents, seven bands raised the war whoop again, ravaging the Pavonia district once more. From Tappan to the Highlands of Navesink the Indians reigned supreme as the Dutch were thrown back upon Manhattan. This first Indian war had lasted for eighteen months and had crippled the scattered bouweries on the west side of the Hudson.

The last director-general, the imperious Peter Stuyvesant, arrived in Manhattan in May 1647. His demeanor was more conciliatory than Kieft's, with the result that until 1655 no serious Indian trouble arose. During this decade a number of Dutch migrated to Pavonia, settling at Hoboken, Horsimus, Paulus Hook, and Communipauw. In that year, when Stuyvesant was engaged in conquering the Swedes on the Delaware,

1,400 Indians attacked New Amsterdam. Driven off, they crossed the Hudson and again laid waste the Pavonia settlements, destroying crops and driving off the livestock. This second Indian war left not a single white settler west of the Hudson.

Stuyvesant revealed considerable ability in developing settlement in the future Bergen County. In 1656, recognizing the impossibility of protecting individual farms, he secured an ordinance requiring all settlers to reside in compact villages, as in New England. Stuyvesant also insisted that all lands already settled or earmarked for settlement be cleared by Indian purchase, and he renegotiated the title to all lands west of the Hudson. The territory thus validated extended from Weehawken to Secaucus on the Hackensack, southward to Kill van Kull, and northward along New York Bay and the Hudson to Weehawken. For eighty fathoms* of wampum, twenty of cloth, twelve kettles, six guns, and a half barrel of strong beer, the Indians agreed to relinquish this territory in which few of them now resided.

Immediately a group of former residents requested permission to return to their "beloved Gemoenepa." They petitioned to be relieved of tithes, taxes, and similar burdens for a period of years. This was granted on condition that they organize themselves in compact villages. Suitable tracks of land were granted to all who applied. In March 1660, Tielman Van Vleck and Peter Rudolphus sought permission to settle on "the maize lands" behind Communipauw. Van Vleck is regarded as the founder of Bergen, the first permanent town in New Jersey. He had originally studied law in Amsterdam and had come to New Amsterdam in 1658. The town itself was laid out by Buyten Cortelyou, who had surveyed New Amsterdam. Bergen was designed as a square, 800 feet on each side, intersected by two main streets, with another circumscribing its palisaded border. Each quarter contained eight lots, and in the center was a small green. Beyond the palisades were "outside gardens," each extensive enough to support a small vegetable and livestock farm. The purchaser was required to occupy his lot within six weeks and each family to have one member capable of bearing arms. Many of the lots were leased.

---

* A fathom was six feet.

In August 1661 Van Vleck was appointed schout or chief administrator, with instructions to bring to justice all violators of the laws and ordinances. Stuyvesant and his council also created a petty court, with all judgments subject to appeal at New Amsterdam. The schout would convene the court, and the schepens or magistrates would conduct it. The schout received three guilders per meeting and the schepens fifty stivers.* Major crimes such as bloodshed, theft, robbery, adultery, whoring, and smuggling were heard in New Amsterdam, but minor offenses such as brawls, slander, scolding, striking with the fist, and the drawing of weapons were left to Bergen Court, with the schout acting as prosecutor. The magistrates of Bergen were men of note—several would serve in Stuyvesant's landtag or assembly of 1664 and later in the first assemblies of proprietary East New Jersey.

The revival of settlement at Bergen aroused interest elsewhere, and there were many newcomers from Manhattan and its environs during the five years before the English conquest. Since Bergen's lots were exhausted, a number of newcomers took up land at Communipauw, now a fortified village, and along Horsimus (Mill) Creek. Because the cruel Indian attack upon Esopus (Kingston) in 1663 alarmed the settlers about Bergen, pressure was brought upon Stuyvesant to penalize those who had not furnished one man for each lot taken up. Stuyvesant and his council also ruled that absentee owners and others not providing a man to keep watch and ward would forfeit their lots. Fortunately tragedy did not strike again, and the Bergen district passed quietly under English control in 1664.

On the Delaware, the southern boundary of New Netherland, the Swedes gained a foothold in 1638. The Dutch never recognized the Swedish occupation, which lasted until 1655. New Haven colony also attempted to plant settlements there, particularly in southern New Jersey. The Maryland proprietor, Lord Baltimore, watched these developments with misgiving, since he claimed by patent the territory on the west bank of the Delaware

---

* The Dutch guilder, or florin, a gold coin, was worth about $2.25; the stiver was a copper coin worth about 3 cents.

as far north as the latitude of Philadelphia. The Dutch in 1624 built a small post, Fort Nassau, on the east bank (Gloucester), which they hoped to use as a base for trading with the Indians living on the Susquehanna. Since the results were disappointing, the fort was abandoned for a period of years. Indeed Dutch interest in the Delaware region was fitful until the arrival of the Swedes. As late as 1633 neither the Dutch nor the English in Virginia had heard of Baltimore's Maryland grant, nor were they aware of the curious patent of Charles I to Sir Edmund Plowden, issued in 1634 for lands in the lower Delaware basin. When in 1634 Captain Thomas Yong, an Englishman, took his ship up the river, he ordered the Dutch watchship there to leave, consoling her commander with the thought that the Hudson was "a better river." The Dutch lack of initiative in the south was but another reflection of the weakness of New Netherland.

Sweden's venture overseas was inspired by Dutch promoters and came at a time when Sweden, under Gustavus Adolphus, rose to military power in Europe. By 1630 the Baltic was seething with maritime activity, though Sweden had few ships or commercial enterprises of her own. Holland commanded two-thirds of Sweden's foreign trade. Peter Minuit, former director-general of New Netherland, and Samuel Bloomaert, two Dutchmen at odds with the Dutch West India Company, interested the Swedish ministry in establishing a New Sweden on the Delaware. With arrangements agreed upon, the *Calmar* and the *Griffen* were sent to the Delaware in December 1637 laden with trading goods and settlers. Half the capital was raised by Bloomaert, who remained in Holland, and half in Sweden by five men, three of whom belonged to the powerful Oxenstierna family. Arriving on the Delaware in March 1638, Minuit, familiar with the river, settled at Fort Christina (Wilmington), and trade with the Indians was begun. At reoccupied Fort Nassau, Commander Peter May notified Director Kieft of the intrusion, but the Dutch were too weak to do anything about it. On the return voyage to Sweden Minuit lost his life in a storm, though his ship arrived safely with its cargo of furs aboard. Twenty-three colonists remained at Fort Christina.

The Swedes were no more successful as colonizers than the

Dutch, despite the backing of the Swedish crown. Though a number of sporadic efforts were made to send supplies and settlers, nothing transpired according to schedule. Both Swedish and Dutch promoters were chary of advancing additional capital. Despite inducements, especially to skilled workers, the response was disappointing. Later some settlers were recruited by sending deserters from the army and Finnish poachers from the forests. In 1641 the Dutch partners persuaded the Swedes to buy them out on the ground that the Dutch West India Company had rendered their position untenable. Bloomaert remained in the service of the Swedish crown.

In April 1640 Peter Ridder arrived as governor of New Sweden. He was accompanied by two Swedish Lutheran ministers, the first on the Delaware. He purchased additional lands from the natives to the north and south from the Falls to Cape Henlopen. Then he acquired territory on the New Jersey side from Raccoon Creek to Cape May. Holland and Sweden were now on friendly terms while, locally, a threat from the English drew them together.

English traders from New Haven had appeared sporadically, but in 1641, under the auspices of the newly formed Delaware Company, their leaders, Governor Theophilus Eaton of New Haven Colony and two fur traders, George Lamberton and Nathaniel Turner, were commissioned to purchase lands on both sides of the Delaware. Turner and Lamberton then began to prepare for a settlement at Varken's Kill (Salem Creek) in southern New Jersey. New Haven's move was motivated by several factors: to find a better climate and to engage in the Indian trade from which she was blocked by Connecticut. Turner and Lamberton erected a fort and brought in twenty families, thus establishing the first English settlement, though not a permanent one, in southern New Jersey.

In January 1643 a newly appointed Swedish governor, Johan Printz, arrived; he was to rule New Sweden for a decade. Described by the English as "furious and passionate" and named "Big Tub" by the Indians (he was alleged to weigh 400 pounds), Printz was a professional soldier, trained in the rough school of the Thirty Years War. Unfairly criticized, as was Peter Stuyvesant, Printz was essentially a man of action; severe but not cruel, strict but not arbitrary, and the ever faithful servant of his sovereign, Queen Christina. He moved swiftly to strengthen his feeble colony. To command the Delaware he built Fort Elfsborg on the east bank just below Varken's Kill and Fort New Gothenburg on the west bank at the mouth of Darby Creek (Philadelphia). The English at Varken's Kill did not bother him, for the inhabitants were wracked by illness.

The story of the decade is a kind of *opéra bouffe*, with the Swedes and the Dutch baiting one another but uniting to thwart the designs of the English. In 1643, after serving several terms in a London prison for debt, Sir Edmund Plowden, holder of a patent to the Delaware estuary, worked his way to Virginia and there prepared an expedition to the Delaware. He succeeded in embarking, but his crew seized the vessel and abandoned him on an island off Cape Henry. On reaching Fort Elfsborg, the mutineers were taken by Printz and returned to Virginia, where they were hanged. Plowden himself was rescued by two loyal followers. By 1648, back in England, this enthusiastic visionary was preparing a more grandiose expedition, but he was unable to find the necessary support.

Swedish relations with the Dutch continued amicable until the coming of Peter Stuyvesant as director-general in May 1647. Like Printz, Stuyvesant was a soldier and a man of action. He issued commissions freely to Dutch ship's captains to trade on the Delaware, predictably giving rise to "incidents." He then began to consolidate the Dutch holdings on the New Jersey side. Both Printz and Stuyvesant could claim identical lands by virtue of purchase from rival Indian sachems. By the spring of 1651, Printz's continual interference goaded Stuyvesant to direct action. He led an expedition across New Jersey and transferred Fort Nassau to a newly built redoubt half a dozen miles below Newcastle. Henceforth Fort Casimir, as it was named, was the Dutch bulwark on the Delaware.

As late as April 1653 there were only twenty-six Dutch families at Casimir, but the Swedes, too, were growing weaker. Since 1643, when Printz arrived, until 1653, when he left, the population of New Sweden had dwindled to less than one hundred. The New Sweden Company was losing money, and the government refused further aid. Printz, who had carried on courageously for a decade, departed in 1653 at the very time when Sweden's interest revived. The attempt to bolster New Sweden was prompted by the appointment of the ambitious Eric Oxenstierna as head of the Commercial College, the ministry of trade. John Rising, secretary of the College, an energetic young man, was appointed director of New Sweden. Persuaded that the colony lacked only an adequate population, more than 200 settlers aboard the *Eagle* arrived in May 1654, increasing the population nearly fivefold. Food became scarce, and disease brought by the passengers created havoc. During the severe winter that followed the colony was dependent on the English traders for food.

New Haven Colony was alarmed when Director Rising threatened to drive her settlers from the Delaware. In New Haven efforts were made to revive interest in Varken's Kill. The General Court sent Vice-Governor Stephen Goodyear to treat with the Swedes, but he left Fort Christina convinced that New Haven's case was not strong. No further attempts were made to settle on the Delaware. Meanwhile Rising made a bad mistake. He took the Dutch fort, Casimir, on May 21, 1654. Immediately Stuyvesant was ordered to drive the Swedes from the river. After a year's delay, for the director was in the West Indies, he led an expedition to the Delaware. On September 14, 1655, the Swedes, reduced to extremity, surrendered Fort Christina. Stuyvesant granted them liberal terms, including the right to return to the mother country. Those who stayed retained the privilege of subscribing to the Augsburg Confession—the Lutheran credal code—and of receiving instruction in it from their own ministers. Their religion gave the Delaware Swedes the tenuous link with the homeland that was to endure until 1786.* By 1663 all of New Sweden was taken over by the City of Amsterdam in lieu of debts owed the city by the failing Dutch West India Company.

---

* As late as 1672, in the last of a number of such attempts, Sweden instructed her minister to England to "try in a polite way" to prevail upon Great Britain to return New Sweden.

From 1655 to 1664 Stuyvesant wrestled against insuperable odds to keep New Netherland afloat. These were not happy years. New England, with ten times the population of New Netherland, was pushing across Connecticut, while the English towns on Long Island were making demands, especially for a landtag or assembly. Indian disturbances began again, with the New Amsterdam outbreak of 1655 and the Esopus wars of 1659–1660 and 1663–1664. Revenue was badly needed, so that the director was forced to make concessions to the inhabitants. Oddly, toward the end, the dangers imperiling New Netherland's existence drew the burghers and their director together.

Little aid was forthcoming from the Dutch West India Company or the Dutch government. The passage of the English navigation act of 1651, following strained relations for many years, precipitated the first Dutch war, 1652–1654, and with the limitation of Dutch commerce with England to direct trade, the Dutch West India Company was plunged into bankruptcy. In Holland, Jan de Witt, who was determined to destroy the company, began his twenty-year ministry. In consequence Clarendon and his ministers in 1664 felt assured that Holland would make no great effort to defend New Netherland. The Dutch colonists in America clearly foresaw the end that would overtake New Netherland.

Swedish and Finnish peasant farmers were the residual element on the Delaware. When Sir Robert Carr seized New Sweden early in October for Colonel Nicolls, he thought it a poor place. Carr's report also confirms the evidence from Dutch and Swedish sources that the New Jersey side was practically uninhabited by white men. Israel Acrelius, in his classic work *A History of New Sweden*, first published in New Stockholm in 1759, wrote that in 1664 "there were as yet no residents upon the east side of the river . . . which was a poor, sandy and abominable country." When the first English Quaker colonists arrived at Salem in 1675, about a hundred Swedes and Finns had crossed over to the New Jersey side of the Delaware.

2

THE PROVINCES OF EAST AND WEST JERSEY

The proprietors Berkeley and Carteret assumed that they had been granted the right of government under their New Jersey patent of June 1664. Thus when they issued their Concessions and Agreements of February 10, 1665, they laid great stress upon this privilege. Actually the grant from the Duke of York was of the soil only and did not bestow the right of government. As later demonstrated, the duke could not delegate to others a power that inherently belonged to the crown alone. In other words, though the grant from the king to the duke was legal, it could not pass to a third party. A major difficulty arose in later years from the duke's insistence, over the protest of the crown authorities, that Berkeley and Carteret, as well as their successors, were entitled to the right of government.

The Carolina proprietorship, the prototype of New Jersey's, was that of a feudal fief rather than a trading company, and it embodied the ideas of a landed nobleman rather than those of a London merchant. New Jersey, like Maryland and the Carolinas, is classified as a proprietary colony; while others, like Massachusetts Bay, whose charters were modeled on those of a trading company, were known as corporate colonies.*

The February 1665 Concessions and Agreements of the

* The proprietorships or proprietaries originated with the English palatine of the fourteenth century, when the crown, in order to protect its exposed northern borderlands, bestowed upon certain powerful nobles powers of government and

proprietors of "New Caesaria" (New Jersey) were practically identical with those of the Carolina proprietors issued only six weeks before. Since their object was to lure settlers from New England, just as the Carolina proprietors hoped to attract settlers from Barbados, the boons found in the Carolina Concessions—a general assembly, freedom of trade, and liberty of conscience— were repeated in the New Jersey Concessions. The New Jersey Concessions provided for a governor appointed by the proprietors and a council named by the governor. Other important proprietary appointees were the surveyor general, the receiver general, and the secretary. The governor, council, and a lower house composed of twelve elected representatives or deputies would constitute the general assembly. This body would enact all laws providing they did not contravene those of England or the proprietors' instructions. Under no circumstances might the assembly violate the article guaranteeing liberty of conscience (for Protestants).

The assembly was also accorded the power of constituting courts and defining their jurisdiction, of appointing certain officers, and of fixing their salaries and fees. It was also empowered to lay equal taxes and assessments upon the inhabitants, but not upon unimproved proprietary lands. The assembly was instructed to raise revenue for the support of government and for defense. The inhabitants were required to swear allegiance to the king and loyalty to the proprietors, thus qualifying

---

soil that amounted to quasi-sovereignty. Durham was the most notable. In America, the proprietorship was employed to reward entrepreneurs who had made substantial capital outlays and incurred great risks in planting settlements. When Lord Baltimore, for example, received his Maryland patent in 1632, he was vested with a full panoply of seignorial and manorial privileges. With the Restoration, the proprietorship was revived, with crown favorites as the recipients. Most of the proprietors never came to America, their authority being delegated to deputies. The colonists resented the outmoded exactions inherent in the proprietorship, such as the oath of fidelity to the proprietor and the quitrent. They would settle for no less than their rights as Englishmen, particularly that of levying their own taxes. Friction between the colonists and the proprietors was predictable and was not limited to the Jerseys. See Charles M. Andrews, *The Colonial Period of American History*, 4 vols. (New Haven, 1934-1938), especially II, 197-240.

as freemen. The guarantees of religious freedom were strong and specific; no one would be punished or called into question for any difference of opinion "in matters of religious concernement," unless he disturbed the civil peace. These provisions were essential if settlers were to be enticed from New England.

Lands suitable for settlement would be divided into tracts of from 2,100 to 21,000 acres, and one-seventh of each would be reserved for the proprietors. Towns would be laid out, with one-seventh of the lots similarly reserved. The remaining lands would be sold subject to a proprietary quitrent of $\frac{1}{2}$d. per acre. Additional inducements to settlers were provided by means of the old Virginia system of headrights. Heads of families would be entitled to 150 acres, plus 150 for each manservant and 75 for each womanservant. After the expiration of his term of three or four years, an indentured servant was entitled to 75 acres. For those arriving a year or more later these allotments were gradually reduced. Indians were to be humanely treated, a policy believed not only beneficial to the planter but advantageous for the propagation of the Gospel.

Neither proprietor had any intention of coming to New Jersey. Since Carteret was anxious to establish a settlement, while Berkeley was indifferent, Sir George bore the expense of the first expedition. His cousin, Captain Philip Carteret, then twenty-six years of age, was appointed governor. The *Philip* with the governor, his assistants, and thirty servants arrived in Newark Bay on August 1, 1665, and anchored off a point called Elizabethport in honor of Lady Carteret. Philip Carteret's assistants were Robert Vauquellin, surveyor general designate, and James Bollen, secretary and register. The servants, French-speaking denizens of the isle of Jersey, were indentured to the governor or his assistants. Thus the governor himself soon claimed the headrights on eighteen of them. From the beginning all three of the party's leaders had an interest in the operation of the land office.

Even before the English conquest, settlers from Long Island had shown a fleeting interest in New Jersey. Most of them, especially the Quakers and the Baptists, had left New England for Long Island because of religious persecutions. Many within the Puritan church, dissatisfied with its demanding tenets, also sought asylum there. Several groups had sought permission from the Dutch to take up New Jersey lands, but they received little encouragement. With the English conquest however, interest revived. In September 1664, Governor Nicolls gave John Bayley, Daniel Denton, Luke Watson, and three others permission to undertake a settlement. On December 1, after purchasing lands from the Indians, as required, Governor Nicolls granted these associates a tract of 400,000 acres on Kill van Kull, near what became Elizabethtown. He guaranteed them and their settlers the usual privileges of English subjects in America, and in turn they agreed to pay an annual quitrent "according to the customary rate," to be first remitted in March 1670.

The associates and the early settlers adjusted themselves quickly to the new proprietary regime of Carteret. In February 1665 sixty-five of them took the oath of loyalty. The settlers were principally from the easterly Long Island towns, and most had migrated there from Connecticut towns formerly in New Haven Colony. All shared the institution of the town meeting and the same religious orthodoxy. Governor Carteret quickly broke up the complexion of this new Zion by purchasing Bayley's substantial interest in Elizabethtown. Home lots of four acres were offered for £4, and the realty business flourished on a modest scale.

The Elizabethtown associates engaged in transactions that resulted in the creation of two new towns. They sold the southern part of their grant for £80 to men from Newbury, Massachusetts, and in 1667 a confirmatory deed was issued by Carteret to eight associates of Woodbridge township, named in honor of the Newbury minister, John Woodbridge. In 1668 thirteen men took the oath of loyalty, and in June 1669 Governor Carteret granted the associates a town charter, stipulating that a minimum of sixty families be settled and that a town quitrent be paid. Subject to confirmation by the governor, a minister might be called, to whose support each freeholder must contribute. The freeholders were permitted to choose their own magistrates and constables.

In December 1666 the principal Woodbridge associate, Daniel Pierce, sold a third of his large holdings to four New Hampshire men who founded Piscataway, named for the stream that divided New Hampshire from Maine. By 1670 at least fifteen families had settled there. Although this was far short of the sixty families specified, Governor Carteret permitted the undertakers to proceed.

As mentioned, a second tract was granted in April 1665 by Governor Nicolls to twelve Long Island men. Known as the Navesink or Monmouth patent, it extended from Sandy Hook to Barnegat Bay and up the Raritan River for twenty-five miles in a large triangle. Nicolls granted the associates and settlers exemption from quitrents until 1672. The patentees, a mixture of Quakers and Baptists, came largely from Gravesend, Long Island. Since the original associates for the most part were interested in the project primarily as a realty venture, the settlers turned to new men like the Quakers Richard Hartshorne, John Hance, and Eliakim Wardwell and the Baptist John Bowne to lead them. Many of the Navesink settlers, eighty in number, were originally from Rhode Island and Massachusetts. In February 1668, twenty-eight Navesink men took the oath of loyalty. The villages of Middletown and Shrewsbury were founded, with town meetings and petty courts under elected magistrates. In June 1667 the Navesink settlers began to convene "assemblies" at Richard Hartshorne's plantation at Portland in the belief that Nicolls had originally accorded them this right. Actually they were entitled to a local jurisdiction only.

The founding of the sixth town, Newark, can be attributed to discontent in New Haven Colony. John Davenport and the other orthodox ministers there had fumed against "the Christless rule of Connecticut," whose clergy had accepted the Halfway Covenant. In 1665 New Haven Colony was annexed to Connecticut, whereupon the diehards decided to leave. Encouraged by Governor Carteret, their envoys, led by Robert Treat, decided to settle in New Jersey. Newark Township lay north of Elizabethtown and comprised an area of roughly fifty square miles. The land was well drained, with bottom land, meadow, and stands of pine and cedar. The town, named in honor of the Reverend Abraham Pierson of Newark-on-Trent, Lincoln County, England, was situated on a bluff. Families from Branford, Guilford,

Artist's representation of colonial Newark. *Courtesy of the New York Public
Library Picture Collection.*

Milford, and New Haven arrived in May 1666 to settle this orthodox Zion. Lots were laid out, and provision was made for a church, a market place, a wharf, and a mill. The settlers agreed that none should be freemen unless they were church members, and that church members only could hold office. The founding of Newark represented the efforts of three men: Robert Treat of New Haven, and Jasper Crane and Abraham Pierson of Branford.

The six towns bore certain resemblances. All were carefully planned before settlement, and each offered the settler a home lot, with some meadow and upland, at reasonable terms. Some lands were distributed by lot, and in other cases they were assigned by the associates. All public matters were decided in town meeting by majority vote of the freeholders. Each town was authorized under the Concessions to send two elected representatives to the provincial assembly. The towns were required to pay quitrents on their "public" or town lands and the individual upon his holdings. Because a period of grace was permitted the towns, this burden did not as yet impede settlement. Unfortunately the quitrent rate in the case of Elizabethtown and Navesink was not stipulated in the Nicolls deeds; presumably it was negotiable with each grant. The duke himself viewed such rents more as a formality than a source of income, because in New York province they were never collected systematically. When the New Jersey towns were called upon by Carteret at the end of the grace period to remit, they resisted, arguing that quitrents did not apply to them because the duke's grant to Berkeley and Carteret antedated the Nicolls grants. This conflict over quitrents colored much of New Jersey's early history.

Within the proprietary was the Dutch settlement of Bergen, incorporated by Director Stuyvesant in 1661. Bergen township lay between the Hackensack and Hudson rivers and ran from Kill van Kull to just north of Weehawken. In November 1665 its thirty-two citizens took the oath of loyalty, and the town agreed to pay £15 per annum on its 11,500 acres. All male inhabitants were accorded the status of freemen, and Bergen was permitted to retain its petty court, nominate magistrates, appoint constables, choose a minister, and elect two representatives to the assembly.

As with other colonies, New Jersey attracted land speculators, and from 1667 to 1670 a group of Barbadians purchased large tracts in Bergen County. The New Barbados tract of more than 15,000 acres was purchased by William Sandford and Nathaniel Kingsland, kinsmen. Sandford took up residence, but Kingsland was represented by his nephew and heir, Isaac. John Berry, who brought his family, two servants, and thirty-two Negro slaves, purchased a huge holding above New Barbados. Other Barbadians were John Palmer, later prominent in New York, Lewis Morris, Sr., Samuel Moore, and Michael Smith. These men, all of whom brought some slaves, both cultivated their holdings and engaged in selling lands, particularly to Dutch immigrants from New York. Several of them became distinguished in East Jersey as members of the provincial council and the Court of Common Right, the supreme court.

The provincial government got off to an unhappy start with the meeting on the first assembly at Elizabethtown in May 1668. The Navesink deputies voted for a provincial tax, only to be repudiated by the Middletown town meeting. The latter body agreed to recognize Carteret as governor only on condition that Navesink's privileges under the Nicolls grant were recognized. The town meeting contended that the proprietors' interest in New Jersey was "obscure" and that the assembly in accepting them as "absolute proprietors" had deprived the settlers of their rights under their Nicolls patent; should their deputies take the oath of loyalty, they alleged, the settlers would be reduced to the status of "absolute tenants," subject to any quitrent the proprietors set. Since the assembly itself broke up because of a quarrel with the governor, no settlement with Navesink was reached.

Trouble also broke out in Elizabethtown, where under the Nicolls patent no quitrent would be collected until March 1670. A falling out with Governor Carteret occurred when he insisted on presiding at the town meeting, admitting whom he pleased as freemen, and selling lots without informing the other associates. Acts of defiance followed, and the offenders were fined. When the rents did fall due, many shirked payment. Carteret warned that they would lose their status as freemen unless their names appeared on the quitrent roll. The town of Newark, which held no Nicolls patent, voted reluctantly to pay its quitrent, but the town meeting resolved that its title derived solely from its Indian purchase—revolutionary doctrine.

The whole situation exploded in the spring of 1672 when Captain James Carteret, the proprietor's heir, appeared unexpectedly in New Jersey. The dissidents shrewdly flattered this gullible young man and used him as their tool. In March 1672, when the assembly could not reach an agreement with Governor Carteret regarding quitrents, the deputies called a meeting, attended by all but the aggrieved Navesink deputies, and elected James Carteret "president of the province." The governor and his council promptly branded those attending the "pretended assembly" of May 14 as mutineers. Seeking popular support, Governor Carteret issued a confirmation of privileges under their Nicolls patent to the Navesink towns. They were granted the right to make "all prudentiall laws" and were given other concessions. Unfortunately Navesink was to place a much broader interpretation on Carteret's concessions than warranted. Woodbridge, also loyal, was rewarded with the remission of a third of its quitrents for seven years.

In June 1672, Governor Carteret returned to England to inform Sir George of this unhappy state of affairs. John Berry, acting governor, and the council sent a delegate to London to testify that their lives and property were being threatened and petitioned Sir George to confirm the governor's authority. The rebellion of 1672 was cut down ruthlessly. The Duke of York declared the Nicolls patents null and void, and the crown itself commanded all persons to yield obedience. Thus reinforced, Sir George laid down the law. All landowners must obtain proprietary patents lest their lands be forfeited, and the constables were ordered to collect quitrents by action of distraint. In a second declaration the proprietor bore down hard on the inhabitants and the house of deputies. No person could vote unless he held a proprietary title. Henceforth the governor and council alone would qualify freemen, establish courts, charter town corporations, appoint provincial officers, and allot lands. They alone would decide what measures would be introduced in the assembly. Those participating in the rebellion must yield submission, and all individuals and towns must pay their quitrent arrears immediately. Though the revolt was put down, the grievances that were engendered festered until the end of the proprietary period in 1702.

Before Governor Carteret returned, a Dutch fleet took New York and with it New Jersey. The brief reoccupation lasted from July 1673 to November 1674. In return for his collaboration with the Dutch, one Samuel Hopkins of Elizabethtown, a revolutionary sympathizer, was appointed a schepens of Elizabethtown and soon after secretary of Achter Kull, as northern New Jersey was named. The oath of loyalty administered by the Dutch officials affords a census of East New Jersey in 1673. Elizabethtown listed 80 men; Woodbridge, 64; Middletown, 60; Shrewsbury, 58; Piscataway, 43; Newark, 86; and Bergen with its outlying district, 78. The total population was therefore about 2,500. At this time the settled area was confined to a small belt bordering the coastal waterways from Bergen to Shrewsbury. New York province had more than double the number of inhabitants.

The Dutch occupation was uneventful. Toward the close, Elizabethtown, Newark, and Piscataway petitioned for a confirmation of their alleged rights, but they were informed that they enjoyed the privileges of Dutch citizens everywhere—quiet possession of their lands and liberty of conscience. Unknown even to the Dutch governor, Anthony Colve, the Dutch in 1674 signed a treaty with England providing for the mutual restoration of all conquered territory.

Meanwhile a significant change had taken place in the New Jersey proprietorship. In March 1674, Lord John Berkeley sold his share to two Quakers, Edward Byllynge (Billing) and John Fenwick, and in 1676 Sir George Carteret agreed to a partition of the province that left him the territory east of a diagonal line extending from the upper Delaware to Little Egg Harbor. Thus East and West New Jersey were created, and they were not reunited until 1702.

Under Governor Carteret, who returned in November 1674,

East Jersey resumed her unhappy course. Between 1668 and 1681 there were in all seven assemblies. The later assemblies merely built upon the basic laws that were adopted in 1668. For example, the revenue act of that year called for a tax of £30 through the imposition of a levy of £5 on each township. Since the payments were made in kind, the table of equivalents reveals the price structure of the economy. Wheat and peas were valued at 3s. per bushel; beef at 2d. per pound; pork at 3d.; bacon at 6d.; tobacco at 4d.; and tallow at 6d. The province budget requirement, £50 by 1676, mounted rapidly until 1679, when it was nearly £200. No provision was made for the governor until 1676, when he was voted an allowance of 2s. for every male over fourteen.

The assembly of 1676 enacted a code of criminal law, most of it suggested by the Duke's Laws of 1665. Penalties for murder, sodomy, buggery, rape, arson, burglary, theft, false witness, vicious children, night revelry, and conspiracy were adopted; and to these in the second session were added penalties dealing with unlawful marriage, fornication, drunkenness, and killing. Murder, sodomy, buggery, and false witness "with the intention of taking a life" were punishable by death. Arson and burglary might also bring the death sentence, but branding was the more common penalty. Guilty persons were required to furnish security against the public charges of caring for their bastards. Those convicted of drunkenness or of taking the Lord's name in vain were fined or placed in the stocks, or both. No man, however, would suffer the death penalty unless his crime was proved by the evidence of "sufficient" witnesses. The East Jersey code represents the southernmost extension of New England criminal law. Combining restitution and corporal punishment, it was more lenient.

The East Jersey assemblies adopted with modification other essential acts based on the Duke's Laws. These dealt with such workaday matters as stray livestock, fencing, pounds, livestock brands, bounties on wolves, weights and measures, the licensing and regulation of inns and taverns, the sale of liquor, Indian trade and relations, and the recording of vital statistics. In 1675 the jurisdiction of petty courts was defined. A feature was a provision granting "time and space" to a defendant who was poor, the origin of New Jersey's vaunted stay of execution. The petty courts would sit monthly in each town, and the magistrates, elected annually, were the most respected citizens.

Following English practice, county and sessions courts were established which met twice yearly, with appeals permitted to the court of assize, the superior court. Court fees, always a sensitive matter in colonial times, were set by the assembly. The judges were elected annually, many serving long terms. Legal training among them was rare. The whole matter of superior courts under Governor Carteret is hazy since they were obscured by the creation of special courts by the governor following the rebellion of 1672. After 1680 these courts were prerogative tribunals pure and simple, controlled by the governor and his council and resented by the people.

Matters of manufacture and trade found their way into the statute books beginning in 1676. Fearing that the province's reputation suffered from the poor quality of the leather exported, each town was ordered to appoint an inspector. Persons exporting green leather or improperly cured hides would forfeit them. To encourage leather making, tanners were granted permission to fell trees for bark on common lands. The assembly of 1679 appropriated £150 to provide reparation to owners of ships and cargoes that were detained or condemned in the port of New York. An act of oblivion for those participating in the rebellion of 1672 brought reassurance to the average citizen, and even the thorny question of quitrent payments subsided temporarily.

With the appointment of Edmund Andros as governor of New York in July 1674, New Jersey was thrown into turmoil. Andros was to be a storm center in the northern colonies until 1689. By training a soldier, he was rewarded by the Stuarts for his loyalty and knighted in 1679. As the soldier-governor of New York, he carried out his orders with a directness that perplexed those of opposing claims. His hand was soon felt in the Jerseys.

Andros was puzzled regarding the New Jersey proprietors' claim to the right of government but showed no hesitancy in collecting customs on cargoes entering the Delaware River. In the case of East Jersey, however, he was cautioned not to demand such payments for fear of arousing Sir George's "choller." But in 1679 when Governor Carteret categorically declared the ports of East Jersey not liable for the payment of customs, Andros decided that failure to act would constitute an acknowledgment of the proprietors' right of government. He commanded Carteret to cease "his distinct government," and when the governor responded with angry defiance that he would resist until Sir George's and the king's pleasure were known, Andros had him arrested and brought to trial in New York for illegally exercising the power of government. To Andros's chagrin, the jurors brought in a verdict of not guilty. Nevertheless, the court ordered Carteret to desist from assuming any authority! Andros then went to Elizabethtown and, after an acrimonious confrontation, dissolved the assembly.

By a curious turn of circumstances that occurred several times during colonial New Jersey's checkered history, the proprietorship was saved. The indomitable Sir George himself died in January 1680 at the age of eighty. Since his widow had no influence at court, Governor Carteret despaired of getting any assistance in England. The Duke of York, however, was in serious political trouble over his Catholicism and could not afford to add to his list of opponents. When his friend William Penn, who was by now deeply involved in the planting of West Jersey, suggested that the claim for customs might be referred for a legal opinion to the distinguished attorney Sir William Jones, the duke seized the opportunity. He of course foresaw that the decision would go against him. When in July 1680 Sir William held that the duke could not demand customs, James on August 6 issued an order extinguishing this claim.

There was meanwhile little opposition to the Andros takeover among the New Jersey inhabitants. A few men who refused to cooperate were arrested but soon released. Sir Edmund was recalled at the close of 1680, and Carteret resumed his post as governor, serving until 1682, the final twelve months as caretaker. For a time he was fully in charge and did much harm. In the assembly of 1681 he engaged in a violent quarrel with the lower house that revealed how little he had learned. The deputies asserted that the proprietors' Declarations of 1672 had subverted the liberties of the people and had stripped the house of many of its privileges. When the leaders demanded redress, the governor refused to discuss their demands, and when the house finally resolved that "the inhabitants . . . are not obliged to conform themselves," New Jersey was again on the verge of rebellion. Carteret's last year was an empty one, for he had lost the confidence of the people and their representatives. Ill-advisedly he had again resorted to the "prerogative courts" created during the rebellion of 1672 by gubernatorial commission. When East Jersey was sold by the Carteret estate in February 1682, one of the first acts of the new regime was to void these hated instruments of oppression.

Philip Carteret had been governor of all New Jersey, then of East Jersey separately, for a period of sixteen years, except for the periods of the Dutch reoccupation and the Andros takeover. Because of the continuous unrest—the meddling of the governor in Elizabethtown's affairs, the quarrel with Navesink regarding its privileges, the rebellion of 1672 followed by the proprietor's Declarations, and the near rebellion of 1681—immigration practically halted, and the province failed to grow. Despite the inadequacies of proprietary government, seven towns had come into existence—a tribute to the associates and the settlers who had grappled with one obstacle after another.

Lord John Berkeley had taken little interest in New Jersey as co-proprietor. There is no record of consultation between the partners. The story of his withdrawal from the proprietorship (briefly mentioned earlier in this chapter) might be termed a typical Restoration comedy. Lord John told a crony, Edward Byllynge, who was deeply in debt, that if he could raise the money to buy his interest, he (Byllynge) could recoup his shattered fortunes. This proposal appealed to Byllynge, "a cunning fellow," who succeeded in persuading a friend—Major John Fenwick, "gentleman" of Binfield, Berkshire, and like Byllynge a Quaker—to put up the necessary £1,000. The indenture, executed on March 18, 1674, acknowledged that the purchase was "in trust for the use of Edward Byllynge" and that "the Deed is Absolute." Though Fenwick, after the two fell out, protested that he had acquired Byllynge's interest "with my own money," the purchase was certainly in trust for Byllynge and his assigns. Byllynge's name could not appear in the conveyance as owner because he was in bankruptcy.

This amazing pair, whether pious frauds or self-deluded innocents, add spice to New Jersey's early annals. Both were ex-soldiers; Byllynge, a Cornishman, had served under General Monck (Lord Albemarle) and Fenwick under Cromwell. By 1659 Byllynge was in London as a brewer and an active Quaker, known as the writer of several tracts advocating civil liberty. Samuel Pepys, the diarist, recorded in 1661 that he saw Byllynge and several other Friends set upon by soldiers, who "did use them sorely."

Despite his role in the founding of West Jersey, Byllynge's reputation was tarnished. In 1673 he was charged with making off with £40,000, a part of which belonged to the Society of Friends. When Byllynge assumed full blame for the defalcation, he announced that the good name of the Society was not involved. Far from disowning him, the Friends' leaders gave ear to his scheme of founding a Quaker refuge in America. Major Fenwick, a stubborn and contentious man, was determined to manipulate his interest in New Jersey independently of Byllynge, whom he regarded as a junior partner. As a Friend, he hoped to enlist members of the Society in his ventures.

What Byllynge and Fenwick had obtained in March 1674 was a half-interest in the as yet undivided proprietorship. Because of the Dutch reconquest of 1673, the proprietary title was invalid unless renewed by the crown. Following the Treaty of Westminster, Charles II issued a confirmatory grant to his brother the Duke of York, but when James learned of Berkeley's sale to Fenwick, he issued a release to Sir George only. This instrument vested Carteret with the ownership of the soil—but with no specific power of government—of all New Jersey lying north of a line connecting Barnegat Bay with the mouth of Pennsauken Creek on the Delaware. All that Fenwick and Byllynge held at this juncture, then, was a claim to the southern part of New Jersey. What they needed desperately was an acknowledgment of the right of government.

While these matters were pending, Fenwick, who held the deeds in his possession, refused to yield them to Byllynge until the latter agreed to give him for his sole use a portion of the territory—in fact, two-thirds of it. Unable to compose their differences, these two were persuaded as Friends to submit their dispute to the arbitration of William Penn. After much haggling, which tested Penn's patience severely, Fenwick agreed to accept one-tenth and £500 in cash that he needed badly to launch a settlement. (William Penn's intervention in this affair marks the beginning of his involvement in America.)

Byllynge's creditors meanwhile were dunning him. The upshot of the matter was that Byllynge and his creditors, principally Quakers, prevailed upon Penn to join with two of them, Gawen Lawrie and Nicholas Lucas, to act as trustees for Byllynge and to fashion a plan to untangle his finances. Lawrie, later a governor of East Jersey, was a London merchant, and Lucas was a maltster from Hertfordshire. By an instrument known as the tripartite deed, signed by Byllynge, Fenwick, and the trustees, the proprietorship was divided into 100 parts or shares, 10 of which were assigned to Fenwick.

The trustees then decided to sponsor a Quaker colony of their own on the Delaware. The Quakers, a small sect of 50,000, were being steadily persecuted because of their refusal to compromise on any principle that would substitute man-made law for that of God; nor would they, like other Dissenters, deign to meet in secret. Such contrariness was regarded as civil disobedience by the authorities and as disloyalty by the people. The Friends went to jail in droves, and many perished in prison. As many as 20,000 suffered fines and imprisonment, including a fifth of those who later went to West Jersey and half of those who migrated to Pennsylvania.

Despite the persecutions, the Society of Friends attracted many influential converts. Their earlier fanaticism was waning. Men like William Penn, Robert Barclay, George Keith, Robert Turner, and Thomas Lloyd joined, not only because of the simplicity of Quaker beliefs, but because of their advocacy of the principle of liberty of conscience. Too, their practice of aiding those in need appealed to many of humanitarian leanings. Of equal importance was the conversion of a substantial group of merchants and artisans in the towns.

William Penn was the foremost advocate of religious liberty in England and the ablest opponent of Stuart persecution. For his outspokenness, he spent a total of two years in prison between 1667 and 1671. All the while he published tracts and petitioned both king and Parliament for relief. With his force of character, his perception of large issues, and his knowledge of the law, Penn had advanced far beyond the modest Quaker doctrine of passive resistance. In 1670–1672 he won a great victory in the Penn-Mead trial when the Court of King's Bench upheld the right of the jury to bring in a verdict contrary to the judge's instructions. This case won him a national reputation. Penn and the other Byllynge trustees strove for the removal of obstacles, none of which deterred Fenwick's early departure for New Jersey. They needed a validation of their title, a recognition of the right of government, and a more meaningful boundary. Sir George, who held the settled part of the province, was prevailed upon to make a new division that gave the trustees control of the eastern bank of the Delaware from its source to its mouth. By this Quintipartite Deed, signed by Carteret, Byllynge, and the three trustees, a diagonal line was drawn from Little Egg Harbor to a point on the Delaware River close to its source at latitude 41°40'N. In signing this document, Sir George, perhaps unwittingly, had strengthened the Fenwick-Byllynge claim. Fenwick was not a party to the agreement, since he had already left for America. In order to obtain additional funds to finance his expedition, he had mortgaged his tenth to John Eldridge and Edmund Warner. These two were persuaded to transfer Fenwick's interest temporarily to the trustees to enable them to treat with Sir George. When Fenwick learned of it, he claimed he was being defrauded. It was sharp practice, but the trustees felt that Fenwick had violated his agreement with them in undertaking a separate settlement. In the division of the province into East New Jersey and West New Jersey, the latter, encompassing 4,600 square miles, was much larger than East Jersey, with 3,000 square miles.

John Fenwick was consumed by a single purpose, to found a

colony of his own. During the summer of 1675 he had signed "articles of agreement" with thirty-odd "adventurers." Those who purchased 1,000 acres of land were designated as "proprietors." He offered headrights of 100 acres to families at a quitrent of 1d. per acre. Indentured servants, too, were welcomed. Fenwick's settlers were Quaker shopkeepers and artisans from London and its environs. Almost miraculously Fenwick succeeded in organizing his expedition. The *Griffen*, with about one hundred passengers aboard, arrived on Salem Creek on November 23, 1675 and planted "Fenwick's Colony," or Salem, the first permanent English settlement in West Jersey. Unhappily, however, the founder was destined to fail because of his personal involvements, his quarrels with the trustees, and his clashes with Governor Andros of New York.

The trustees were highly disturbed by Fenwick's actions. They appointed Richard Guy, Richard Hartshorne, and James Wasse to visit Fenwick and insist that he honor his agreement with them. Guy, already in Salem, had fallen out with Fenwick; Hartshorne was the leading East Jersey Quaker; and Wasse bore the trustees' instructions with him. Wasse was also instructed to locate a site further up the Delaware for the trustees' settlement. On reaching Salem, Wasse informed the settlers of Fenwick's breach of faith. The chief proprietor could not defend himself since he was imprisoned in New York.

Fenwick's nemesis was Governor Andros, who refused to acknowledge that he had any right of government. When Fenwick failed to answer a Newcastle court summons, he was taken to New York in January 1677 for trial. As he was unable to produce his deeds, which were held by his mortgagors, the court of assize fined him £40 and compelled him to give security of £500 not to act in any public capacity. Andros then permitted him to return to Salem. By the spring of 1678 Fenwick was again in trouble for refusing to pay the small tax levied by the Newcastle jurisdiction and for dispossessing those who would not acknowledge him as lord proprietor. Again he was taken to New York, where he was held in custody until March 1679. On his return he found his affairs in chaos. William Penn, acting for the trustees, bought up the Eldridge-Warner mortgage, and in 1683, just six months before Fenwick's death, Penn himself, who bore Fenwick no animosity, purchased his remaining interest in Salem Colony.

During the Fenwick interlude the trustees perfected their own plans. They decided they must go ahead, even though the duke had not recognized their title. They formed a joint stock company of 100 shares or proprieties valued at £350 each, thus converting the Fenwick-Byllynge purchase of £1,000 into an equity worth (on paper) £35,000. The purchaser of one full share was entitled to 1/100 of the province lands. Fenwick had received ten shares, and ten more were used to satisfy Byllynge's creditors. The trustees then undertook to sell the remaining shares. By August 1677 when their ship, the *Kent*, arrived, they had disposed of thirty, and by 1683 the residue had been sold or assigned.

The great majority of the West Jersey purchasers were Quakers, principally small merchants, merchant craftsmen, or shopkeepers with some fluid capital. A little man could invest in a fraction of a share; in fact a $\frac{1}{7}$ share at £50 was common. The most notable purchasers were affluent Quaker leaders like Penn; Robert Turner, a wealthy Irish linen draper; John Bellers, a noted philanthropist and social reformer; Arent Sonmans, a Dutch-born merchant of Edinburgh; and Thomas Rudyard, one of Penn's lawyers.* Of the 120 individual purchasers, seventeen were Irishmen, actually English Quakers who had moved to Dublin, and three were Scots. The English purchasers were "south country people" from London and Middlesex, Northampton, Hertford, and Leicester, or "north country people" from York, Nottingham, and Derby. Wealthy Quakers supported the New Jersey venture, regarding all Friends undertakings in America as a duty. The largest single purchasers, with five shares each, were Benjamin Bartlet, Byllynge's son-in-law, and John Hind, a Quaker. The only known speculator was Dr. Daniel Coxe, a non-Quaker of London.

---

* For the complete list see Pomfret's *The Province of West New Jersey* (Princeton, 1956), Appendix, 285–289. As Sonmans was a foreigner, his share is listed under Thomas Rudyard, his legal trustee.

Before sending their expedition to the Delaware, the trustees issued the famous West Jersey Concessions of March 3, 1677, proclaiming them "a foundation for after ages to understand their liberty as men and christians, that they may not be brought into bondage but by their own consent." Originally attributed to William Penn, who knew their contents, they were written by Edward Byllynge, the chief proprietor.* Formulated in 1676, the Concessions were not immediately published for fear of disturbing the boundary negotiations with Sir George and of prejudicing Penn's efforts to obtain a confirmation of title from the Duke of York. The language of the Concessions was neither legal or feudal but was addressed to plain people who could understand the privileges and responsibilities set forth. Throughout there is revealed the sincerity and high-mindedness of those of the Quaker faith. The Concessions were signed in England and America by both proprietors and settlers.

The Concessions of 1677 provided for an elected assembly with power to enact laws providing they were in conformity with the laws of England and the Concessions themselves. All adult males, with few exceptions, were entitled to vote on measures of the assembly. The first duty of an assemblyman was to present the recommendations or grievances of his constituents, and should he fail to do so he could be challenged by the other members of his district. All bills could be amended, and a two-thirds vote was required for passage. Until the assembly met—the first meeting was scheduled for March 25, 1681, the beginning of the year, old style—the province would be governed by appointed commissioners who would also serve as magistrates. The Concessions also contained a carefully prepared code of law, embodying Quaker notions of justice which were adopted with little change.†

---

* In February 1685 Thomas Budd and Samuel Jennings, two influential men at odds with Byllynge, wrote, "the frame of government prescribed in the Concessions were of his [Byllynge's] preparing. . . ." Byllynge's authorship is also alluded to in Jennings, *Truth Rescued from Forgery*, published in 1699. Byllynge's tract *A Mite of Affection . . .* (1659) contains proposals strikingly similar to some in the Concessions, such as dividing lands into tenths and hundredths. Finally, the style of writing is that of Byllynge, not Penn.

† The Concessions of 1676–1677 are published in Leaming and Spicer, *Grants, Concessions, . . .* (Philadelphia, 1752; reprinted Somerville, N.J., 1881), 383–

Since the trustees expected to dispose of all 100 shares, there could be no proprietary system of overlordship. The commissioners were instructed to purchase large tracts of land from the Indians and to divide each purchase into 100 parts. The first dividend of land was stipulated at 5,000 acres per full share, with the fractioner receiving land in proportion.* The quitrent system did not take root in West Jersey, because the shareholder imposing quitrents would have had little chance of selling his lands. The unit of settlement became a medium-sized farm cultivated by the owner and his family. The Concessions provided a headright system, and liberal terms—50 acres and freedom dues—were offered indentured servants at the expiration of a three- or four-year term.

There were similarities and differences between the East and West Jersey Concessions. Both were liberal and designed to attract settlers, guaranteeing the basic rights of Englishmen, easy access to land, freedom of conscience, freemanship, and participation in local and provincial government. Both, importantly, established a general assembly with an elected lower house and with power to share in law-making. The West Jersey Concessions were superior, not only in spelling out the powers of the assembly, but in their concern for the liberties of the individual— among them trial by jury, security from arbitrary arrest, secret ballot, and an exemplary code of laws.

In a tract written by Penn, the trustees in September 1676 invited members of the Society of Friends to emigrate to New Jersey. Penn advised his readers not to make a decision rashly but to first consult with relatives, friends, and members of their meeting. The *Kent*, with Gregory Marlow as master, sailed with 230 passengers aboard and arrived at Newcastle on August 16, 1677, after a tedious crossing. The north country Friends were taken aboard at Hull and the others at London. The *Kent* called first at New York in order that the commissioners might inform

---

411, and conveniently in Julian P. Boyd, ed., *Fundamental Laws and Constitutions of New Jersey* (Princeton, 1964), 71–104.

* By 1714 each full propriety or share had yielded its owner 16,500 acres in four dividends.

Governor Andros of their mission. They wished to avoid the troubles that Fenwick had encountered. Andros obligingly appointed the commissioners as magistrates under him, with the privilege of establishing a petty court, appointing constables, and disposing of their lands. After paying the 5 percent customs at Newcastle, the *Kent* sailed upstream and discharged her passengers at the mouth of Assiscunck Creek. For security reasons the Yorkshire and London groups decided upon a single settlement, Burlington. While engaged in assigning lots and planning a town, the commissioners made three purchases from the Indians spanning the considerable territory from the Falls (Trenton) to Oldman's Creek. Burlington lay halfway between. The natives were treated with all consideration since the settlers needed all the goodwill they could muster against the coming winter. Other ships continued to arrive, and by 1681 a total of 1,400 Quakers (including those of Salem) had made the long journey. In the spring of 1682 a group of Quakers from Ireland settled on Newton Creek, south of Burlington. The commissioners designated the territory north of Burlington as the First Tenth; that extending from Burlington to Pennsauken Creek as the Second Tenth; that assigned to the Irish group from Pennsauken to Timber Creek as the Third Tenth; and that from Timber to Oldman's Creeks as the Fourth Tenth. The undeveloped lands below Oldman's Creek were known as the "lower six tenths," but only the Salem Tenth achieved an identity before the system of tenths gave way to the county system.

William Penn was unremitting in bringing pressure on the Duke of York to recognize West Jersey's title and right of government. In his quest he was aided by Robert Barclay, the Scots Quaker of Edinburgh. Here the duke was temporarily in exile because of the hostile feeling aroused regarding his succession to the throne. Barclay enlisted the good offices of his kinsman, the Earl of Perth, an influential Scottish adviser of James. As mentioned earlier, the "inspired" decision of Sir William Jones of August 1680 was the consequence, and after seven years of uncertainty it appeared that West Jersey had finally obtained the guarantees of quiet possession and the right

William Penn, 1696, by Francis Place. *Courtesy of the Historical Society of Pennsylvania.*

of government. Unfortunately, as it turned out, the duke had no power to convey the right of government.

In acknowledging that the right of government went with the soil, the duke unfortunately vested that right in Edward Byllynge as chief proprietor. Penn, preoccupied with the Pennsylvania charter, withdrew from the trusteeship, and in September 1683 it was dissolved because Byllynge, through the sale of his proprieties, was presumed to be solvent. Byllynge lost no time in proclaiming himself governor, and in so doing he had in effect repudiated his Concessions. He appointed Samuel Jennings, formerly a Londoner, his deputy governor in residence. The settlers, liking the man and trusting Penn's recommendation, accepted him.

The commissioners governed ably until the assembly met in November 1681. The West Jersey assemblies, meeting from 1681 to 1685, also handled matters effectively, but the distrust of Byllynge cast a long shadow. Indeed the first order of business of the assembly of November 1681 was to adopt ten "fundamentals" designed to keep the power of government in the hands of the inhabitants. In freely subscribing to the Fundamentals, Jennings showed himself in full accord with the settlers. Despite the fact that Byllynge was abhorred by many Friends in England, George Fox and other Quaker leaders continued to support him. Jennings, now convinced that the power of government was vested in the people, put into force the laws adopted by the assembly. In the session of May 1683 when it was rumored that Byllynge was coming as governor, the assembly adopted additional precautions to protect its guarantees of self-government under the Concessions. At midnight of May 14, when the assembly was on the point of adjourning, William Penn, John Fenwick, and five others, delayed by a storm, arrived from Salem. On Penn's advice, for he regarded Byllynge's arguments for abrogating the Concessions as specious, the assembly elected Jennings governor, in effect usurping the government.* A committee of fourteen was appointed to petition

---

* Penn had succeeded in persuading the recalcitrant Fenwick to represent Salem in the assembly for the first time. Byllynge's agent, Thomas Mathews,

George Fox and other leading Friends for an acknowledgment that the proprietors had purchased "the land and the government together." In March 1684 the assembly delegated Samuel Jennings and Thomas Budd, a councilor, to treat with Byllynge in London, voting £1,200 to contest their case; pending the outcome, the assemblies of 1684 and 1685 adjourned immediately after convening.

In England Jennings and Budd, getting nowhere with Byllynge, agreed reluctantly to a binding arbitration by leading Friends, including George Fox, Alexander Parker, and George Whitehead. This was not a hostile jury *per se,* and all had examined the assembly's petition. The conferences lasted from July 31 to October 11, 1684, with the assembly's appeal rejected by a vote of eight to six. The "award" stated that though Byllynge had promised the right of government with the soil, until the Jones decision it was not his to give, and moreover he could not be divested of it without his own consent. The arbitration had bitter repercussions in West Jersey. Thomas Budd in two pamphlets published in London sought to discredit Byllynge, thereby disturbing George Fox. Penn, more urbane, merely commented that "Thomas was rash in a passage or two, yet the book is universally liked in American matters." *

The assembly of November 1685 and that of May 1686 prepared to resist all of Byllynge's instructions and overtures, especially the suggestion that absentee proprietors be allowed proxy votes in the assembly for each full share they owned. West Jersey's struggle for self-government was terminated suddenly with Byllynge's death in January 1687. His heirs, two daughters and his son-in-law, Benjamin Bartlet, in February sold Byllynge's remaining shares together with the right of government to Dr. Daniel Coxe, the court-favored speculator-extraordinary.

The West Jersey assemblies from 1681 to 1686, with Thomas Olive as the perennial speaker, promulgated many laws imple-

---

wrote, "Never man was more minst and run down than E.B., not being there to spake for himself, and old dirt throne upon him by W.P." He was disgusted with Fenwick's role, "reserving to hisself his Lordship of the Right of Government (in Salem) and yett was one of the Assembly men."

* *Good Order Established in Pennsylvania and West Jersey* (London, 1685).

menting the Concessions of 1677. In 1685, with Salem represented for the first time, the assembly numbered fifty with full representation from the first four tenths and Salem. Fifteen acts reiterated almost verbatim the settlers' legal rights. In all judicial actions the testimony of reliable witnesses was accepted as proof, and false witness was severely punished. Except in capital offenses the plaintiff was master of his process, with full power to forgive the offender. Persons imprisoned for criminal offenses must work for their bread. Those guilty of assault would be punished as determined by the jury, while those guilty of stealing must make a twofold restitution or work off the penalty. If a settler brought in a charge against an Indian, six Indians would serve on the jury; this stipulation was in part responsible for the exemplary relations with the natives. On the whole, the penal code of West Jersey, reflecting the ideals of the Friends, was less severe than that of East Jersey.

Among the large series of normative laws adopted, several are of interest. A penalty of £3 was imposed for furnishing strong drink to the Indians, and to give the law teeth, half the fine would go to the informer. For indentured servants the "custom of the country" was fixed at four years, with freedom dues of ten bushels of corn, two horses, an axe, and necessary apparel to be furnished by the master. The first revenue act imposed a tax of £20 on each settled tenth, but, with a debt accumulating, the assembly levied a tax of 5s. per 100 acres on all surveyed lands.

A cluster of laws dealt with the disposition of lands. Commissioners for the Settling and Regulation of Lands were appointed and given broad powers. *Inter alia* they were instructed to mark the bounds of the several tenths and to lay out 64,000 acres in each for ultimate distribution to the proprietors or their assigns. Actually, with the creation of the Gloucester Court in May 1686, a typical county court, the system of tenths was gradually abandoned in favor of the county system, and by 1693 the county system of local government was fully established. Beginning with Burlington and Salem, township governments were instituted, with power to adopt local ordinances, assess local rates, and elect town officials. The commissioners also adopted regulations to forestall the creation of large estates and the accumulation of choice tracts by speculators. Except for Dr. Coxe's later feeble efforts at Coxe's Hall on Delaware Bay, there were no mesne lords following John Fenwick. Since most Quakers came as fractional owners or with some funds, the number of nonowners was small. Land was plentiful and relatively inexpensive.

The creation of West New Jersey as a refuge for persecuted Quakers was a noble undertaking. Although it ended in failure, the years 1676 to 1686 were illustrious. Three sensible men—Penn, Lawrie, and Lucas, as trustees for Byllynge—had formulated a comprehensive plan for a Quaker colony. William Penn played the role of the great persuader. Not only did he succeed in keeping John Fenwick within bounds, but he undoubtedly influenced Byllynge to write the Concessions of 1677. His considered advice on emigration to Quaker families carried great influence, with the result that within a half-dozen years a number of small settlements were planted.

The local West Jersey leaders, too, deserve great credit for creating an orderly government in the wilderness. Lacking influence in London, they were unable to cope with such external factors as Byllynge's resumption of the chief proprietorship and his repudiation of the Concessions. Though they made their peace with the prickly Governor Andros, they were not equipped to deal with the ever-nagging problem of the right of government, upon which they had placed great expectations. With Byllynge's resumption of the chief proprietorship and, ultimately, with the sale of his interest to Dr. Daniel Coxe, their zeal and motivation were sharply eroded. Destined for a slow growth, West New Jersey quickly yielded to Pennsylvania as the Quaker commonwealth in America.

What was left was the Quaker heritage of New Jersey—an exemplary way of life that gave south Jersey a unique identity into the nineteenth century and beyond. And to American history was bequeathed "The Concessions and Agreements of the Proprietors, Freeholders, and Inhabitants of the Province of West New-Jersey, March 3, 1676/1677," whose architects saw eye to eye with Oliver Cromwell that "in every government there must be Somewhat Fundamental, Somewhat like a Magna Carta, which should be standing, be unalterable."

3

PROPRIETARY GOVERNMENT

With Daniel Coxe as chief proprietor in West Jersey and with the sale of East New Jersey by the Carteret heirs, both provinces fell into the hands of proprietors more interested in profits from the sale of lands than in the welfare of settlers. Since the right of government remained in doubt, despite the confirmation issued by the Duke of York, the Jerseys ceased to attract settlers. Internally there was dissatisfaction and unrest because the inhabitants, convinced that they were being deprived of privileges vouchsafed them by their original Concessions, regarded their proprietors with suspicion.

The Carteret heirs, after several attempts to sell East Jersey, put the proprietary up for auction. It fetched a disappointing £3,400, instead of an anticipated £10,000, from a group of twelve headed by William Penn. All were Quakers living in and about London, with the exception of William West, a lawyer. By deed of lease and release dated February 1–2, 1682, the purchasers bought the soil, with all arrears of quitrents, and the right of government. The Twelve Proprietors were well-to-do merchants or "gentlemen," and four were citizens of London.

Before William Penn left for Pennsylvania in August, the twelve partners agreed to take in twelve associates, and the whole body of entrepreneurs was henceforth known as the Twenty Four Proprietors of East New Jersey. Of the new men, five were Londoners, two were Dublin Quakers, and six were Scots, three of them Quakers. Familiar faces were Edward Byllynge, now legally solvent, and Robert Turner, the Dublin merchant.

49

Among the Scots were Robert Barclay; his kinsmen, the Earl of Perth and his brother James Drummond, later Viscount Melfort; and Arent Sonmans, the Dutch-born Quaker merchant then residing in Edinburgh.

The East Jersey purchase was a shrewd move on the part of Penn and his Quaker associates. The Friends already controlled the east bank of the Delaware, and with Penn's grant of Pennsylvania of 1681 the Quaker interest was extended to the west bank as far north as New York province. With Penn's acquisition of the "three lower counties" (Delaware) from the duke, his territories also encompassed the south side of Delaware Bay. Thus by the end of 1682 Quaker proprietors held all the lands from New York to Maryland. Any grandiose ideas they may have had, however, were shelved because of Penn's complete absorption with Pennsylvania.

The entrance of Robert Barclay, the great Scottish Quaker apologist, into the East Jersey enterprise forecast a new opportunity, that of wooing not only Scottish Quakers but the far larger number of unhappy Scottish Dissenters. Perth and Melfort, wealthy men high up in the Scottish government, though hardly interested in providing a haven for the persecuted, were willing to speculate in New World lands. It was almost by default that the Scottish proprietors seized the initiative in East Jersey colonization, and the enterprise was soon regarded as a Scots undertaking.

In September 1682, Perth and Melfort nominated Robert Barclay as governor for life. They purchased a whole propriety for him and, in addition, gave him a bonus of 5,000 acres. Though it was well understood that Barclay would not reside in the province, his appointment was well received there. Among the Friends, Barclay ranks with Fox and Penn, and intellectually he was their superior. A learned man, he became the Friends' leading advocate. From 1670 to 1676, he published a dozen tracts including the famous *Apology*, but he wrote little in later years because of the demands made upon him as governor and because of his efforts (with Penn) to win the Duke of York, heir apparent to the throne, to a policy of religious toleration. Like many Scottish Quakers Barclay had suffered persecution and imprisonment. By contrast his cousins, Perth and Melfort, were among the most self-seeking and unscrupulous politicians of their age. Throughout 1683 Barclay was in London or in Scotland attending to proprietary business. He wrote the instructions for Thomas Rudyard, his deputy governor, and disposed of several proprieties in Scotland as their London owners withdrew. Many fractions of shares were sold there to a half-dozen men in political circles and to Barclay's large coterie of relatives and friends. In the end forty-five of a total of eighty-five East Jersey proprietors and fractioners were Scots.* Unfortunately Barclay's early death in 1690 at the age of forty-two, coupled with the cessation of religious persecution in Scotland, halted Scottish emigration to East Jersey.

The Scots proprietors formulated Fundamental Constitutions that were never put into effect. Because of their complex legislative provisions they were ill adapted to the American environment and admittedly inferior to the Carteret Concessions. They are of interest only in revealing what the feudally oriented Scots proprietors regarded as a model of government.† What was deemed essential in the old Concessions was retained. Since the Scots proprietors were competing for settlers, stress was laid upon provisions such as trial by jury and religious liberty. Nothing in the Fundamental Constitutions could be construed to condone "atheism, irreligiousness, swearing, drunkenness, whoring, adultery, murder or other violence, or indulgence in stage plays, masks, revels, or suchlike abuses"—good Calvinistic tenets.

Meanwhile the Scots proprietors were concerned about the right of government. On March 14, 1683, the duke, to oblige his political allies Perth and Melfort, issued a release to the Twenty Four Proprietors similar to that granted Sir George Carteret in 1680. Four deputy governors served the proprietors: Thomas Rudyard, 1682–1684; Gawen Lawrie, 1684–1686; Lord Neil

---

* The Proprietors and fractioners of East Jersey are listed in John E. Pomfret, *The Province of East New Jersey, 1609–1702* (Princeton, 1962), Appendix, 397–400.

† The Fundamental Constitutions are published in *New Jersey Archives*, I, 395–410; and in Julian P. Boyd, ed., *Fundamental Laws and Constitutions of New Jersey* (Princeton, 1964), 109–125.

Campbell, 1686–1687; and Andrew Hamilton, who governed with several interruptions until New Jersey became a royal colony in 1702. Rudyard was a Friend and a well-known lawyer. Like other affluent Friends he was a proprietor of West Jersey, East Jersey, and a First Purchaser of Pennsylvania. He left for New Jersey in November 1682. Through him the proprietors gave assurances to the inhabitants that they would work zealously for the welfare of the province and appealed to them for their cooperation. Only the stubborn and the obstinate, they asserted, would be suppressed.

The proprietors embarked upon a promotion campaign, publishing two "Brief Accounts," followed in 1685 by George Scot's more ambitious *Model of Government.** Aside from the first "Brief Account," issued by the Twelve Proprietors in 1682, all were directed toward prospective Scottish settlers. These tracts contrasted the advantages of East Jersey with the bleak outlook in Scotland. A skilled craftsman in East Jersey, for example, was guaranteed a year's work at good wages. Indentured servants would serve only three or four years, not the five or six years as in Scotland, and they would receive land and other severance benefits. A prospective settler could purchase land from the proprietors for £10 per 100 acres at a quitrent of 2d. per acre (later reduced to 1d.). Headrights of 50 acres for heads of families and 25 acres for "weaker members" were offered those transporting themselves.

Fairly accurate descriptions of East Jersey were written. This community embraced seven towns inhabited by "a sober and industrious people." From Scot's *Model of Government* we obtain population estimates for 1685: 400 in Shrewsbury township, 500 in Middletown, 400 in Piscataway, 600 in Woodbridge, 500 in Elizabethtown, 500 in Newark, and 350 in Bergen; a total in excess of 3,000. Several brochures describe the project of building a capital city at Ambo Point at the mouth of the Raritan (later named Perth Amboy in honor of the Earl of Perth).

---

* Scot was associated with Dr. John Johnstone, an Edinburgh druggist, in the promotion. Both received gifts of land for their efforts. *The Model of Government* is printed in full in William A. Whitehead, *East New Jersey under the Proprietary Government* (rev. ed., Newark, 1875), Appendix, 365–475.

The Scottish migration took place between 1683 and 1688. It was not a Quaker exodus. There were only a thousand Friends in Scotland's population of 1 million; there Calvinism was the national creed and Presbyterianism the religion. The repression of Presbyterianism had been going on since Charles II ascended the throne in 1660, and by 1679 persecution was rampant. A third of the dissenting clergy had been ejected, and the deprived ministers were forbidden to reside near their parishes. Heavy fines were imposed for nonattendance at the state church.* The authorities used a heavy hand, quartering troops in the recalcitrant districts in the southwest. There were bloody outbreaks, the prisons were crowded, and the death penalty was decreed for those attending conventicles and for those aiding the lawless. Those who were hanged were regarded as martyrs by the people. Such was Scotland's "killing time."

Economic conditions, too, were poor. Ambitious Scots were fleeing the country: "The best roads in Scotland were those leading out of it." There were other handicaps. Evictions were common, and justice was perverted. Since Scotland was politically backward, it was easy for the Stuarts and their henchmen to maintain control of the country. The English regarded the Scots with dislike and contempt, a feeling that was fanned by colonial officials in America who regarded the Scottish traders as smugglers.

The Scottish emigrants were for the most part Calvinists. Contrary to popular belief, there were few Covenanters. Most came from the eastern district, from places such as Edinburgh, Montrose, Aberdeen, and Kelso; it is clear from their letters that as many sought economic opportunity as wished to escape from religious persecution.† All four major expeditions were sponsored by Governor Barclay. The first left Scotland in August 1683 and arrived late in December. The proprietors' agents, representing six whole proprieties, took up 6,000 acres of land and a fourth of the 150-acre lots laid out in Perth Amboy. The 6,000-acre tract

---

* The Presbyterian congregations resented especially the requirement imposed from above that their ministers must receive collation by a bishop.

† Many letters are published in Whitehead, *East New Jersey*, 410–472.

was located on Chingeroras Creek on the Raritan opposite Ambo Point. The proprietors' agents were commissioned to sit on the provincial council as proxies.

Two expeditions left in 1684, one from Aberdeen and Leith and the other from Montrose; passage for an adult was £5 and for a child, 40s. The Leith party encountered a heavy storm off Hampton Roads, leaving her 150 passengers to make their way from Virginia to New Jersey directly. The 1684 settlers scattered; some remained in Amboy, and those with servants settled at Chingeroras, while others located on the proprietors' lands at Cedar Brook (Plainfield) along the south bank of the Raritan and in the Blue Hills (Watchung Mountains).

Governor Thomas Rudyard arrived in Elizabethtown in November 1682. Acting with tact and moderation, he appointed a provincial council that included a number of prominent resident owners: Lewis Morris, Sr., John Berry, William Sandford, and John Palmer. William Penn, the only proprietor then in America, journeyed from Philadelphia to assist his friend Rudyard in organizing the government. Penn aided in establishing an attitude of conciliation in the council and among the old inhabitants.

The assembly of March 1683 was the first since the unhappy session of October–November, 1681. John Bowne was again elected speaker, and the fourteen deputies, two from each township, included a majority who had sat in the last assembly. All were dedicated to maintaining the privileges of the Carteret Concessions. A first order of business was to pay off old scores. For their role in the 1681 dissolution and for abetting Carteret in erecting courts by special commission, Robert Vicars, former provincial secretary, and two councilors, Henry Greenland of Piscataway and Samuel Edsall of Bergen, were declared guilty of "divers misdemeanors and Arbitrary Actions," and were debarred from holding public office. A grand jury later condemned Robert Vicars as "a Common Nusance." Governor Rudyard diplomatically did not interfere in these proceedings.

The most disturbing occurrence during Rudyard's administration was the rift that developed between the council and the deputies. It was a pity that those who had united to rid the body politic of venal men and who forged a much needed legislative program could not have managed to prevent the opening of old wounds. The lower house submitted a bill relating to the public debt that was amended by the council. Instead of considering the amendments, the deputies brought in an entirely new bill, creating confusion. They also insisted that in all conference committees the house be represented by five members to the council's four. To guard against exciting the inhabitants, the council proposed that matters relating to quitrent collections from the towns be discussed in secret, but when Speaker Bowne objected, the altercation accelerated with ominous swiftness to a consideration of "the pretended rights" of the towns. After tedious harangues it was agreed that the towns could not infringe laws adopted by the assembly; thus, hopefully, conflict between provincial and local authority might be avoided.

A sharper struggle with the towns involved Governor Rudyard as agent of the proprietors. A claim was advanced by the Navesink towns that they had been exempt from quitrent payments on their township lands, but Rudyard, himself a lawyer, insisted that no patents had ever been issued free of quitrents. He offered to refer the whole matter to the courts, a tender that the Navesink deputies dared not accept. Rudyard deftly avoided being drawn into a similar controversy with the Elizabethtown deputies by bluntly informing them that the machinery to put things right was in their power. Though he succeeded in avoiding rebellion, obviously old wounds still festered.

Their business far from finished, the assembly threatened to adjourn. The lower house demanded a complete review of the Concessions themselves in order that the province "might bee at some certaintie of the Ground & Foundacon on which we stand." Smarting from the council's criticism, the deputies declared that if they must own or deny the Concessions, "they disowned them." When the council offered to review any changes the deputies had in mind, the deputies backed down.

Much fundamental legislation was adopted despite the incessant wrangling. To provide a system of courts, East Jersey was divided into four counties: Bergen, Essex, Middlesex, and

Monmouth. These county courts dealt with both civil and criminal cases. The Rudyard assembly also took pains to safeguard the legal rights of the individual. Justice would "neither be sold, denied, or deferred"; no man would be deprived of his liberty save by a jury trial; no man's goods would be distrained without a fair appraisal of their value; and the courts were forbidden to levy costs in excess of damages. The accused might plead his case in person, through a friend, or through an attorney. There were but few lawyers, and it was not until 1698 that the legal profession was fully recognized.

A supreme court, the Court of Common Right, was created by the assembly of 1683 to hear appeals in excess of £5. It sat four times a year and was vested with civil, criminal, common law, and equity jurisdiction. The court was fashioned in the light of colonial needs and experience. Composed of from six to twelve justices, the court included councilors, deputies, and prominent townsmen. Eventually the deputies disappeared, and from 1692 to 1700 only one noncouncilor sat. The governor, who appointed the justices, presided. The Scottish newcomers added strength to the bench in providing men like David Barclay, John Campbell, Dr. John Johnstone, David Mudie, and George Keith. Though one finds merchants, surveyors, physicians, and even a craftsman, most justices were men who had picked up a practical knowledge of the law. Rudyard himself was a lawyer, while his successors, Lawrie, Campbell, and Hamilton, were highly informed men. But aside from John Palmer, who soon became attorney general of New York, there was no lawyer on the bench until 1700.

Since the Carteret code of law had all but lapsed in 1681, the Rudyard assembly adopted a new general code. The Puritan-influenced laws were mitigated, and punishments were made less harsh. And though it followed more closely the law of England, the new code was influenced by the Quaker laws of West Jersey and Pennsylvania, for William Penn, sitting on the council, had a hand in the revision. For some offenses the fines were increased, and since prisons were lacking, the stocks were freely used. A more sophisticated council intervened to halve the fines for worshipping in private and profaning the Sabbath, and it halted the obnoxious use of informers. As before, stage plays, revels, cock-fighting, and the like were still outlawed as exciting people to "rudeness, cruelty, and irreligion." The general laws of 1683, with little modification, served the province until the end of the proprietary period in 1702. Among the other laws adopted were those imposing heavy fines for purveying liquor to the Indians and a set of regulations governing Indian conduct, now merely precautionary, since there were few Indians and little Indian trade. A militia act required all males from sixteen to sixty to possess arms and to drill two days a year. The tax system was revised, and instead of the £12 tax on each township, county assessments were laid on the basis of population. Bergen would pay £12, Essex £14, Middlesex £10, and Monmouth £15 in winter wheat, summer wheat, corn, or pork at the going prices.

Meanwhile Barclay and his Scots associates renewed their efforts to obtain more colonists. Lord Neil Campbell, who as brother of the ill-starred Earl of Argyle was suspect, was permitted to remove to East Jersey and to take as servants a number of political prisoners. Exploring this possibility, Barclay petitioned the Scottish Council for leave to transport a large cadre of such men, but only a few were recruited. The most ambitious expedition to East Jersey was led by George Scot, author of the *Model of Government*. In 1685, chartering a ship, his agents rounded up a hundred passengers, described by an unkind contemporary as a mixture of debtors, the poverty-stricken, "whoores and prodigal wasters," prisoners, and some of "phanatical principles" and dissatisfied with the government. The voyage of the *Henry and Francis* ended in tragedy, with more than seventy (including Scot and his wife) perishing from malignant fever. There were no further Scottish expeditions. Emigration, as such, had no great appeal to the Scottish people, especially when the religious persecutions began to wane. The proprietors, too, were losing interest because of poor land sales. In addition, Perth Amboy had failed to develop. Much of East Jersey's surplus of grain and livestock found its way to New York to augment the cargoes shipped from that major port.

Gawen Lawrie, the newly appointed deputy governor, was of Scottish ancestry but had resided in London for many years as a merchant. As a former Byllynge trustee, he had gained some knowledge of American colonization. The Scots proprietors provided him with comprehensive instructions that were frequently augmented. He would continue land purchases from the Indians, resurvey patents in dispute, collect quitrent arrears, and reexamine the validity of the Nicolls titles. He was also charged with urging the assembly to provide for the charges of government and to adopt the Fundamental Constitutions. Lawrie arrived in East Jersey in January 1684.

Wisely the proprietors decided to turn the disposition of lands over to the resident proprietors and fractioners acting in their own interest and as proxy to the absentee proprietors.* Thus came into existence in April 1685 the Board of Proprietors of the Eastern Division of New Jersey. It included the fourteen proprietors and fractioners in residence, all Scots save the Irish Quaker Thomas Warne. The board (still in existence) was endowed with sweeping powers: it could approve acts of the assembly until reviewed by the British proprietors; it could settle matters at issue between the proprietors and the inhabitants, especially pretenses to land, arrears of quitrents, and the validity of titles; it could lease proprietors' lands, purchase land from the Indians, and determine the boundary lines with West Jersey and New York. The board was ordered to pay the deputy governor £180 annually from the sale of lands and the quitrent receipts.

As instructed, the board strove to perfect the orderly laying out of the proprietors' lands. They would be sold at not less than £10 per 100 acres, with a quitrent of 6d., or leased at not less than 2d. per acre. To prevent engrossing, no one might buy or lease more than 1,000 acres on one site. On individual holdings the quitrent was reduced to 1d. per acre. When huge tracts were purchased from the Indians, such as the 24,000-acre holding at Barnegat,

---

* By now the system of land conveyancing was causing untold confusion in both Jerseys. For instance, the transfer of $\frac{1}{32}$ of $\frac{1}{16}$ of $\frac{1}{2}$ share (of 24) by Nicholas Brown of Shrewsbury to Stephen West of New England is a prime example of the process in East Jersey; while the sale of $\frac{1}{32}$ of $\frac{3}{90}$ of $\frac{90}{100}$ shares by George Hutcheson to Anthony Woodhouse is typical of West Jersey. (Fenwick's 10 shares were handled independently by the Salem proprietor, leaving the trustees 90 shares to dispose of.) *New Jersey Archives*, XXI, lists countless examples of such cumbersome transactions.

they would be divided into twenty-four parts, and smaller purchases would be assigned in rotation to a few proprietors in turn. Assessments of £5 and £10 were levied from time to time for land development on all proprietors. The early board members were overwhelmingly Scots.*

The Lawrie assembly did not meet until April 1686 because of the efforts of the governor to settle a dispute with the towns that had been going on since 1668 over quitrent payments. He demanded of the towns, as instructed, an unqualified acknowledgment of the proprietors' rights of government and soil and a recognition that the duke's grant to Berkeley and Carteret superseded all claims under the Nicolls patents and all titles purchased from the natives. The Navesink towns of Shrewsbury and Middletown fought Lawrie tooth and nail. The test case, however, involved John Berry, the councilor, who refused to pay the quitrent on his vast New Barbados holdings. He was sued in the Court of Common Right under the writ of *scire facias*,† and though he defied the court, in the end he was forced to take out a proprietary patent and pay his quitrents. It was only then that the towns gave in. These disputes did not help the governor in his relations with the assembly.

Lawrie's assembly convened in April 1686, with a second session in October under Governor Lord Neil Campbell, who succeeded Lawrie. The Lawrie assembly was not memorable for its legislation—its acts were extensions of existing laws—but rather for the measures it rejected. Both houses rejected the proprietors' Fundamental Constitutions, with the council commenting, "It was the sense of this board that the same did not agree w'th the Constitucon of these *American* parts." The proprietors wisely abandoned the matter. Lawrie then urged the house to adopt a revenue bill, as no consideration had been given taxes since December 1683. The lower house balked, with

---

* For example, at one meeting presided over by Lawrie those present were David Barclay, Thomas Gordon, John Campbell, Robert and Thomas Fullerton, David Mudie, Dr. John Johnstone, George Willocks, and Thomas Warne, all but Warne Scots.

† An ancient writ requiring anyone proceeded against to validate his title.

Speaker Richard Hartshorne contending that there was no reason for the inhabitants to pay the officials' salaries since they did not appoint them. All Lawrie could obtain was a promise of reconsideration at the second session.

The proprietors were dissatisfied with Lawrie, declaring that he had not given them full information. In March 1686, they had commissioned Andrew Hamilton, an Edinburgh merchant and a fractioner, to make an on-the-spot investigation. In September, Lawrie was replaced by Lord Neil Campbell, then residing in the province. In October the assembly rejected Campbell's tax proposals, arguing that the inhabitants had spent as much money on the province as the proprietors and that the towns themselves had paid the costs of all public improvements. It then adjourned. In December, Campbell obtained leave to visit Scotland and decided not to return. His ad interim deputy, Andrew Hamilton, was appointed governor, and his first term lasted until August 1688 when Edmund Andros, governor of the newly created Dominion of New England, was given jurisdiction also over New York and the Jerseys.

The Scots attained a position of prominence in East Jersey out of all proportion to their numbers. Many were men of high native ability. They manned the provincial council and the Court of Common Right, and they dominated the resident Board of Proprietors. Few sat in the lower house, since Perth Amboy was the only Scots town. The Scottish settlers fanned out wherever the proprietors located their lands and were pleased with their prospects. The Indians they encountered, though few, were friendly and could be hired to cut timber and do similar chores. One could also contract with them to furnish venison, deerskins, corn, and other commodities. Their weakness was strong drink. Indeed their chiefs requested that drunken Indians not be driven from the farms but tied up until sober! The Scots begged the proprietors to send them a minister, since Archibald Riddel, who came on the *Francis and Henry*, had returned to Scotland. Lacking ministers, the Scots met on the Sabbath to read the Bible, pray, and sing hymns. There was no antagonism between the "old inhabitants" and the Scots, though the newcomers preferred to live apart.

Like those of East Jersey the West Jersey proprietors, following Byllynge's death, emphasized the sale of lands. Dr. Daniel Coxe, who by 1692 had amassed twenty full shares, had established himself unquestionably as the chief proprietor. A man of grandiose ideas and one of the great American speculators of his age, he won recognition as a scientist and was admitted to the Royal Society. With a Cambridge degree and a training in medicine, Coxe became a court physician, treating among others Charles II and, later, Queen Anne. About 1680 he became intensely interested in the New World. Before his death in 1730, his projects extended from Maine to the Gulf of Mexico.

In 1687 Coxe informed the resident proprietors of his purchase from the Byllynge heirs and declared himself zealous of promoting the welfare of the province. Though not legally bound by the 1677 Concessions, he stated that he would ratify such fundamentals as liberty of conscience and trial by jury and he would accord the assembly "all powers consistent with the ends of good government." He spoke of coming to West Jersey but never did so. Aware of the discontent in the province, he asked that "instead of factions and divisions, there be a generous emulation among you who shall promote the welfare of our community." Coxe was formally announced as governor in February 1688 at the Burlington court meeting.

Reaching the conclusion that the administration of lands was too burdensome for men elected annually, the assembly in 1687 requested the resident proprietors to assume the management of all proprietary lands. A group of fifty-nine resident proprietors, each owning a $\frac{1}{32}$ share, organized as the Council of Proprietors of West Jersey in September 1688. From their number they elected nine commissioners, five from Burlington and four from Gloucester County.* The principal responsibilities of the council were to record all proprietary rights, supervise the distribution of dividends of land, issue warrants of survey, and administer unappropriated lands. The resident proprietors now felt in a position to safeguard their property interests vis-à-vis Coxe and

---

* Prominent among them were Thomas Olive, president, John Reading, Francis Davenport, and Andrew Robinson.

the other English proprietors. With the establishment of the West Jersey Council on September 1, 1688 and the East Jersey Board on April 19, 1685, the two colonies, in matters of land management, were running a parallel course. There was one difference. The former was the work of the resident proprietors themselves, while the latter came about through the initiative of the Scottish and English proprietors. The situation in West Jersey led to a conflict with Coxe, who as chief proprietor had no patience with the newly created council.

To placate Coxe the council waived its restrictions forbidding the formation of great estates. It authorized his agent to take up great tracts, one of 36,000 acres between Crosswicks and Assinpink Creek and another embracing a large part of Cape May County. In 1692 Coxe estimated that as owner of more than twenty proprieties, he held more than 1 million acres. He attempted to develop his holdings, building Coxe's Hall on his manor at remote Town Bank, just above Cape May, complete with servants, feudal services, and quitrents. He imported Frenchmen skilled in the arts of panning salt, curing fish, and viniculture. His visions were inexhaustible: harvesting forests of oak and pine to make boards, spars, and even ships; marketing pitch and tar; using sand and clay to manufacture pottery; and from warehouses in Philadelphia shipping his products to the West Indies and southern Europe. But because of the Andros takeover in 1688 and the inflexible attitude of the crown regarding the right of government, Dr. Coxe sold his holdings on March 4, 1693 to the West Jersey Society, a newly formed company of London men, for £9,800—£4,000 in cash and £5,000 as a mortgage. The new proprietors were even less concerned about the inhabitants than Coxe; they were interested solely in the sale of lands.

Daniel Coxe was anxious to reach a final determination of the East–West Jersey boundary line. The quintipartite deed of 1676 had provided a diagonal boundary line from Little Egg Harbor to a point on the upper Delaware at 41°40'N. New York, too, wished to ascertain the exact location of this "north station point," especially with a view to keeping it as far south as possible. After several efforts, the West Jersey line was shifted 50' westerly, thus favoring slightly East Jersey's claim. George Keith of East Jersey was delegated to run the line, but he carried it only sixty-two miles, from Little Egg to John Dobie's plantation on the Raritan, the terminus of the settled area. Dr. Coxe unexpectedly disowned the Keith line, claiming that West Jersey had been deprived of much land. Insisting that the line be run as a straight diagonal to the station point, he contended that the East Jersey proprietors, of whom he was one, had never claimed more than one-third of New Jersey. A year later he reversed himself and agreed to accept the more southerly station point, 41°N. The West Jersey Council assented reluctantly, grumbling that the resident proprietors had been deprived of several hundred thousand acres of "the very heart and cream of the Country." In December 1689 the East Jersey Board also accepted Coxe's proposal, only in 1695 to withdraw its action. The controversy was allowed to drift until 1715, when the pressure of settlers in the disputed territory brought the matter forcibly to a head both in New Jersey and New York.

In summary, during the early sixteen-eighties the New Jersey proprietorships experienced radical changes in ownership. The Twenty Four Proprietors replaced the Carteret interest in East Jersey, while Dr. Coxe obtained the chief proprietorship of West Jersey. In East Jersey, owing to the zeal of Robert Barclay, an effort was made to enlist more settlers. Though the dream of creating a Nova Scotia failed, the Scottish efforts provide a fascinating episode. After their experience with Carteret the East Jersey towns were watchful of their new deputy governors Rudyard, Lawrie, Campbell, and Hamilton. The assembly, unhappy with the proprietors' insistence upon exercising their prerogatives, was in a mood to challenge the validity of the Concessions themselves. They were at pains to mold their new supreme court, the Court of Common Right, so that it could not become the tool of the proprietary interest.

In West Jersey no one had any confidence in the motives of the chief proprietor, Dr. Coxe. The settlers distrusted him, rightly supposing him to be interested only in financial benefits for himself. To defend themselves the West Jersey resident proprietors and fractioners formed the Council of Proprietors. For decades this body was to struggle with indifferent success to protect the inhabitants from the greed of the absentee proprietor interest.

The sudden intervention of the crown in 1689 in including both Jerseys in the Dominion of New England was to bring home to the resident proprietors and the inhabitants of New Jersey just how tenuous was their claim to the right of government. The crown's intransigence on this point was one factor in Dr. Coxe's sale of the West Jersey proprietorship. Following Barclay's premature death in 1690, the Twenty Four Proprietors of East Jersey turned from their interest in promoting immigration to a consideration of how best to exploit their land monopoly. Their stubborn preoccupation with the collection of quitrents—a quarrel that West Jersey, fortunately, was spared—was for decades to fan the animosity of the inhabitants.

Despite the Jones decision of 1680, the question of the right of government continued to nag. In 1684 Governor Thomas Dongan of New York urged that New Jersey be reunited with New York, a hope that was shared by Sir John Werden, the duke's secretary. When Perth and Melfort got wind of this, they bluntly informed Dongan that the duke had assured them that none of their proprietary rights would be disturbed. Nevertheless Werden wrote Dongan to keep an eye on New Jersey and Pennsylvania since both "are apt to stretch their privileges." A boundary should be run on the upper Delaware lest East Jersey, like Connecticut, would soon lay claim to the South Seas. Dongan also stated that it was harmful to have two governments on the same river, the Hudson, and recommended that it be made clear that New York embraced the Hudson and all its arms, including Kill van Kull! He requested confirmation that all ships passing Sandy Hook first make entry at New York. Significantly, Werden hinted that an action of *quo warranto* would soon be brought against the Jerseys and Pennsylvania to compel them to prove their claims to the right of government.*

---

* *Quo warranto* was a writ issued in behalf of the crown by which one was required to show by what right he (or they) exercised any franchise, liberty, or office.

In February 1685 the Duke of York ascended the throne as James II. Pressure mounted for action against the proprietary charters. The crown authorities were convinced that the colonies must be better administered and the proprietary colonies eliminated. This view had sympathetic reverberations in America: from William Blathwayt, auditor general of the royal revenues in America; from Edward Randolph, the place-hunting collector general of customs for New England; from William Dyer, customs collector at Philadelphia who claimed that New Jersey's Court of Common Right twice ruled against his officers in their efforts to enforce the Navigation Acts; and from the mayor of New York, who claimed that as a result of New Jersey's separation from New York the trade of that port, as well as His Majesty's revenues, had fallen by a third. As a result, writs of *quo warranto* were served on Rhode Island, Connecticut, and the Jerseys, and in April 1686 the Privy Council instructed the prosecutions to proceed and added Maryland to the list.

Alarmed by this new turn of affairs, the proprietors of East Jersey submitted their rejoinder to the writ *quo warranto* in June 1687. They stated that they had spent more than £12,000 in developing the colony and that they had received no return on their investment. But if the king now deemed it wise to place all the colonies under his more immediate jurisdiction, they felt they were entitled to certain guarantees: the sole power of purchasing land from the Indians; power to issue land patents and collect quitrents; and retention of the privilege of free ports, with an officer of the crown in residence to collect the customs and enforce the navigation laws.

In the spring of 1686 while the *quo warranto* prosecutions were getting under way, the crown set up an improvised amalgamation of certain colonies. The Dominion of New England first included Massachusetts, Plymouth, New Hampshire, Maine, and the "Narragansetts Country" (Rhode Island). Sir Edmund Andros, who was appointed governor, arrived in December. In the fall of 1687, as instructed, he annexed Connecticut, and in the spring of 1688 New York and the Jerseys. Sir Edmund governed with the aid of an appointed council, on which the Jerseys had no representation. The New Jersey proprietors were in no position to object, since they were discussing terms of surrender with the crown. In August 1688 Andros paid ceremonial visits to his newly assigned colonies. He appeared briefly in New York City, Elizabethtown, and Burlington. There was little opposition to the Andros takeover: "They showed their great Satisfaction in being under his Majesties immediate government," Andros reported. He continued the local officials in office "to their high content."

On April 30, 1688, fifteen East Jersey proprietors—headed by Perth, Melfort, Barclay, and Penn—signed a document of surrender to the crown. Undoubtedly the Lords of Trade, advisers on colonial matters, had satisfied the proprietors with respect to certain reservations. Coxe and the West Jersey proprietors in London surrendered under similar terms at the same time.*

Meanwhile, in East Jersey Governor Hamilton was in charge. Since he knew that the proprietors were negotiating the surrender, there seemed little point in calling council or assembly meetings. With a war against France imminent, he did convene the assembly in May 1688 at Governor Dongan's request. Dongan had requested aid from the neighboring colonies for the defense of the Albany frontier. Actually war did not break out until 1689.† Richard Hartshorne was again elected speaker, and the eighteen deputies constituted a veteran body. The lower house criticized Hamilton's request for a tax to assist New York because it had not been requested directly by the crown or the proprietors. But on the council's insistence it did agree to a modest bill of £500. Since all dominion assemblies were suspended during the Andros regime, which lasted until April 1690, the East Jersey assembly did not meet again until September 1692. The deposed Governor Hamilton, until he returned to

---

* Leaming and Spicer, *Grants, Concessions*, . . . (Philadelphia, 1752; reprinted Somerville, N.J., 1881), 604–605. For West Jersey, see Carlos E. Godfrey, "When Boston Was New Jersey's Capital," *Proceedings of the New Jersey Historical Society*, LI (1933), 1–18 *passim*.

† King William's War, 1689–1697, was part of the continental struggle against Louis XIV of France.

England, served as a judge on the Middlesex County Court and presided over the Board of Proprietors. In West Jersey, too, the machinery of government continued to function, but the chief proprietor, Dr. Coxe, was incommunicado. The Council of Proprietors met only sporadically; and, as in East Jersey, there was no assembly until November 1692.

Fortuitously, the Glorious Revolution of December 1688 favored the New Jersey proprietors with an unexpected moratorium of twelve years. Since with the dethroning of James II and the accession of William and Mary *quo warranto* proceedings had been postponed, the proprietors reasserted their right of government. The king's advisers, with the French War on their hands, were intent only upon organizing a centralized defense, and New York, with her exposed Albany frontier, was regarded as particularly vulnerable. The influential Dr. Coxe assumed the role of spokesman for the proprietors of both Jerseys, and when he learned that Colonel Benjamin Fletcher, newly appointed governor of New York, was empowered to unite the Jerseys with New York, he appeared before the king's council, where "after long debate" he succeeded in having this instruction killed.

After the withdrawal of Dr. Coxe the proprietors of both Jerseys acted in concert. Since Robert Barclay had died in 1690, William Dockwra, the powerful secretary and agent of the East Jersey proprietors, worked closely with Paul Docminique, secretary of the West Jersey Society. Andrew Hamilton was reelected governor of East Jersey on March 27, 1692 and governor of West Jersey on April 11, by their respective proprietors. His combined salary amounted to £300 per annum. Hamilton returned in September 1692 and served until 1702 as governor of both Jerseys, with the exception of the year 1698–1699. He was also in charge of the colonial postal service and was briefly deputy governor of Pennsylvania in 1701. He was the last proprietary governor of New Jersey. Hamilton was endowed with tact and judgment, but as the representative of a none-too-popular absentee government, his position was difficult in both divisions, as East and West Jersey were now called. As his deputy in West Jersey he appointed Edward Hunloke, influential merchant and judge, and sometime attorney for Dr. Coxe;

Hunloke was one of the few non-Quakers there to hold high office. Until 1700, the West Jersey Society was too preoccupied with its projects in West Jersey to pay much attention to its East Jersey holdings represented by the two shares purchased of Dr. Coxe.

From 1692 to 1702 only seven East Jersey assemblies were convened, six under Hamilton and one in 1699 under Governor Jeremiah Basse. The house now comprised twenty-two members: two from each of eight towns; two from New Barbados district; one each from the outplantations of Bergen (Hackensack); and one from the "Raritan Plantations," the newly created Somerset County. A new district settled by Scots, Wickatunck-Taponemus, named Freehold in 1694, elected two members. The veteran Richard Hartshorne was elected speaker in 1692, 1695, and 1696; William Lawrence of Hackensack in 1693; the Reverend John Harriman of Elizabethtown in 1694; and Samuel Dennis of Shrewsbury in 1698. The assemblies of the 1690s were experienced bodies, since half the membership had sat previously. Nor had the composition of the house changed. The old towns returned staunch Puritans; Bergen and New Barbados sent men of Dutch extraction; Shrewsbury and Middletown, a succession of Quakers; and Perth Amboy and Freehold, Scotsmen. The council, too, was a veteran group and remarkably stable. The most prominent new man was Lewis Morris II, nephew of Lewis Morris of Tinton, who had left Barbados because of the Quaker persecutions to become a large landowner, founder of the Tinton iron works, and a former councilor. The young Morris, only twenty-two, was destined to become chief justice of New York and New Jersey's first royal governor. As the ward of his uncle, the younger Morris inherited his New Jersey lands, together with the 2,000-acre Bronk estate in New York. Young Morris grew up a headstrong youth who not only quarreled with his uncle, but broke with the Friends because of his impatience with their strict discipline. He was a stormy petrel in New Jersey affairs until his death in 1746. Like Morris, the other members of the council were affluent men, many with business interests in New York City. The legislation of these years reveals little that is new;

consequently it is not in the statutes that one finds the clue to East Jersey's troubles.

There were some laws of general interest. In 1693 the counties were formally divided into townships, and in 1694 the court fees—ever a sensitive subject—were reviewed and changes were made to speed up the work of the courts. Because of "the great Exorbitances and Drunkenness," the liquor laws were strengthened, as were those restricting the sale of liquor to the Indians. Declaring that education was being neglected, the townships were authorized to maintain teachers, but unfortunately little resulted. The assemblies of 1696 and 1698 were "crisis" sessions, and there was no assembly in 1697.

In 1692 Hamilton, as instructed by the proprietors, proposed a revenue measure of £400, in part to aid New York. The assembly complied, altering the head tax from 10d. to 4s. on householders; 2s. on nonhouseholders; and 1s. on all females over sixteen. The following year, when the governor asked for the support of thirty militiamen, the house allowed twenty, appropriating only £430. Ominously, during the debates, the deputies railed against New York's interference with New Jersey's commerce. In 1694, instead of voting a defense appropriation, the house provided £30 to prosecute the New York customs collector for hindering the use of Perth Amboy as a free port. The crown was in no mood to consider the niceties of New Jersey's quarrel with New York, and in February 1698, Solicitor General Thomas Trevor declared bluntly that New Jersey "remains a part (of New York) and dependent upon the Government and protection of New York against any Enemys."

In 1695 Hamilton stirred up a row by informing the deputies that he would recommend certain "proposals" to the assembly: one of them was a demand for the payment of quitrents, which aroused their ire, especially since several key quitrent cases were pending in court. The house treated the governor's request for an annual revenue coldly, finally passing a measure for a meager £150. The house then announced to Hamilton that it would consult with the proprietors directly regarding quitrents, free ports, and other matters at issue. The new tax schedule reveals the relative importance of several township and county districts near the close of the proprietary period; for example, Monmouth County was assessed £47 9s. 6d.; Bergen, £14 8s. 6d.; the new Somerset County, £4 16s. 6d.; New Barbados and Aquackanonk (in Bergen) £12 6s.; Piscataway, £10 5s., and Perth Amboy, £3 18s. These levies were based on wealth and population.

The assembly of 1695 ended unhappily, with Speaker Hartshorne informing the governor that the house would take no action on his other "proposals." East Jersey, he stated, had done enough for defense; moreover, the inhabitants were burdened with quitrent arrears. If the inhabitants were to pay quitrents, the proprietors must bear the expense of validating their claim to free ports. So the wrangling continued until Hamilton adjourned the assembly. He refused to sign six bills.

As president of the Board of Proprietors, Hamilton proposed that Thomas Gordon, its secretary, be sent to London to urge the proprietors to insist upon a recognition of free ports, work out an agreement enabling individuals or towns to purchase their quitrents, and brief them on the quitrent cases in court. Hamilton reconvened the assembly in February 1696, apprised them of Gordon's mission, and urged them, since the right of government itself was in danger, to make some appropriation for defense. When his request was denied, he dissolved the assembly. Interest in defense was waning as the frontier danger receded. Nevertheless Governor Fletcher of New York commented that he could "obtain no assistance from adjacent colonies, except the Jersies," a compliment to Hamilton's unceasing efforts. Owing to Gordon's absence Hamilton called no assembly in 1697. The next year it was learned that Hamilton would be replaced, owing to a misunderstanding of a provision of the Navigation Act of 1696 that was thought to require that all places of trust and emolument in the colonies be restricted to native-born subjects of England. Many Scots in the colonies, including Hamilton, were disqualified. A year later the crown reversed its decision, and Hamilton returned.

The quitrent problem constituted a running sore throughout New Jersey's colonial history. Hamilton as governor in 1692 had insisted upon the payment of the rents and their arrears. This renewal of policy gave rise to lawsuits in the Court of Common Right. As before, the patentees of Elizabethtown led the opposition, abetted by those of Middletown and Shrewsbury. In earlier days, rather than see their lands forfeited, many settlers had taken out proprietary titles. Others, however, had avoided having their lands on the quitrent rolls by merely obtaining warrants of survey, thus protecting title to their lands. Actually the revenues from quitrents had not increased appreciably from 1685 to 1696.

In 1693 the Board of Proprietors attempted to evict one Jeffry Jones, occupant of a 180-acre farm in Elizabeth township, for lacking a proprietary title and paying no rent. At the trial in the Court of Common Right the board was represented by its former secretary, James Emott, and Jones by the ablest New York lawyer, William Nicolls. The case of Fullerton vs. Jones dragged on for months, with the court finally giving judgment against Jones, whereupon Nicolls moved an appeal to England on the ground that the jury had been overruled by the justices. The bench, consisting of members of the provincial council, refused to grant an appeal, so Nicolls petitioned the crown.* In February 1697 the king in council—acting on the recommendation of its judicial committee—set aside the verdict. The associates and inhabitants of Elizabethtown were forever convinced that their patents, issued by virtue of Governor Nicolls's grant of 1664, had been validated. The proprietors, in turn, claimed that the reversal was owing to an error in procedure.

The case of Noews vs. Ball over the proprietors' claim that quitrents in arrears might be recovered by restraint was also originated in 1693, but it did not come to trial until May 1695. Again the opposing attorneys were Emott and Nicolls. Formerly the proprietors had resorted to the writ *scire facias,* which required that the patentee show cause why his rent had not been paid. Since the results had been indifferent, the board abandoned its use and instructed Hamilton, as president, to bring an action of distraint. Thus one Peter Noews, an Elizabethtown associate, sued Edward Ball, the proprietors' bailiff, for distraining his

---

* The only case ever appealed from the Court of Common Right to England.

livestock for £18 arrears. Despite substantiating arguments by Emott, the jury brought in a verdict for the plaintiff, Noews, and the proprietors were thus deprived of this means of collecting arrears. Another case, Hallewood vs. Smith, also argued in May 1695, concerned the *habendum,* or nature of the estate, of the East Jersey owners. The wording of the original Carteret patents limited their holders to a life interest instead of an inheritable estate in fee simple, an obvious error. A decision in favor of the proprietors, however, gave the board a powerful weapon in enforcing its alleged proprietary rights. Hamilton offered to substitute new patents with the desired *habendum* on condition that the quitrent arrears, if any, be paid.* When Jeremiah Basse succeeded Hamilton as governor for the year 1698–1699, he fell heir to a full-fledged political issue. The resident board contended that the proprietors should not be blamed for endeavoring to collect quitrents if the inhabitants were unwilling to provide for the support of the government; and, if the people persisted in their obstinacy, they believed that the proprietors were warranted in surrendering their right of government to the crown, securing the best terms they could. Following the reversal of the Jones decision, the Elizabethtown associates, sixty-five in number, petitioned the crown to rid the province of proprietary government.

Meanwhile, in West Jersey, the West Jersey Society was making efforts to develop its interests. With Sir Thomas Lane, alderman and in 1693 Lord Mayor of London, as president, the society issued 1,600 shares of stock with a par value of £10 per share. As many as 1,430 shares were sold in a single day, and the price rose rapidly to £50. As late as 1695, when interest was declining, they brought as much as £20. The society's business was transacted by an executive committee, usually presided over by the treasurer, Robert Hackshaw. Its enterprises in West Jersey, such as the export of tar, pitch, and knee timber, were not

---

* The wording of the Carteret deeds was *heirs or assigns forever,* instead of, as in English law, *heirs and assigns.* East Jersey owners believed, with reason, that their ownership was not limited to a life estate. The Court of Common Right followed English law. Not until 1750 did Chancellor Lord Hardwicke rule that *or* in such cases had the same meaning as *and.*

successful, therefore it was compelled to concentrate on the sale of its huge land holdings.

The society appointed Jeremiah Basse, an erstwhile Baptist preacher with high ambitions, as its agent, and as instructed he sold lands freely in Cape May County and above the Falls. Coxe had valued these lands at £10 an acre, but except for the choicest parcels they brought only £5. By 1699 230,000 acres of an estimated 577,000 had been disposed of. Though the society persisted for decades, it reaped no great windfall from the sale of its lands. Moreover, it was never happy in its choice of agents and factors—Nathaniel Westland, Thomas Revell, and Basse. In 1697 Basse and Revell were ordered to call Westland to account. Basse then became surveyor general, with no better result, despite the fact that the society sponsored him for the governorship the following year. To complete a long story, in 1699 Hamilton was appointed the society's agent with instructions to prosecute Basse, and on Hamilton's death in 1703 Lewis Morris was appointed agent, with orders to bring Basse to account.

The West Jersey Council of Proprietors was in a delicate position in its endeavors to safeguard the interests of the resident proprietors. To their consternation, the society chose to ignore them. The council had reorganized in 1693 with a distinguished membership, all Quakers. Thomas Gardiner was elected president and John Reading secretary. Basse alarmed the council by surveying vast areas without consulting it. He then appeared before the council and demanded to act as proxy for seventy of the hundred original proprieties, a monstrous claim! The council took no action, but in May 1695 it made an attempt at conciliation by electing a society man, John Tatham, as president. Basse then demanded membership. The council agreed, but on condition that the society furnish evidence that the English proprietors owned as many as thirty shares. Instead, Basse left for England, leaving unresolved this matter of highest importance to the stability of the province. The greatest blow to the council was his appointment as governor shortly after.

During the years 1692 to 1697 Hamilton governed West Jersey with a steady hand, and much useful legislation was passed. Francis Davenport, a leading Quaker, had replaced the elderly

Thomas Olive as speaker, and the assembly met regularly in May and November. Among its reforms were the delineation of county bounds, the incorporation of a number of towns, and provision for the annual election of local officers by the freeholders. Democratic self-government was on occasion put to a strain, for example when the constable of Maidenhead (Lawrenceville) township neglected to appoint collectors, or when the constable of Springfield attested that the town meeting had refused to elect assessors or collectors. The court system was overhauled, with additional justices chosen by the assembly to assist the councilors who had doubled as county court justices. Many served long terms, and these able men were, with rare exception, Quakers. The criminal code was revised, and a supreme court composed of county justices and councilors was established. It was reorganized as a court of county justices and three others chosen by the lower house. Because of a wise policy of postponement exercised by the bench, many cases were settled out of court.* Throughout the proprietary period easy, open, and inexpensive justice prevailed, a heritage of the Quaker Concessions. For the willful, the machinery of justice was adequate. When West Jersey was incorporated into the royal province of New Jersey in 1702, her relatively mild sanctions were supplemented by the harsher English criminal code. A new tax system similar to that of East Jersey was adopted, substituting a schedule based on real estate and personal property for the old head tax. That on improved land was set at 1d. per acre, that on unimproved land at ½d. Noteworthy was the impost of 2s. 6d. placed on Negro slaves ten years of age or older.

With the election of the forceful Samuel Jennings as speaker in May 1697, trouble developed. Because of Hamilton's tact all had gone reasonably well. However, Revell, Tatham, Barkstead, and Westland, together with Basse, formed a small but well-organized anti-Quaker clique. Unfortunately, too, there developed a doctrinal split among the West Jersey and Pennsylvania Quakers

---

* Thomas Olive's practice of settling disputes on his farm, plow in hand, when he was a commissioner (1677–1681) gave rise to the term "Jersey justice"—simple, swift, and direct.

created by the apostate George Keith, a division that had unsettling repercussions throughout West Jersey. When the air cleared following several years of strife, a number of prominent Friends who cast their lot with the Keithian faction joined the Basse faction.*

Basse had returned to England in 1695, and learning of the impending decision to disqualify Scots like Hamilton, he determined to obtain the post of governor for himself. Seeking to ingratiate himself with the Board of Trade and particularly William Popple, its influential secretary, he intimated that Hamilton had favored the Scots traders, who, he alleged, were flagrantly violating the Navigation Acts. Basse urged that all provincial officers and assemblymen be required to take an oath to uphold the Act of 1696 and that vice-admiralty courts be established in all the colonies. Violations, he asserted, were not being properly tried in the colonial courts. In April 1697 a royal proclamation was issued virtually accusing the proprietary colonies of negligence in enforcing the acts of trade.

Basse succeeded in persuading the English proprietors to appoint him governor, but before recommending the required approbation to the Lords Justices the Board of Trade insisted that Basse post the usual bond of £1,000. Since Basse did not have the money and the proprietors would not furnish it, Secretary Popple refused to act. However, with the tacit approval of the proprietors and gambling that a final plea would win him an exemption, Basse returned to New Jersey as governor, arriving in April 1698. In West Jersey he at once appointed his cronies to the council. The lower house, with Jennings as speaker, refused to accept Basse until he produced the approbation. Basse then stacked the courts with his judges and sent Peter Fretwell, a provincial treasurer, to prison for refusing to surrender his records. Jennings convened a secret meeting that drew up a petition against the governor and later told Basse to his face that he would throw him out of the government. Pamphlet warfare ensued, with the publication of

---

* See Chapter 5 for a fuller discussion of Keith and the controversy surrounding him.

The Case Put and Decided, published by Tatham, Revell, and Westland in January 1699, and *Truth Rescued from Forgery and Falsehood* . . . by Jennings in June. Jennings in his tract charged that first Byllynge had betrayed the inhabitants; that Coxe, when opposed by the people, had cravenly sold out; and that the West Jersey Society had usurped not only the distribution of land but the government itself. The society's minions, he asserted, were Basse and Tatham. Obviously, then, by 1699 the discontents in both divisions had grown to explosive proportions.

4

THE SURRENDER TO THE CROWN
AND THE TRANSITION TO
ROYAL GOVERNMENT

The passage of the Navigation Act of 1696 and the replacement of the Lords of Trade with a vigorous Board of Trade was of major import to all the colonies. Among other provisions, the Act of 1696 tightened the customs service, erected vice-admiralty courts in the colonies, and put pressure on the governors to enforce the trade regulations. Alarmed by the feeble support of the colonies during King William's War, the board had urged a consolidation of the colonies and especially the eradication of the proprietorships. There was little chance that *quo warranto* and *scire facias* proceedings would be forgotten. In the colonies prerogative men led by Edward Randolph, now surveyor general of customs in America, made it their business to inform upon the colonies.

The proprietors of both New Jersey divisions petitioned the Board of Trade to recognize their claim of free ports and especially to restrain the New York authorities from practices injurious to them. In September 1697 the board advised that it had not issued regulations forbidding the Jerseys the use of their own piers. Collectors had now been stationed at Perth Amboy and Burlington for the collections of duties. Of necessity, it added, certain revenues had been allocated to New York during the French war to assist her with her defense.

An opinion rendered in October caused the proprietors great consternation. Attorney General Sir Thomas Trevor and Solicitor General Sir John Hawles ruled that the power of designating ports had never been granted by the Duke of York; therefore the duke's grant to Berkeley and Carteret could not convey it. New York harbor had been designated as the port for all the duke's territories, and as the keystone of defense for several colonies New York was entitled to special privileges. In November the king's council rejected the proprietors' petition and ordered that the instructions of Lord Richard Bellomont, newly appointed governor of New York, contain the usual provision not to permit goods to land in East Jersey unless the duties were first paid in New York.

Bellomont issued a proclamation forbidding the establishment of ports in New Jersey and ordered the New York collector to seize any vessel entering Perth Amboy without first calling at New York. New York's position was that she depended on her trade to support her heavy defense expenditures, that New Jersey was too weak to suppress smuggling, and that the latter's shipping, four or five sail, did not warrant a port. In July 1698 when George Willocks, the East Jersey board's agent, returned from England, he and Governor Basse proposed to the provincial council that a test case be made of East Jersey's right of port. The same day the New York collector attempted to seize a ship unloading at Perth Amboy. He and his assistants were attacked by a mob, arrested, and kept in custody by a justice of the peace. The commissioners of customs supported New York's position that the collecting of customs at Perth Amboy was not intended to exempt New Jersey from any duties she was obligated to pay at New York. The proprietors, not satisfied, submitted a new petition to the king's council.

The London proprietors, meanwhile, had instructed Governor Basse to propose a number of measures to the East Jersey assembly; foremost among them was an appropriation for the support of government and reimbursement to them for the expense they had incurred in seeking to gain recognition of Perth Amboy as a free port. Anticipating that Basse would soon receive the crown's approbation, he was instructed to call an assembly in two months' time. Actually, with no approbation forthcoming, it did not meet until February 1699.

In East Jersey opposition to Basse coalesced quickly because he lacked the promised approbation. Trouble first showed up in the courts and was led by young Lewis Morris, whom Basse had dropped from the council for questioning his credentials. On May 9, 1698, at a meeting of the Court of Common Right, Morris rose and asked by what authority the court sat. Basse, presiding, replied, "By the king's." Morris denied it, and when Basse demanded to know who else was dissatisfied, Morris shouted, "One and all!" with several others joining in. Morris, when ordered arrested, drew his sword. He was fined £50 for contempt and was imprisoned. With the aid of friends he escaped, and while in hiding he sent out "Red-Hott Letters" to all the town meetings attacking the proprietors—"base, inconsiderable persons who really have not the right to govern." He excoriated quitrents as an unjust tax "upon us and our heirs forever" and charged that the surveyor general went about "pinching pieces of land from honest men." The English proprietors, he asserted, had threatened to place East Jersey under New York unless the people paid their quitrents and accepted "some lousy fellow they would send for a Governor." He urged the towns to retain the able William Nicolls as counsel, and if Nicolls were too busy, he would represent them himself.

The *Hester* affair, of Basse's doing, complicated matters with the British authorities. Late in November 1698 Basse began to unload this small ship, owned jointly with John Lofting, his brother-in-law, at Perth Amboy. Bellomont ordered her seized and taken to New York. Basse was told that if she paid the New York duties, she would be restored. Basse refused, stating that he wished to test the claims of New York before the Court of King's Bench, the highest court of common law, and that the proprietors had instructed him not to recognize any commands from Bellomont. Though Basse's council had unanimously resolved that the governor should not accede to the demands of Lord Bellomont, it advised him not to use force to retake the *Hester*. Failing with the council, Basse carried the matter to the assembly in February 1699, hoping to elicit its support. Addressing the house in a flattering manner, he contended that many English merchants would trade directly with East Jersey if the assembly supported free ports. Surprisingly, the house voted £675 to aid with the prosecution.

The assembly's action aroused great resentment. Meetings prompted by Lewis Morris were held in Newark, Elizabethtown, Perth Amboy, and Freehold. The assembly was criticized, and Basse was accused of prostituting his office for private purposes. Basse's enemies signed a petition to the proprietors requesting his removal, unaware that the latter had decided to restore Hamilton if the Board of Trade agreed. On May 9, 1699, Basse announced that he would go to England to consult with the proprietors and that Andrew Bowne, a councilor, would act as his deputy. Only a month before, Morris and several others had been accused by the council of seditiously assembling for the purpose of subverting the government. George Willocks, now receiver general, and Thomas Gordon, prominent Scots who heartily disliked the Scot-baiting Basse, now joined Morris. On May 10, at Basse's last council meeting, Morris and Willocks were summoned to appear before the Court of Common Right. Basse then departed for England. Two days later a grand jury indicted Morris, Willocks, and Gordon for stirring up opposition to the government, and they were imprisoned. On May 13 a large band of men from Elizabethtown freed Morris and Willocks from Woodbridge jail. These two then sent a threatening letter to the council.

When the assembly reconvened on the 15th, with Morris himself a newly elected member from Perth Amboy, Acting Governor Bowne called for a bill to suppress insurrection, but in the face of mounting opposition, and being somewhat cowed, he pleaded for any measure that would promote public safety! The assembly leaders informed him that no revenue bill could be adopted because of the opposition of Morris and his faction. The speaker—John Harriman, the able Elizabethtown minister—and seven other members left without awaiting adjournment, and soon there was no quorum.

Though Basse returned to East Jersey in August 1699, the proprietors had had enough of his antics. Hamilton was recommissioned governor. By December, when he arrived, the province was in a state of rebellion that not even he could cope with.

Lewis Morris, blamed by many for the disorders that followed, was determined that the proprietorship must end if the inhabitants were to have tranquility. Orderliness, in his judgment, could be established only by the crown.

In March 1699 the proprietors suddenly relinquished their claim to free ports as a right and reiterated that East Jersey would willingly pay the same royal duties as levied in New York. New York's claim that Perth Amboy was part of the mouth of the Hudson, they stated, was specious; actually it was on the Raritan River, well outside of New York Bay. They requested the Board of Trade to permit a test case, else the inhabitants would charge that the proprietors were remiss. In April 1699 the board recommended that the king's council consent to a trial at the Court of King's Bench of the right of free ports and of the right of government itself! The proprietors, alarmed, hotly contended that their right of free port did not depend on their right of government. This, in justice to themselves and the inhabitants, they could not acknowledge.

Not wishing to face a full-fledged defense of the right of government, the New Jersey proprietors in July 1699 submitted a précis of the terms upon which they would surrender the proprietary to the crown. Of the thirteen stipulations one was the recognition of Perth Amboy as a free port. The board took its time in considering the terms proffered, satisfied that its decision to link the right of port with the right of government was a master stroke. The board was also aware that the proprietors hoped, by obtaining an approbation for Hamilton, to gain a tacit acknowledgment of the right of government. This request too was refused. Since there were a number of objections to the proposals of surrender, the board decided "that the business may hang yet some time longer in suspense." In January 1700 the anxious proprietors made it known that if the right of port were granted, there would be no further difficulties about the terms of surrender.

The *Hester* case came before the Court of King's Bench for the purpose of reaching decisions on the right of port and the right of government. Basse was now out of office. Surprisingly the court found for Basse and Lofting, who were awarded damages of

£1,000. In commenting, the chief justice stated that the court was not convinced that New York possessed any independent jurisdiction over the Jerseys. Perth Amboy was confirmed as a free port. This triumph was of no value to the proprietors who had already offered to surrender the proprietorship.

Meanwhile Secretary William Popple of the Board of Trade was warding off petitions from proprietors of both Jerseys for an approbation for Hamilton. Not waiting for it, Hamilton arrived in New Jersey in December 1699 only to find the colony in a state of confusion. In March 1700 when the justices attempted to open the Middlesex County Court at Elizabethtown, there were disorders. In July, Andrew Bowne and Richard Hartshorne, on behalf of the assembly, appealed to the Board of Trade for aid. Hamilton, they asserted, had restored Lewis Morris to the council as "a strong man," and Morris had declared that the people must submit to Hamilton or be drenched in blood. Since whole towns were rising, they pleaded that the crown appoint someone to keep the peace until a governor with an approbation was chosen. The next major disturbance took place at the Essex County Court at Newark. When the constable was ordered to apprehend a malefactor, he was attacked. The presiding judge, William Sandford, was set upon by three men, whereupon the bench adjourned the court. A mob of sixty rode over from Elizabethtown, forced the sheriff to give them the keys, and took the prisoner away. Shortly afterwards more than one hundred inhabitants of Elizabethtown and Newark petitioned the king to appoint a legitimate governor.

Hamilton, hoping that matters would settle down, did not call an assembly until the end of May 1700. He sorely needed a revenue measure but had little hope of obtaining its adoption. He explained to a doubting house that the crown had withheld its approbation only because it was awaiting the result of the trial or the consummation of the surrender. He charged the house with using his lack of approbation as a pretext for taking the government out of the proprietors' hands. In frustration, Hamilton dissolved the assembly.

Secretary Popple transmitted to the proprietors a copy of the remonstrance of the inhabitants, requesting a rejoinder without delay. Their "Answer" came too late to influence the Board of Trade; in fact the final paragraph reminded the board that they had already agreed to a surrender under terms they deemed equitable and that their revised terms were ready for delivery. The "Answer," after labeling the remonstrance of the towns as the work of a few malcontents "impatient of any Government," simply defended their conduct through the years. Since they wished to obtain the best terms possible from the crown, the document's tone was highly respectful.

The last disorders of the proprietary period took place in March 1701 at the Monmouth County Court at Middletown. The pattern of revolt was now well established. Here the authority of the court was challenged; militiamen drilling conveniently nearby broke up the court proceedings; and a mob seized the justices, one of whom was Lewis Morris. On the following day, having taken proper precautions, the court (with a newly appointed bench) haled the offenders before it and levied fines upon them. Individuals and groups continued to send petitions and pleas to England begging that something be done to counteract this state of anarchy. By now all regarded Hamilton's administration as a lame-duck operation.

Incredibly enough, the former acting governor Andrew Bowne appeared before the council in June 1701 and exhibited a commission, signed by a number of English proprietors, superseding Hamilton as governor. Hamilton immediately invited several members of the resident Board of Proprietors to meet with the council. All declared the commission surreptitious, since it was signed only by members of the William Dockwra faction in London, a minority. Lewis Morris wrote the board that the commission was signed by men who were disgruntled with those proprietors who had removed Basse. It was his opinion that proprietary government in New Jersey was a shambles and that the only remedy was for the crown to appoint Hamilton as the first royal governor.

West Jersey's final years under the proprietorship were similarly marred by confusion and disorder, and though the issues and personalities were different, it was the appointment of the despised Basse as governor in 1698 that ultimately precipitated the violence. The West Jersey Society soon recognized its mistake in turning its interests over to men like Basse. The resident council was drawn largely from the old Quaker leadership, men who were trusted and supported by the people and who also dominated the elective assembly. When Hamilton returned as governor late in 1699, the Quaker faction determined to support him, approbation or no, and to quash the Burlington "ring." The latter fought back with all the power it could muster, locally and among the London proprietors. Freedom of ports, navigation laws, and New York's interference were not factors in the West Jersey disorders.

In May 1701 the West Jersey Council, resident proprietors, and members of the lower house petitioned the crown to grant Hamilton an approbation. The name of Samuel Jennings headed the list. The opposing faction, led by Revell, Westland, and other anti-Quakers, accused their enemies of having challenged the authority of Basse during his term; they charged further that when Hamilton returned, not only had he taken no steps to punish them, he had appointed several leading Quakers to office. The petitioners alleged that because of their closely organized meetings the Quakers were able to beat them in elections and so control the assembly. On their part Samuel Jennings, Francis Davenport, William Biddle, and Mahlon Stacy dispatched to William Penn in London an account of the abuses to which West Jersey Friends were being subjected and asked him to use it as he saw fit.

The Board of Trade was in no hurry to act upon the proprietors' memorial of surrender, submitted in July 1699. It had not liked certain of the proprietors' reservations and believed, correctly, that in the fullness of time they would abandon them. Meanwhile the board and other crown authorities were studying suggestions from many sources. Edward Randolph recommended that, because of her small population, East Jersey should be united with New York and West Jersey with Pennsylvania. Both divisions, he stated, had done a poor job in policing smugglers. Ex-Governor Basse, too, was fishing in these troubled waters. He favored Randolph's recommendation and urged that a governor be appointed who would put a stop to violations of the Navigation Acts. By August 1701, Lewis Morris had arrived in England as the agent of the East Jersey Board of Proprietors. A Hamilton man, he won from the Board of Trade a degree of confidence never approached by Basse. He upheld Hamilton's actions and recommended that those who had participated in the disorders be punished. For the moment he urged the governor, whoever he was, be given an approbation.

On August 12, 1701, the proprietors of both divisions submitted their final memorial of surrender to the crown. Though their claim to free ports had been upheld, they were willing to surrender all rights of government. The proprietors asked certain reservations, which may be summarized as follows: (1) A united New Jersey, with an elective assembly meeting alternately at Perth Amboy and Burlington; (2) a house of representatives of thirty-six members, half from each division, with the qualifications for voting to be 100 acres of land and for membership in the house 1,000 acres; (3) a full complement of courts, with a supreme court meeting alternately at Perth Amboy and Burlington and with appeals to the king limited to actions of £200 or more; (4) all Protestants to be eligible to hold public office and to serve on the council and adoption of a law enabling Quakers to substitute a proper declaration for the oath; (5) a grant of those privileges deemed necessary for good government, trade, and prosperity, with freedom of port for Perth Amboy, Burlington, and Cohansey on the understanding that crown collectors would receive the customs and enforce the navigation laws; (6) the liberty of maintaining markets and fairs at Perth Amboy and Burlington; and (7) the allocation to the proprietors of important powers now enjoyed by them: confirmation of their lands and quitrents; the sole right of purchasing lands from the Indians and the monopoly of the Indian trade; and the power of appointment of the surveyor general and his assistants. Finally the proprietors requested an approbation for Hamilton until the surrender terms were finalized.

Lewis Morris in London advanced rapidly to a position of leadership among the proprietors. In September 1701, he submitted a further petition to the Board of Trade signed by himself in behalf of the majority of the resident proprietors. They requested the privilege of nominating the first royal governor, believing that without this concession their estates in the colony would not be secure. They recommended Hamilton, who, with the exception of the Dockwra faction in London and a small number of the "meaner sort" in New Jersey, enjoyed the confidence of practically all the inhabitants of West Jersey and five-sixths of those of East Jersey. For members of the council the proprietors suggested Morris, William Pinhorne, William Sandford, Samuel Leonard, Miles Forster, and Samuel Dennis of Woodbridge, "men of the best Estates," from East Jersey; and Samuel Jennings, George Deacon, Peter Fretwell, Thomas Gardiner, and Francis Davenport, all Quakers, together with Edward Hunloke, Daniel Leeds, and Thomas Revell, non-Quakers, from West Jersey.

In a separate communication to the board, Morris dealt with the proprietors' reservations. He saw little that should cause concern. Free ports were necessary to place New Jersey on a parity with other colonies. If the proprietors were allowed to choose the governor, the inhabitants would respect their property rights. He expressed the hope that the qualifications for freemen and their representatives would not be tampered with, otherwise "those persons of best Estate . . . and proprietors' Interests would be at the disposall of the tag, rag and Rascality."

The negotiations for the surrender were set in motion on October 2, 1701. The Board of Trade reviewed the events leading to the proposals of surrender. It noted that all factions wished to surrender the right of government but were divided over the appointment of Hamilton as governor. It recommended that the crown constitute a government immediately by royal commission because of the disorders in New Jersey. The board further advised that the governor's instructions, not the terms of surrender, set forth the frame of royal government, together with articles needed to secure the proprietors in their property rights and the inhabitants in their civil rights.

The authorities moved with unusual swiftness. On October 5 the Lords Justices directed the board to prepare drafts of the governor's commission and instructions; on January 6, 1702, the drafts, now accepted unanimously by the proprietors, were laid before the King's Council with the recommendation that someone "wholly unconcerned in the factions" be appointed governor. On January 29 a draft of surrender was sent by the council for the signatures of the proprietors of both divisions. The death of King William in March 1702 delayed the execution of the surrender until April 15; it was signed by Queen Anne two days later. The formal surrender contained a recital of the chain of title, the signatures of fifty-two proprietors, and a confirmation of their willingness to surrender their "pretended" title to the right of government. The concessions to the proprietors appeared in the instructions to the new royal governor.

Edward Hyde, Lord Cornbury, a cousin of Queen Anne, was appointed New Jersey's first royal governor. He was already in America as the newly appointed governor of New York and would administer both colonies. His instructions, dated November 16, 1702, did not reach him until July 1703. Several of the 103 instructions were of importance to the proprietors. The assembly was instructed to adopt a measure confirming their right of soil, together with all quitrents reserved or due them, and all other privileges contained in their original patents save the right of government. The governor and the assembly were forbidden to lay a tax on the proprietors' unimproved lands, a great boon. The proprietors alone were permitted to purchase lands from the Indians. Their surveyors alone could survey the lands held by them, and their agents were empowered to receive aid in collecting the rents due them. The proprietors had reason to be satisfied, failing to obtain full advantage in only one proposal, the naming of the governor. When Morris returned to New Jersey, he was handsomely rewarded by the resident board with new patents for his lands at a nominal quitrent, the cancellation of his quitrent arrears, and a lease of an enormous acreage between the Shrewsbury and Manasquan Rivers, with the privilege of cutting timber and of manufacturing pitch, resin, tar, and turpentine.

As a means of preserving the peace, Morris was also appointed acting governor until Cornbury assumed office. Hamilton was now ill, and he died in April 1703. As president of the council Morris would be able to build up a following. Robert Quary was added to the council as an ex-officio member to enable him the better to discharge his duties as an admiralty judge.

As proposed, the assembly would meet alternately at Perth Amboy and Burlington. It would consist of twelve members from each division (reduced from eighteen), with two each from the capitals, Perth Amboy and Burlington. In addition, Cornbury was instructed to institute a full system of courts, with appeal allowable to the king in council in cases involving more than £200.* Liberty of conscience was guaranteed to all but Roman Catholics, and it was recommended that an act be adopted permitting Quakers to substitute an affirmation for the oath. Quakers were also declared eligible for public office. Upon the moot question of free ports, the governor was directed to inform the assembly that the customs and other impositions must be equal to those of New York.

After a tortuous period of thirty-seven years, New Jersey's proprietary period came to an end. For years, through their assemblies and their resident boards, the inhabitants strove to hold the successive absentee proprietary interests in check by controlling their governors, preventing the enlargement of pro-prietary interests in the assembly and the boards, and by keeping close watch on the manipulations of the land monopolists in the provincial councils. In such an environment, factionalism con-tinued without cease. Yet in both divisions, self-government flourished at the provincial and the local level. So long as their vital interests were not disturbed, the proprietors were not inclined to interfere. Their most sensitive concern was the latent fear of having their vast holdings of unimproved land taxed. Here they were afforded some protection by the original Concessions, just as the inhabitants were guaranteed certain rights. The result was a kind of *modus vivendi*.

By 1696 there was increasing discontent and restlessness. The

---

* Implemented by an act of 1704 providing a system of county courts: common pleas, quarter sessions, and oyer and terminer. A supreme court had both appellate and original jurisdiction, while the highest tribunal, the court of errors and appeals, was composed of the governor-in-council. The governor as chancellor presided over equity cases. The judicial system came under the royal prerogative except for petty courts established by the assembly.

land monopoly was being challenged in the assemblies, the proprietary governors were unable to gain the confidence of the lower houses, and, significantly, the crown was determined to bring New Jersey into the royal system. For the historian the situation is complex, if not bewildering. Permeating the whole period was the uncertainty of the right of government, that right having been challenged by the crown almost from the beginning. This controversy was raised and dropped with exasperating frequency. Events like the Andros interlude of 1688, not to speak of the persistent interference of New York, plagued the Jerseys. An important factor, too, was the procrastination and indeed the indifference of the agencies of the crown. New Jersey was small, and London was 3,000 miles away; but by 1696 the crown had taken up the issue in earnest, and the surrender was inevitable.

Only a few important leaders emerged during the proprietary period. In East Jersey, Richard Hartshorne and the Reverend John Harriman achieved prominence, and in West Jersey, Thomas Olive and Samuel Jennings were highly esteemed, but they were essentially local men. New Jersey's settlers were for the most part farmers who were content to till their lands and were only rarely interested in the factional politics that absorbed the assemblies. New Jersey's issues were provincial, dominated largely by the relationship with successive proprietors. Overshadowed by New York, which was important in overseas trade and in matters of imperial defense, the Jerseys received little attention from the crown; her proprietorships more and more irritated its officials as time wore on. Few Jerseymen were called to London; the authorities made their wishes known to the proprietors, who acted through their deputy governors. Lewis Morris was the exception. Prominent in New York as well as East and West Jersey, he acted in what he considered New Jersey's best interests. Highly independent, he shifted his course as circumstances dictated, making enemies as he did so. From 1699 to 1702, for example, he was anti-Basse and pro-Hamilton; he fought the Dockwra faction of the London proprietors; and by 1701, through sheer ability, he attained the position of spokesman before the crown for the majority of the proprietors of both East and West Jersey.

In perspective, the surrender had broader than local implications. It was part and parcel of a new imperial policy to bring the colonies more closely under the crown. Powerful men acquainted with the colonies, such as Governor Francis Nicholson and Edward Randolph, as well as observers like William Penn, saw only chaos in the existing system of haphazard relationships that had grown up. The Whig majority in Parliament was determined to support the merchants and shippers in their efforts to control the overseas trade.

The approach was tangential. In 1696 an important trade and navigation act was adopted by Parliament. Though it contained little that was new, it did codify legislation extending back to 1651, and it provided specific means of enforcement. Taken with later acts encouraging the production of certain commodities and prohibiting the manufacture of others, the navigation laws made up "the old colonial system." The Act of 1696 created the Board of Trade, successor to the Lords of Trade and Plantations. Led by William Blathwayt, its most knowledgeable member, and William Popple, its indefatigable secretary, it soon won and retained the confidence of crown officials from the king in council down. Its recommendations were sought by virtually all departments and agencies. Its most impressive early achievements were the extension of the royal authority through a strengthening of the customs administration, the creation of admiralty courts in the colonies, and the adoption of the principle that newly appointed governors, in both royal and private colonies, must have the crown's approbation.

The board's cherished ambition was to bring about an amalgamation of the colonies and particularly to get rid of the proprietorships. The Jerseys stood out as the most absurd of the private colonies. Progress was halting, in part because the Andros experiment of 1688 had left a bad taste at home and in the colonies. King William's War was a boon in that it pointed up the need for more centralized defense and imperial administration. Though there were many attempts at unification, the board's achievements were meager. Its designs of bringing New England closer to New York and of uniting West Jersey with Pennsylvania and East Jersey with New York failed, as did those of reclaiming Pennsylvania and Maryland for the crown. Actually its single victory was the New Jersey surrender. From an historical point of view, New Jersey never again during colonial times would receive as much attention as it did during the surrender negotiations.

5

NEW JERSEY IN 1702:
A PORTRAIT OF SOCIETY

New Jersey at the beginning of the eighteenth century was small in population as well as area. The combined population of the two divisions was probably no more than 10,000. At the outside there were 7,500 in East Jersey and 2,500 in West Jersey. In the American colonies as a whole the population had doubled since 1660, with 92,000 in New England, 104,000 in the South, and 53,000 in the recently established Middle Colonies. New Jersey's neighbors had outstripped her, with nearly 20,000 in New York and 15,000 in Pennsylvania.*

In both of New Jersey's divisions farming was the principal means of livelihood, and the one-family farm of 50 to 150 acres predominated. By 1700 the great majority were homeowners, even in East Jersey, where many indentured servants had been imported from Scotland. The Indian natives supplied a few servants and an occasional slave, but their population was by now static and their labor not regarded as dependable. About 300 Negroes had entered New Jersey, principally from New York, either as servants or as slaves. In New York, where labor was in demand, there were more than 2,000 slaves, the largest number in the northern colonies. The New Jersey black was a freeman, a servant, or a slave. In the East Jersey law of 1683,

---

* For these population statistics see W. Frank Craven, *The Colonies in Transition* (New York, 1968), especially 15–16, 60, 288–290.

mention is made of Negro slaves in conjunction with indentured servants and Indian slaves, and additional references to Negro slaves appear in the laws of 1694 and 1696 dealing with runaway slaves, their possession of guns, and thefts of livestock. As yet there was no slave code, nor was there mention of Negro slaves in the West Jersey laws.

Since New Jersey's soil was relatively fertile, a great variety of crops, fruits, and livestock flourished. Surplus crops and forest products were beginning to make their way to New York and Philadelphia. Despite these advantages, immigration had slowed by 1700. There were no more immigrants from Scotland, and few from Long Island or New England. In West Jersey immigration from Britain had practically halted. Meanwhile there was a drift of the young and ambitious from New Jersey to New York City and Philadelphia, partially compensated for when, near the turn of the century, a group of wealthy "Yorkers" began to speculate in lands about the headwaters of the Raritan, with a number settling in East Jersey. This development, several decades later, led to a secondary migration from New York, Long Island, and New England.

There were nine towns in East Jersey worthy of mention: the six original Puritan towns, the old Dutch settlement of Bergen, the Scottish-oriented Perth Amboy, and the emergent town of Freehold, also of Scottish origin. No East Jersey town had a population of 1,000. The West Jersey towns were smaller and more widely separated. As late as 1707 Burlington had only 800 inhabitants, Salem 500, and Gloucester 400. Haddonfield, just east of Gloucester, was a rising village. The typical New Jersey town was a township or county seat where the local court met, where produce was exchanged and other business transacted, and where there was a congregation or, in West Jersey, a Quaker meeting.

In East Jersey the town meeting and the Puritan congregation were similar though not identical to those of New England. As land was plentiful, there was no need to hold the meadow in common. Moreover, since the East Jersey township extended from ten to fifteen miles into the country, individual families tended to leave the village and reside upon the land. The division

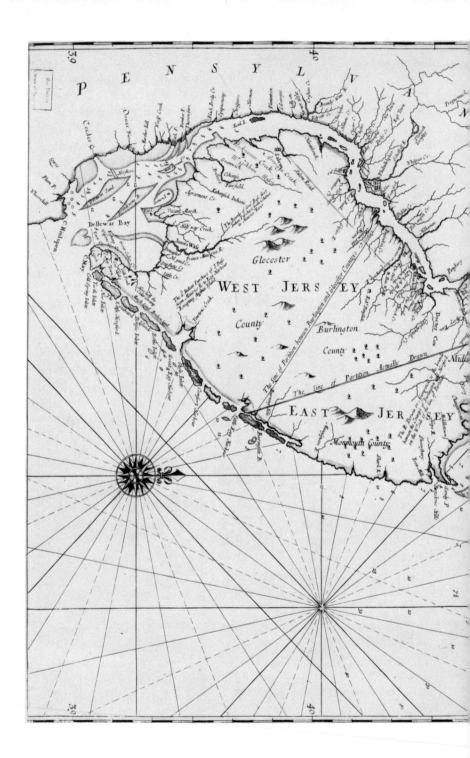

Map of East and West Jersey by John Thornton (c. 1700). *Courtesy of the Library of Congress, Geography and Map Division.*

of township lands was handled first by the associates, later by the "town's men" or selectmen. The first drawing was for home lots, the second for meadowland, and the third for upland where staples such as wheat, rye, and maize were planted. The size of the owner's holding varied from town to town, with home lots for house and garden of from six to ten acres and larger allowances for meadow and upland. Most towns held reserve lands for newcomers, and the freeholders voted themselves additional meadow or upland as needed.

Class distinctions, as in New England, were maintained for a time, but greater social mobility was soon manifested. Though at first the associate or the magistrate was given modest preferment, it was soon recognized that essential tasks such as the erection of the meetinghouse, the wharf, and the market required the efforts of all. Each town strove for economic independence, and from time to time craftsmen were offered special inducements to settle. The townsman produced necessities such as vegetables, fruit, milk, butter, and meat and traded his surplus for the items he needed. Lacking specie, the "current pay of the country" was reckoned in measures of pork, wheat, and other provisions used by all.

The East Jersey freeman refused to yield control of the town to magistrates holding office for life, and soon all local officials were elected annually. As the town meeting debated the control of the disposition of lands, of admitting new settlers, of levying taxes, or of amending the fundamental agreement, the powers of the associates and later of the selectmen were gradually limited. The freeholders also elected the township's representatives to the assembly. There was broad participation in public office save for the traditional exclusion of women, indentured servants, and slaves.

During the first decade of settlement the inhabitants of East Jersey resided in villages, for compactness was both a convenience and a necessity. As the Indian menace abated, the system broke down because of the owner's need to utilize his meadow or upland, frequently located four or five miles away. With the second generation many young adults had no choice but to erect their houses in the country. There were marked disadvantages. It was difficult for the farmer and his family to attend church; his children suffered for the lack of schooling; long trips to town had to be made for supplies or medical aid; and during the winter, life was strenuous. In time, however, hamlets appeared among the farmlands, and the multiplication of villages began.

East and West Jersey afforded significant contrasts. The population of East Jersey was more compact and had a greater diversity of national origins. Bergen, "the Dutch country," harbored a mixture of Reformed folk from the Low Countries and a few Huguenots who had moved into the upper Passaic and Hackensack valleys. Essex County, the seat of Newark and Elizabethtown, was predominantly Congregationalist. Elizabethtown also included a scattering of Baptists, Quakers, and Anglicans. Middlesex County, comprising Woodbridge and Piscataway townships, embraced many denominations. Woodbridge contained Congregationalists, Anglicans, Quakers, and Scotch Calvinists, while Piscataway bore a New England Baptist stamp. Perth Amboy, the capital, was Scottish in origin. In Monmouth County, Quakers and Baptists predominated in Middletown and Shrewsbury and Scotch Presbyterians in Freehold. Lewis Morris in 1700 observed that the towns were peopled from New England, the inhabitants being generally independents (Puritans), and that each had a meetinghouse. "They have some few churchmen (Anglicans), Presbiterians, Anabaptists, and Quakers settled among them." West Jersey, by contrast, was a Quaker community, despite Daniel Leeds's prejudiced estimate of 1699—"832 freeholders, whereof Quakers, 266." By the end of the century there was a small, politically oriented group of Anglicans in Burlington.

New Jersey's early culture was commonplace rather than élite, and she lacked the advantage of an educated aristocracy. One searches in vain for unique economic or commercial achievements or for arresting esthetic, intellectual, or educational innovations. There was no printing press, and regular schooling was rare. The inhabitants were a simple, unsophisticated people of good morals and great industry, intent mainly upon establishing a means of livelihood.

Woodrow Wilson in his address to the New Jersey Historical

Society in 1908 commented that the history of America was the history of its villages writ large. He was thinking of colonial New Jersey, where peoples of many national origins and many creeds were able to work out the adjustments to enable them to live together as neighbors. Their town meetings, with practically all adult males qualified to participate, and their representation in the general assembly by elected delegates contributed much to their satisfaction. Despite great diversity, there was surprisingly little discord among the towns.

Undergirding this respect for order and decency was the guiding strength of the denominations and sects. As in New England, in East Jersey the meetinghouse was the fulcrum of the town's activities. In the early decades, the town meeting and the sessions of the petty court as well as of the overseers or selectmen took place at the meetinghouse. Only the commercially oriented fair, held once or twice a year, and the market lay outside its orbit. Thus in relating the story of the several religious denominations one closes a gap in the colony's history not filled by the recital of its political activities.

The New England Puritans gave East Jersey her congregational churches. Indeed during the early years events in the New England churches had direct repercussions in East Jersey. Its settlement by the Puritans coincided with the great controversy in New England over the adoption of the Half-Way Covenant. Many New England leaders felt that the church was losing ground because the attainment of "saving grace," the *sine qua non* of full membership, was beyond the reach of the average Christian. Church members were unhappy because their children were not automatically accorded full membership status as a birthright; while a portion of the clergy was concerned lest such restrictions curb the growth of the church. The issue hinged upon the status of the children of members. The "half way" view, a compromise, was adopted in 1682 after five years of strenuous debate. Children were permitted the sacrament of baptism but were barred from the Lord's Supper and from a vote on ecclesiastical matters when grown—a second-class membership. To become a full-fledged member one must still experience a complete profession of faith. This type of religious awakening was of such intensity that only a few could hope to attain it. Yet a number rejected the Half-Way Covenant as being too liberal. In some towns the church divided, and in others the orthodox minister and his flock departed. Among the latter was the Reverend Abraham Pierson of Branford, Connecticut, who in 1666 led his congregation to the wilds of New Jersey.

A determined effort was made to reproduce the New England Way in pristine form by Abraham Pierson and Robert Treat in Newark. The Newark associates—like those of Massachusetts Bay—had adopted a covenant, voluntarily subscribed and morally binding. It, too, embodied the Puritan's notions of good and evil, society and damnation. A Puritan covenant was absolute and placed opposition outside the law. In Newark the minister and his associates hoped to attain, above all, a harmony that no longer seemed possible in the New Haven Colony they had departed. As in early Massachusetts, the minister and the magistrate, the elder and the selectman, the tithingman and the constable would act as the "watchmen of the Lord." Parents would safeguard their children from evil, and neighbor would watch over neighbor. This projected Zion, with its bleak emphasis upon damnation and its concern with salvation, was not destined to succeed in New Jersey any more than in John Winthrop's Massachusetts or in John Davenport's New Haven.

The Reverend Pierson, a Cambridge-educated Yorkshireman, had been minister at Lynn, Massachusetts; then, unhappy with the liberal tendencies there, he had moved to Southampton, Long Island, and finally to Branford, New Haven Colony. An unshakable Puritan, he was at home in John Davenport's orthodox New Haven Colony, where only church members were admitted to freemanship. But when John Winthrop, Jr. connived to annex New Haven Colony to Connecticut, Pierson, in company with Robert Treat of Milford, left for Newark. Treat and Pierson united in organizing Newark as a refuge for orthodox Puritans, with freemanship reserved to the elect. Treat himself was elected one of Newark's two magistrates and as township secretary had great influence in screening those admitted to the town. In 1673, this respected and illustrious man returned to Connecticut, where he was to serve long terms as governor and deputy governor.

The Newark church flourished. In 1669 Pierson's son Abraham, first of a succession of Harvard graduates, was elected assistant pastor and, on his father's death in 1678, his successor. He was granted a good salary (£80), free firewood, and exemption from local taxes. Unhappily in 1687 the taxing of all residents was "desisted from," with the result that the younger Pierson returned to Connecticut. With others he founded the Congregational college at New Haven, later Yale University, and he was chosen its first rector. He was succeeded in Newark by John Prudden of Milford whose father, also a minister, was a founder of Milford. Prudden was a Harvard classmate and close friend of the younger Pierson. Since his salary, on the voluntary basis, was only £50, after eleven years of relative privation he resigned to found a much-needed school. His successor, John Wakeman of Fairfield, also a Harvard graduate and son of a minister, served from 1700 to 1704, dying prematurely. His death was eulogized by the great Cotton Mather. So popular was Wakeman's ministry that a gallery was added to accommodate the congregation, and his salary was increased to £80.

Elizabethtown was never so solidly a Puritan community as Newark, though for forty years its meetinghouse, built in 1671, was the only religious edifice. There was no regular minister until 1668, so that the services were conducted by the deacons. Then Jeremiah Peck, Harvard-trained and minister at Guilford, served for a decade until called to Greenwich, Connecticut. His place was taken by Seth Fletcher, the Southampton minister, who met an untimely death two years later. Fletcher was remembered for his hysterical attacks upon the Quakers, whom he believed to be engaged in a conspiracy to create a vast hegemony in America centered in New Jersey and Rhode Island. He confided his fears frequently to Cotton Mather.

The Elizabethtown pulpit remained vacant until 1687. With the departure of Woodbridge's preacher about the same time, there was no minister in East Jersey save Abraham Pierson, Jr., a situation deplored by the incoming Scots. The Elizabethtown vacancy was finally filled by the Reverend John Harriman of East Haven who, like Fletcher, had preached at Southampton. A man of many talents, Harriman was at Harvard with Pierson and Prudden and was later appointed a surveyor by the Connecticut General Court. His career in East Jersey was notable, for he not only served as minister until his death in 1708 but was elected to the Elizabethtown town council and the East Jersey assembly, eventually becoming speaker. All the while he cultivated his 100-acre farm, ran a flour mill, a cider press, and a glass business, and dealt in real estate. He also founded a school where a score of pupils were taught reading, writing, and the practical arts.

Woodbridge and Piscataway, too, attempted to establish churches. These smaller communities had financial difficulties in attracting ministers. Woodbridge offered a salary of £40, then £50, but in vain. Finally in 1677 James Allin, Harvard-educated and the son of the Dedham, Massachusetts minister, accepted the post. While in England, he had lost his church under the Non-Conformity Act of 1662, and at the time of his Woodbridge appointment he was studying medicine in London. After serving at Woodbridge for five years he was succeeded by Archibald Riddell, a survivor of the pest-ridden *Henry and Francis* expedition of 1685. This first Scottish minister, after five years, returned to Scotland. His successor Thomas Shepard, son of the famous Cambridge divine, was persuaded to fill the vacancy in 1695, but he departed in 1704 because his wife, the former Alice Parker of Boston, was "so advers to Setling in such a poor place." Shepard was a tolerant man, permitting George Keith, then an Anglican minister, and others to use the Congregational meetinghouse.

At Piscataway the lead was taken by the Baptist group originally from Maine. John Drake and Hugh Dunn, "an exhorter," had early preached there, and in 1689 Thomas Killingworth, the pioneer West Jersey Baptist missionary, visited the town. We know little of the early Baptist ministry at Piscataway, regarded as the font of that denomination in New Jersey. In 1700, when one Edmund Dunham broke with his fellow worshippers during a familiar squabble among Baptists over whether Sunday was the true Sabbath, he and others laid the foundation of a Seventh Day Adventist church, the first in New Jersey.

The efforts of the Puritans to establish a new Zion in East Jersey failed because of the heterogeneity of the populace. The inhabitants, too, were well aware of the proprietors' guarantees of religious liberty. Moreover none of the proprietary governors or early royal governors were Puritans, and the assembly was less and less dominated by Puritan influences. The rulers of Newark made strenuous efforts to preserve the Puritan orthodoxy by forbidding "foreigners" to lease or buy a home there or even remain in town without a permit. Soon, however, settlers were being admitted without even signing the Fundamental Agreement, and by 1700 church dues could be levied only with the consent of the taxpayer. In 1713 specially called town meetings transacted the business of the church in behalf of the members, and after the congregation split over the issue of Presbyterianism, neither faction cared to entrust its interests to the town meeting.

In the other towns the citadel fell more easily. In Elizabethtown, Governor Carteret through purchase became an associate soon after his arrival. Then and there the ideal of a Puritan town was lost. The Reverend Seth Fletcher labored to keep out Quakers, but the provincial law stood in his way. The accounts of John Harriman reveal that by 1704 the minister was paid on a voluntary basis. In 1703 George Keith, the first Anglican missionary, preached at Elizabethtown, and in 1706 the Anglicans laid the foundations of old St. John's Church. In 1711 an Anglican missionary named Thomas Halliday reported great success in converting Quakers and Anabaptists but confessed that the Congregationalists were too confirmed in their ways. By 1717, when its congregation adopted Presbyterianism, the Elizabethtown Congregational church was completely divorced from town government.

In Woodbridge, a poorly circumstanced town, religious conformity was doomed. In 1695 one William Webster, a Quaker, mounted a campaign against compulsory support of the minister, and in 1700 the town meeting freed Quakers from paying church dues. Thereafter support was by voluntary contributions only. In Middletown and Shrewsbury, where there were Quakers and

Baptists from the start, there is no record of compulsory support. Likewise Bergen, the Dutch town, and Perth Amboy, the Scots town, relied upon voluntary subscription. The latter, as the provincial capital, supported a Presbyterian kirk, but with the appearance of wealthy "Yorkers" on the Board of Proprietors and, after 1702, of royal governors and other English officials, Anglicanism flourished.

During the latter years of the proprietorship, the Congregational churches were subject to Presbyterian influences. To the Congregationalist the Puritan church was based upon the individual congregation, while to the Presbyterian the church universal transcended it. To the Congregationalist the control of membership was all-important, with the congregation alone deciding whether the candidate had received true "saving faith." The Congregationalist also held that only the congregation could ordain its minister, while the Presbyterian believed that the pastor was a minister of the church universal. The Presbyterians held that the elders, men peculiarly fitted, were the voice of the congregation and, with the minister as moderator, exercised the "power of the keys" in the name of the church universal. The Presbyterians were less restrictive regarding membership, believing that the Lord's Supper was meant to be participated in by most of the congregation, whereas in the Congregational church, where few had achieved the "saving grace," it was celebrated less and less frequently.

The two also differed widely regarding church governance. Although the Congregational churches convened councils, their findings were not binding on the congregation, while the Presbyterian churches were gathered into "courts" called presbyteries and these into higher "courts" or synods. In England, where central organization was imperative, Presbyterianism gained rapidly within the Puritan church. In New England, where the need for unification was not so pressing, no one wished to carry the difference to the point of separation, though as early as 1642 men like Francis Doughty were driven from Massachusetts for their Presbyterian views. The opposing parties were finally brought together in England, where in 1690–1691 a plan of union known as the "heads of agreement" was formulated,

with Increase Mather representing the New England church.
The Congregationalists won an important point: the decisions of
the church councils or courts were recognized as advisory only.
However, the equally important right of ordination was taken
from the congregation and delegated to a council of ministers.
Conciliation was achieved by permitting the congregation to
decide for itself whether it would have ruling elders, and each
was allowed to formulate its own rules of membership. In New
England, because of theological squabbling, the plan of union
was lost sight of—to the chagrin of liberal Congregationalists
who were dedicated to the proposition that "Congregationalists
and Presbyterians were brothers under the skin."

By 1700 new forces were at work in America, especially in the
middle colonies, that were to effect major changes in church
polity. The impetus came from Scotland and Ulster. During the
sixteenth century, with the adoption of the Calvinist Confession
of Faith by the Scottish Parliament, the General Assembly of
laymen and clergy proceeded to organize the congregations into
presbyteries and the presbyteries into synods. The Scots accepted
this system as the only means of coping with the oppressions of
the crown and the aristocracy. Wherever the Scottish church
went—first to Ulster, then to the American colonies—it carried
with it this powerful, centralized ecclesiastical governance. In
England the Reformation took a different course, for under
Queen Elizabeth the Anglican creed was fixed by the Thirty-
Nine Articles that the Scottish James I, to the disappointment of
the Presbyterians, refused to abandon. Thereupon began the
national church of England. Diehards like Robert Browne
espoused separatism and formed separatist congregations. The
main body of the Dissenters, the Puritans, decided to strive in
concert to change the system. Failing in this, they would
emigrate.

With the founding of Massachusetts in 1629 the Puritans,
controlling the civil government, saw no need of adopting the
Presbyterian system. They simply decreed that none save
communicants could vote and that no new congregation could be
founded without the consent of the neighboring churches. In
1648, under the Cambridge Platform, the ministers and elders

ruled that if any congregation proved obstinate, its magistrates could use their coercive powers. This pronouncement took care of recalcitrants like the Brownes, Roger Williams, and Anne Hutchinson. To the congregation was reserved a large degree of independence: each church chose its own pastor, teacher, and elders, and these men were accorded full authority. In time the rule of the elders was challenged, since "free-born" Englishmen everywhere were to question such a large surrender of individual rights.

As the settlers fanned out beyond the borders of Massachusetts, changes were manifest. Thomas Hooker, Connecticut's founder, granted the franchise to some who were not full communicants. In freer Connecticut too there was more willingness to consider adjustments; thus in 1703 its churches adopted the Saybrook Platform enabling neighboring churches to form consociations with some power over congregations and ministers and to unite for the purpose of ordination and licensing. The consociations stressed mutual assistance, not, as in the Presbyterian system, the disciplining of congregations.

With the drift of settlers into Long Island, Westchester, and East Jersey, Congregationalists suffered from handicaps in that they lacked central guidance. The duke's government of New York and that of the East Jersey proprietors could hardly subscribe to the support of the church. Nor could the New Jersey Puritans hope to control the government, as in Massachusetts. Thus a stronger form of church organization was needed. Leadership and assistance came from an unexpected source, the newly formed Presbytery of Philadelphia. Francis Makemie, a Scotch-Irish minister, with the encouragement of Increase Mather, convened a meeting of seven ministers in Philadelphia in 1706. The second meeting was deemed a presbytery, with the assumed right to require the minister's attendance. All factions were satisfied, the Scotch-Irish because Presbyterian standards were adhered to and the Congregationalists because the presbytery did not violate the Heads of Agreement. Makemie's dramatic acquittal in New York in 1706 of the charge of preaching without a license enhanced the status of Presbyterianism in the middle colonies. Since these churches could not affiliate with the government-established churches of New England, they turned naturally to the Philadelphia Presbytery, soon designated a synod.

The isolated little congregations of East Jersey early sought membership in the presbytery because they realized they could not stand alone. In Newark, the New England Way gave ground grudgingly, but by 1706 a majority favored the stronger type of organization. The farmers on the outskirts, unreconciled, finally withdrew, forming the Mountain Society that flourished for thirty years before joining the New York Synod. When the New Jersey congregations joined the Philadelphia Presbytery, they had no notion of embracing the highly centralized system of church governance. Fortunately Makemie gave them assurances; thus, for a time, they thought of the presbytery as akin to the consociation of Connecticut, with limited power over the individual church. All this was to be scuttled when, from 1718 to 1730, the Scotch-Irish poured into Newcastle and Philadelphia during their great migration.

The Dutch population of New Jersey after 1675 enjoyed a noticeable growth. As the Indians were pacified and no longer constituted a problem, new lands were thrown open, and thousands of acres were made available on the upper Hackensack and Passaic above the swampy meadowlands. Speculators like Sandford, Kingsland, Berry, and Governor Carteret hoped to attract Dutch settlers from nearby Bergen, Long Island, and New York. Nor were these owners disappointed, for within a decade they had disposed of much land. Dutch villages grew up as settlers moved in from Manhattan, Harlem, Brooklyn, and other Long Island towns. A number of French Huguenots from Harlem joined them. Land was cheap and fertile, with easy transportation by water to the Puritan East Jersey towns and to New York City. The Raritan Valley, a second Mecca for the Dutch, was opened up when John Inians began to develop the 10,000 acres he had purchased near his ferry at Raritan (New Brunswick).

Deeply religious, the Dutch early formed congregations. At first some endured a hard day's trip from Hackensack-Passaic to Bergen to worship, while others depended upon the infrequent visits of preachers from New York. Soon congregations appeared at Hackensack, Aquackanonk, and Old Tappan, followed by others at Raritan, Six Mile Run (Franklin Park), Schraalenburgh (Bergenfield and Dumont), Paramus, and elsewhere. The earliest churches were plain and octagonal in shape, following in design the Albany church—"the shape being mostly that of an eight-cornered mill"—built by order of the patroon, Kiliaen Van Rensselaer. The first New Jersey churches, Bergen in 1680 and Hackensack in 1696, were octagonal, a style employed in Calvinist churches in the Low Countries.

The Leisler Rebellion of 1689–1691 in New York had repercussions among the East Jersey Dutch. A number of Leisler's Dutch and Huguenot followers fled to New Jersey, for in supporting him they were led to believe that they were espousing the Glorious Revolution of 1688. Conversely, since the Dutch aristocrats and their pastors had opposed Leisler's outburst, New York's Dutch preachers were no longer welcomed in East Jersey. Those of Hackensack courted the poor, pious Dutch teacher from Manhattan, William Bertolf, befriending him and ultimately bearing the expense of sending him to Holland for ordination. He was the organizer of the Dutch congregations in East Jersey.

The Friends, who constituted the majority of West Jersey settlers, were closely knit through their meetings of worship and their monthly and quarterly meetings for business. Policy decisions were made by the Burlington-Philadelphia Yearly Meeting, whose authority was supreme. Thus West Jersey Friends were kept well informed on all matters of importance, lay and spiritual. Basic concepts were renewed, fortified, and redefined by the society's leaders. Close attention was given all matters that impinged upon daily living—morality, rectitude in business, attire, care of the poor, and the education of youth, to cite a few. There were not only meetings for worship, but meetings for men, women, and youth.

The settlement of West Jersey can be traced through the establishment of the meetings for worship. The land was soon dotted with Quaker meetinghouses, satisfying in their simplicity. Plain in appearance, modest in size, these rectangular structures were built of pine or cedar and later of brick or stone. The

Stony Brook Meetinghouse of the Society of Friends, Princeton, founded 1726.
Courtesy of Alan W. Richards, Princeton, New Jersey.

interior was ceiled with boards and furnished with long benches cushioned with brown holland. Those in charge sat in front on a slightly elevated platform. With the passage of years a grove of trees relieved the plainness of the exterior, and the well-ordered burial ground added to the dignity of the meeting.

Salem, Burlington, and, after the arrival of the Irish Quakers, Gloucester organized the first meetings for worship. Soon there were indulged meetings for those who had taken up lands too far removed from the village. The earliest meetings were held in the houses of members, later in the meeting house, the fruition of years of patient planning. The monthly meeting directed all secular affairs. The Salem Monthly Meeting was organized in 1676, that of Burlington in 1678, and that of Gloucester in 1682. The Burlington Meeting early sanctioned meetings for worship on the Rancocas, at the Falls, and at Cooper's Creek, fifteen miles below Burlington. With the coming of more than one hundred Irish Friends, the Cooper's Creek meeting was shifted to Newton, where a monthly meeting was sanctioned by Burlington Quarter in 1686.

As early as 1685 the trend of settlement was apparent. The colonists from Assinpink to Alloways creeks sought the rich stream bottoms and avoided the marshy lands bordering on the Delaware. By 1698 the path of settlement to the north had reached Stony Brook, a fork of the Millstone near Princeton. To the east, in both Burlington and Gloucester counties, settlement was abruptly limited by the pine barrens of the interior. Eventually three villages ten miles inland—Pemberton, Vincentown, and Medford—marked the outposts of settlement. Mount Holly Meeting, on the upper Rancocas, later became famous as the home of the saintly John Woolman.

Newton Monthly Meeting was the parent meeting of the middle area from Pennsauken to Oldman's Creek. During the eighteenth century Newton was to lose in importance to Haddonfield Meeting, founded in 1695. Salem, of course, was the focus for the expansion of settlement in the far south. Its monthly meeting antedated that of Burlington, and its quarterly meeting was as old. As settlers moved out of Salem new meetings sprang up. To the north of Salem the movement was sluggish because this area along the Delaware was occupied by the residual Swedish population. In distant Cape May a meeting for worship appeared as early as 1700, and eventually others were organized on the coastal side of the pine barrens as far north as Little Egg Harbor.

The first Yearly Meeting of the Society was organized in London in 1678. Friends along the Delaware soon felt the need for a central organization, with the result that a committee of prominent Friends including Penn, Olive, Jennings, Budd, and Mahlon Stacy originated the Burlington-Philadelphia Yearly Meeting in 1685. Until 1784 when it was "settled" exclusively in Philadelphia, it alternated between the two places—a tribute to the historic primacy of West Jersey Friends. The relative strength of the several Quaker communities associated with the Yearly Meeting can be gauged by the assessments laid upon the several quarterly meetings in 1696: Philadelphia, £10; Bucks, £4; Chester, £4; Burlington, £5; Gloucester and Salem, £3; and Shrewsbury, £1 10s.

Unlike the Calvinists, the Friends did not emphasize a highly educated ministry. Their ministers or "public Friends" were deeply religious laymen who felt a call—a manifestation of the "inner light"—so compelling that they traveled without compensation from meeting to meeting to give testimony. Many of their ablest men were public Friends; even the boisterous Samuel Jennings was counted among them.

The cardinal virtues extolled by the early Quakers, wrought from suffering and persecution, still challenge the imagination. The Children of Light, as they called themselves, recalled to men and women at a crucial time the necessity for exercising brotherly love and kindness, human dignity and liberty, plainness and simplicity in living, and peace among men. In colonial West Jersey the experience of those "in scorne called Quakers" was not only an affirmation of faith in the essential liberty of conscience but also a reminder that "when men and women meet to wait on the Lord, they depart strengthened and refreshed together."

In the waning years of the seventeenth century George Keith, a Scot, caused a rent in Quaker unity that had grave repercussions in America. His defection was a serious blow, coinciding with attacks upon Quaker hegemony in West Jersey and Pennsylvania.* Keith was forty-six years of age in 1682 when he arrived in East Jersey as surveyor general, appointed by his friend Governor Barclay. He was a highly educated man, steeped in philosophy, mathematics, and the ancient languages. Deeply religious and seeking a faith divorced from worldliness, he had espoused Quakerism, which—though vague to him—promised a God of Love, with emphasis upon a fellowship of man with man. For his faith, he had suffered fines and imprisonment in Scotland, thus winning the admiration of William Penn, George Whitehead, and other Quaker leaders. Keith was primarily a theologian and a questioning disciple, fascinated with the notion of reducing Quakerism to theological orderliness; by contrast, William Penn was a pragmatist and Robert Barclay a humanist.

The religious diversity of East Jersey alarmed Keith, and he resented the "Airey Notionists" among the Friends themselves. In 1689 Keith left East Jersey for Philadelphia, the font of Quakerism in America, ostensibly to preside over the Quaker school there. By 1690, although he did not seem to realize it, he was attempting to reform the tenets of Quakerism, moving away from a sole dependence on the "inner light" to a larger emphasis upon the authority of the Scriptures. But when Keith proposed the adoption of articles of creed, his suggestions were coolly received. Yet his skill in confounding its enemies made him valuable to a sect that by now had little taste for the rough and tumble of debate. Nevertheless the opposition mounted. Some feared Keith's dogmatic subtleties, while the more conservative believed him capable of jettisoning the keystones of Quakerism. Attacks were made upon him in the meeting for worship, and in January 1692 at the Philadelphia Monthly Meeting Keith and his followers withdrew, protesting that Keith was denied the opportunity of defending himself. Keith then published *A Plea for the Innocents*, printed by his staunch adherent William Bradford, the first printer in the middle colonies.

---

* The best account of Keith and the Keithian heresy is found in Ethyn W. Kirby's readable biography *George Keith* (New York, 1942).

This disturbing quarrel came before the Yearly Meeting in September in Burlington when the public Friends submitted a testimony against Keith. Among the signers were William Cooper and Thomas Thackary, two prominent West Jerseymen. Keith defended himself ably, but no bridge of reconciliation was found. The Keithians, a fourth of those present, withdrew as the meeting resolved, condemning his "evil Practices and Wicked Separation," that it "could not have unity with George Keith." An epistle denouncing him was sent to London Yearly Meeting and to monthly meetings throughout America. Keith then founded the Christian Quaker sect, a mixture of Calvinism and Quakerism, that met with indifferent success. He decided to plead his cause in London before the leaders of the Society. His friend Bradford had had enough of wrangling and embarked upon an eventful career as a printer in New York City.

Keith's mission to London was a failure, for he had overlooked the Friends' love of unity and their cold implacability toward apostasy; in fact, Philadelphia Yearly Meeting had testified that Keith had "trampled their judgment as dirt under his feet." At the London Yearly Meeting of 1693 Keith was censured, and in 1696 the London Meeting disowned him. He founded a meeting of Christian Quakers in London that attracted throngs but few Quakers. The same year, Philadelphia Yearly Meeting reported that the Keithians were fewer and had splintered. A number, influenced by the appeals of William Penn, returned to the fold. Others, like George Hutcheson, a West Jersey follower, attacked the public Friends at the Yearly Meeting at Burlington in 1697 but to no avail. Keith's apostasy, however, left scars.

The Anglician Church at the close of the seventeenth century became a church militant, waging war against deism and teaching a positive Christianity. It would stand erect, without benefit of fine, persecution, or official sponsorship, and it would carry its message to the people. In 1699 the Society for the Promotion of Christian Knowledge (S.P.C.K.) was organized, and the church set out to regain its lost membership.

George Keith had all along insisted that religion must be clothed with authority, and here he sensed an opportunity. A number of influential clergy were convinced that he could play an important role, especially in winning back the Quakers. With the assent of Henry Compton, Bishop of London, who was in charge, Keith was courted. At the first meeting of the S.P.C.K. his zeal was praised, and it was decided to enlist him in the church's efforts in America. In 1700 Keith joined the Anglican Church and was ordained a priest.

Meanwhile the remarkable Reverend Thomas Bray, at the request of Governor Nicholson, was sent to Maryland as commissary.* His report on the state of the church in America led to the formation of the renowned Society for the Propagation of the Gospel in Foreign Parts (S.P.G.) in June 1701, with Thomas Tenison, Archbishop of Canterbury, as president. It recommended that missionaries be sent who were able to cope with the hostility of Dissenters. The Society must also assume the costs, else the Quakers, with their unpaid ministers, would regard its missionaries as hirelings.

Bishop Compton then invited influential churchmen in America to contribute their views; among them were Colonel Joseph Dudley, governor of Massachusetts; Colonel Lewis Morris, the most prominent New Jersey layman; and Keith himself. Dudley urged that missionaries be sent to the Jerseys, Pennsylvania, Rhode Island, and the Carolinas. Unless they were mature men, he added, they would be held in contempt. Morris, who confined his comments to East Jersey, wrote with characteristic hyperbole, "The young people, because of a lack of concern, were debauched and ignorant." He recommended that none but churchmen be appointed governors, councilors, or magistrates! Keith, concerned with winning back the Quakers, stressed the need for missionaries and churches.

On February 27, 1702 Keith was appointed the first S.P.G. missionary, with instructions to make a study of colonial needs. As a consequence, the Society decided eventually to send three missionaries to the Jerseys, three to Pennsylvania, and one to

---

* A commissary, though endowed with far less than full episcopal powers, had a general supervisory authority over the church and clergy. The first American commissary, appointed in 1692, was the colorful James Blair of Virginia.

Rhode Island, all Quaker strongholds. With Keith's aid it hoped to win them back, an ambition the Quakers were determined to thwart. After three months in New England, Keith in October 1702 was preaching in the middle colonies. The Quakers, alarmed, sent their "traveling ministers" to trail him and counteract his influence. The combatants rushed into print, with Bradford placing his press at Keith's disposal. In November Governor Nicholson called a meeting of churchmen in New York City to plan grand strategy. It was agreed unanimously that the church was severely handicapped in her ability to ordain candidates for the ministry. They requested, for the first of many times, the appointment of a suffragan bishop for the colonies—a plea that was never honored.

When Keith preached the first sermon at the newly erected St. Mary's in Burlington, he wrote optimistically that plans were afoot to build churches at Perth Amboy, Newcastle, and Chester. Under the patronage of Governor Nicholson he traveled into Maryland, Virginia, and the Carolinas, working indefatigably. In June 1704, after two years, he returned to England. Now too old for preferment, he was granted a modest living and spent much of his time on S.P.G. matters, dying in 1705.

En route to America in 1702 Keith had enlisted as his assistant the ship's chaplain, one John Talbot, who accompanied him everywhere. On his departure Keith recommended that Talbot be made minister of St. Mary's, the only church in New Jersey. Since the slim congregation was unable to provide its share of support, £50 per annum, it was not until 1706 that Talbot became the fixed minister. As was to be expected in an intolerant age, he took a prejudiced view of the Quakers, Presbyterians, Congregationalists, and Baptists. He actually charged that the Quakers would take to the sword when they were strong enough! Talbot was assisted by the Reverend John Sharpe until the latter was appointed chaplain to the troops at Fort George in New York City. The future seemed bright in 1702 with the appointment of Lord Cornbury as royal governor of New York and New Jersey. In the latter, churches were being projected for Salem, Hopewell, Elizabethtown, Perth Amboy, and Middletown. In 1704 and 1705, additional conferences were held in New York

City, with Talbot espousing in vain the appointment of a suffragan. Cornbury was to prove a severe disappointment; he was no Nicholson.

Keith and his successors, aided by Lewis Morris, made ceaseless efforts to establish the church in East Jersey. A valuable ally was the Reverend Alexander Innis, a Scottish Anglican who was denied the backing of the S.P.G. because he was suspected of Jacobite* leanings; for years Innis had been conducting services in the East Jersey towns.

Though Morris insisted that there were only twelve communicants in all East Jersey, baptized members could be counted by the score. From earliest times there were church followers in Elizabethtown, Piscataway, Woodbridge, and Perth Amboy, just as in West Jersey there were Anglicans in Burlington, Salem, and Crosswicks (Chesterfield). As a result of Keith's zeal there were stirrings at Elizabethtown, Woodbridge, Shrewsbury, Middletown, and Freehold. Talbot took up the work where Keith left off, and in 1705 East Jersey received its first S.P.G. missionary, the Reverend John Brooke, stationed at Elizabethtown. Innis plowed his lonely furrow until his death in 1717, obtaining sites for churches at Middletown and Shrewsbury and sponsoring the formation of a congregation at Freehold. He bequeathed his small estate and his library to the church. Anglicans in East Jersey owed a great debt to the labors of Keith and Innis.

During the 1680s, impetus to the growth of the East Jersey Baptists came from the south. A Baptist group at Cohansey (Greenwich) was led by Obadiah Holmes, son of the great New England preacher of that name, but it was Thomas Killingworth, an emigrant from Norwich, Connecticut, who organized the first congregation. As a missionary he was in close touch with Elias Keach and John Holmes of the Philadelphia area, both renowned evangelists. Keach, minister of the famed Pennepack church, brought a number of south Jersey Baptists, including those of Burlington, into affiliation with his church. After Holmes moved to Alloways in Salem County in 1694, he joined up with Killingworth, and both proselytized throughout New Jersey,

---

* Followers of the dethroned James II and his descendants.

rallying the Baptists in the north. In the south, Cumberland and Cape May counties proved rewarding districts. The growth of the Baptists received its greatest stimulus with the formation of the Baptist Association in Philadelphia in 1707. Represented in this body from the beginning were the New Jersey congregations of Cohansey, Burlington, and Piscataway.

The Congregationalists, too, recognized opportunities for service in the south. In 1698 young Harvard graduates were sent to plant the seed there. With the founding of the Philadelphia Presbytery, southern New Jersey looked to it for direction. As early as 1697 a group from Connecticut founded New Fairfield, north of Cohansey, and by 1708 it was able to call a fixed minister, a young Harvard graduate. Within the decade Presbyterian congregations, all linked with the Presbytery, sprang up at Trenton, Maidenhead (Lawrenceville), Pennington, Pittsgrove, Cold Spring, and elsewhere.

Until 1690 there was a drift of Swedes from the west bank, augmenting the scattered groups that Fenwick encountered there in 1675. Though the West Jersey Swedes were welcomed at the Christina (Wilmington) Church, they pleaded for a minister. In 1701 finally the Christina rector, Eric Björk, sent Hans Stalt to be schoolmaster and reader at Penn's Neck. Not satisfied, the Raccoon Creek Swedes to the north invited Lars Tolstadious to be their minister. Until his accidental drowning, he served all the West Jersey Swedes. In 1712 Björk sent his assistant, Reverend Jonas Auren, as a replacement. Henceforth the West Jersey Swedes did not lack for spiritual guidance.

Undergirding education in New Jersey, as in other colonies, was the tradition of the Renaissance and the Reformation, with their relatively high levels of culture.* In Great Britain these standards of piety, civility, and learning had by the eighteenth century trickled down in varying degrees among the fairly literate populace. Since religion was a universal concern, devotional works circulated most widely. The rendering of the Bible into the vernacular by William Tyndale, followed in 1611 by the

---

* Lawrence A. Cremin, *American Education: The Colonial Experience, 1607-1783* (New York, 1970), especially the early chapters, contains the best general account of colonial education before 1700.

King James authorized version, were notable events. In the wake of these accomplishments appeared the great devotional books initiated by Foxe's *Book of Martyrs* (1653). The most widely diffused books in the colonies were the Bible, the *Book of Martyrs*, and John Bunyan's *Pilgrim's Progress* (1674). Works of learning such as Erasmus's *Praise of Folly*, Thomas More's *Utopia*, and Francis Bacon's *Essays* were known to the educated colonist. Before the seventeenth century was out, a stream of indigenous works had appeared—sermons, religious tracts, school primers, and almanacs—beginning with Michael Wiggleworth's *Day of Doom* (1662).

Colonial education followed the British pattern, while non-English groups such as the Dutch and Swedes, also heirs to the Renaissance-Reformation tradition, reveal similarities. All gave lip-service, if not an expenditure of effort, to the necessity of educating the young. But performance was honored in the breach rather than in the observance, regardless of provincial laws. Though everywhere the churches were involved, some ministers were not as interested in schooling as others. The Anglican Church was handicapped by the lack of a bishop to give the effort direction, while other denominations were handicapped by a lack of funds. Despite the hit-or-miss system, there was a concern for the education of orphans and apprentices, and a number of denominations evinced efforts in behalf of the Indian and the Negro. Little was accomplished for the latter until the eighteenth century because of the belief that baptism would confer freedom upon the slave. New Jersey's efforts were typical, though she was behind New England. The total achievement throughout the colonies was not great, with only twenty-three schools in all New England in 1700, eleven in New York, and three in Virginia.

In the school, the reading of the Bible was a *sine qua non*, a corollary of the Protestant tradition. A second force was the determination of parents that their children should not be reared in ignorance. The citadel of education was the family or extended household, soon followed by the neighborhood school. The child began with the ABC primer or the hornbook. From reading, writing, ciphering, and the catechism he moved on to works of piety. The petty or dame school had small, ungraded classes, and the teacher—whether the minister or a female—served on a part-time basis. The parent, the apprentice master, and the overseer of the poor were soon content to leave the substantive matter to the school while they concentrated upon moral values or the teaching of a skill or trade.

The community, the household, and the school all played roles in education, especially in New England with its compact towns where the young were in close contact with their elders. But everywhere population mobility was high, and the challenge of adjustment great. The East Jersey towns were in close proximity to New York City, and the West Jersey villages, as part of Philadelphia's hinterland, were subject to ever-freshening influences. Few flourishing New Jersey communities were far from the hustle and bustle of the New York–Philadelphia axis of commerce, destined to be one of the busiest in America. The impact of commerce, trade, and transportation at the beginning of the royal period reduced considerably the natural isolation of the New Jersey communities.

In proprietary West Jersey common school education was an aspiration rather than a reality. No comprehensive system of public instruction was established until the nineteenth century. The greatest obstacles were the diversity of nationalities and sects and the dispersion of the people from the villages to the farms. Yet, isolated or not, parents wanted their children instructed in reading, writing, and arithmetic.

The earliest New Jersey settlers came from New England. There the Puritans, determined to establish schools,* adopted the necessary legislation—in New Haven Colony in 1638 and in Massachusetts in 1647. It is not surprising that New Haven's laws requiring that children be taught to write legibly and that every town provide a teacher were imitated in East Jersey.

---

* Puritan education was dedicated to overcoming the evil will—original sin—in children. The catechism was ground into them even though they were not expected to understand it. With its emphasis upon depravity, damnation, and death, New England schooling was bleak. Regardless of the aspirations of the Puritan-oriented East Jersey towns, the New England system of schooling never took root in these ever mobile and increasingly heterogeneous communities.

By agreement with Governor Carteret the towns were empowered to set aside land for the support of schools, free of quitrent,
and several of the early town charters provided for the support of
teachers. In 1693 the Puritan-influenced assembly encouraged
the selectmen to enter into agreements with schoolteachers to
teach the three Rs to children, and in 1695 this intention was
reiterated. Lacking school buildings, the teachers taught in their
homes. This early school movement failed, however, because of
the lack of homogeneity among the settlers. And in West Jersey,
where the Puritan influence was slight, only New Fairfield
attempted to support a New England–type school.

The Dutch had similar aspirations, since in Holland, with the
backing of both state and church, every child was taught the
three Rs and the catechism. The first teaching license in New
Netherland was issued by the Classis of Amsterdam in 1637, and
in time most of the Dutch communities provided some schooling.
The responsibility for primary education was shifted gradually to
the self-governing village, and this system reached New Jersey
with a school at Bergen in 1662, before the English conquest. As
in Holland the schoolmaster, to round out a livelihood, doubled
as church reader, sexton, or court messenger. From Bergen,
especially after the Dutch migration of 1675, elementary education spread. It had the hearty endorsement of ministers like
Bertolf and those who came after. Yet schooling was handicapped among the Dutch also because of the dispersal to the
farm. The term was all too short, the hours long, and the
discipline harsh. The Dutch farmer was unwilling to release his
children during the planting, growing, and harvesting seasons.

In West Jersey the Quakers and the Swedes made efforts to
provide elementary and religious education. Though the Quaker
founder, George Fox, laid no store on an educated ministry, he
admonished parents not to neglect the education of the young;
thus in England a number of Quaker schools sprang up.* The

---

* Little notice has been given the influential Quaker primer, *Instructions for
Right Spelling, and Plain Directions for Reading and Writing True English* (London,
1673), written by George Fox and Elias Hooke. It ran through many editions,
including one printed by Benjamin Franklin in 1737. It also included sections
on arithmetic and religion.

Society of Friends urged "guarded instruction," with emphasis upon the Bible and Quaker tenets; to their credit, they also espoused free tuition for orphans, apprentices, and poor children.

William Penn encouraged common schooling for all. Convinced that the home was the font of all moral teaching, he urged parents to inculcate good in their children. More liberal than most, he was not concerned over guarded instruction as a means of preserving orthodoxy, but he held, with other Friends, that whoever learned a trade had an inheritance. A West Jersey Friend named Thomas Budd, in *Good Order Established in Pennsylvania and West Jersey*, published in 1685, proposed a program that included not only reading, writing, arithmetic, and elementary Latin, but also instruction in a trade or "mystery." Boys would be taught joinery, shoemaking, and weaving, and girls would learn knitting and sewing. Such schools would be available to all, including the poor and the orphan.

Among American Quakers piety, practicality, and philanthropy became watchwords of education. Educated men like Robert Barclay and George Keith supported Penn. The Burlington-Philadelphia Yearly Meeting through its epistles to local meetings warned against lapses in providing schooling. In West Jersey, although there are fleeting references to teachers and schools and especially to the education of orphans and apprentices lodged in Quaker homes, the maintenance of schooling proved too formidable an undertaking for the meeting. In consequence the Quaker child patronized whatever neighborhood schooling was available. The teacher in many instances was poorly qualified and taught the three Rs in his or her own home. The bequest by Robert Stacy in 1682 of Matinicunck Island (Burlington) to the town for a school to serve the First and Second Tenths was not acted upon for a long time.

The aspirations of the Swedes rose from their experience as children in the homeland. There the system of education nurtured by state and church was so successful that people were shocked if a child could not read. Even Finland, then part of Sweden, benefited. Like the Dutch, the Swedes were convinced that schooling was essential in bringing an understanding of the

Reformation to the people. The Swedish Lutheran pastor gave instruction in the three Rs and the Bible. Thus the settlers of New Sweden were loath to have their children grow up in ignorance. From the instructions given Directors Johan Printz and Johan Rising, it is obvious that the company had every intention of sponsoring schools; but little was achieved, for the ministers were few and overburdened, and the colony was declining. Even with a belated resurgence in 1655, the three ministers could do little more than encourage a primitive system of household instruction by parents. After the English conquest, as English settlers poured in, the Swedes felt themselves forsaken, and not until 1691, after years of pleading, was there a response from Sweden. Then the interest of the warlike and eccentric Charles XII was enlisted, and the famous Bishop of Skara was placed in charge. His patronage endured for forty years. Despite the arrival of ministers and teachers, the task was arduous, for the 900 Swedes and Finns on both sides of the Delaware were widely scattered. As with the Dutch, many parents neglected to send their children to the parish school, and the children, worn out with the chores of farm and house, were handicapped.

In proprietary New Jersey, with its melange of religious denominations, there was a deep concern for morality. East Jersey received its concepts from Puritan New England, where the means of enforcing moral standards was finely honed. Surveillance there was maintained through the system of "the Lord's watchmen" and public censure. Censure was dreaded, with atonement possible only through public confession accompanied by sincere repentance. In West Jersey also a high moral standard was upheld. The Quaker discipline was as strict as the Congregational, for the Quaker meeting impinged upon every facet of behavior. "Weighty Friends" reasoned with the erring member, reminding him of the discipline. The threat of being read out of meeting usually brought the offender into line. The Scotch Presbyterians, the Dutch Reformed, the Swedish Lutherans, and the Baptists also nurtured strict codes of morality. The Scotch Presbyterians, the Congregationalists, and the Quakers harbored an historic antagonism toward the Anglicans, whom they regarded as harbingers of moral looseness. Because of the power exerted by the Dissenters, proprietary New Jersey exhibited a morally well-ordered society.

In 1702 New Jersey, now united under the crown, was a relatively poor colony. Until 1738 it was to share its royal governor with New York, which had a first claim upon his time. The crown, occupied with imperial commerce and colonial defense, gave New Jersey even less attention. In imperial policy-making only New York was important. Yet this very neglect afforded New Jersey an opportunity to make large advances in self-government. Internal discord and factionalism were to be her principal handicaps.

Economically and culturally her people were backward. The initiative to provide schooling was lacking, and interest in higher learning, literature, and the arts was negligible. There was neither printer nor publisher; thus men like Daniel Leeds of almanac fame, Thomas Budd, author of *Good Order Established . . .* , and George Keith and Samuel Jennings, polemicists, turned to London or to printer William Bradford of Philadelphia for publication.

Too many of New Jersey's potential leaders were drawn off to New York or Philadelphia; even the few who remained were only part-Jerseyans, using the colony as pied-à-terre or as a refuge from political or personal misfortune. Her chief speculators, too, originated in the two neighboring cities; with their large-scale manipulations in land they contributed to the drain produced by the absentee British proprietors. In East Jersey, the removal of the public support for the minister, town by town, was perhaps commendable in one sense, but it did deprive New Jersey of its only nucleus of highly educated men.

New Jersey's inhabitants tended to exaggerate their poverty—a pretext, too often, for avoiding essential taxes. Religion was their consolation; the meeting or church their spiritual home; and the soil their staff of life. The people were tolerant, kindly, hospitable, and, thanks to strong Dissenter influences, highly moral. Only when they were outraged by absentee proprietors or exploited by grasping monopolists did their resentment overflow into violence.

6

THE UNION PERIOD, 1703–1738:
RISE OF THE ASSEMBLY

Despite the advantages of his background—he was a grandson of Lord Clarendon and a member of Parliament for sixteen years—Lord Cornbury had learned little of the art of governing. In the end the queen herself concluded that "his near relation to her . . . should not Protect him in Oppressing her Subjects." Anne's father, King William, had allowed the improvident Cornbury £10 a week; he then gave him the governorship of New York, to which the queen added New Jersey.

After a decade of confusion and disturbance in both divisions, New Jersey awaited with great anticipation government by the crown. There was hardly a faction that did not welcome the change. No one conceived that matters could possibly be worse than they had been. In many respects they were mistaken.

Cornbury first appeared in the colony in the summer of 1703. His deputy, Lieutenant Governor Richard Ingoldsby, a military man, did not arrive until the following year. Since Cornbury did not trust his ambitious assistant, New Jersey, more frequently than not, found neither in residence. Cornbury was self-centered, avaricious, and unwise. A transvestite, this "detestable magot" embarrassed his supporters and brought ridicule upon himself. On assuming his post Cornbury was forty-one years of age and married, though by 1706 he was a widower.

New Jersey's historic factionalism came to the fore immediately in a fierce contest to win the governor's favor, for the colonial executive enjoyed substantial powers. In East Jersey, the "Scotch" proprietary clique centered about Perth Amboy was led by Dr. John Johnston, a wily old man susceptible to bribery; George Willocks and Thomas Gordon, two highly successful placehunters; and the wealthy, strong-willed, always independent Lewis Morris. All supported the East Jersey Board of Proprietors' monopolistic policy of high-priced lands. Opposition to the resident proprietors came from the group of English proprietors headed by William Dockwra, long-time secretary and register, and from Peter Sonmans, son of the Dutch-born Arent Sonmans, who in his family's name claimed $5\frac{1}{4}$ of East Jersey's 24 shares. Sonmans soon presented himself in New Jersey as a troublemaker. The Dockwra group, abetted by Sonmans, wanted quick profits; hence they urged the rapid disposal of proprietary lands through the distribution of large land dividends. This faction cleverly allied itself with the Nicolls patentees of Essex and Monmouth counties. The Dockwra group was willing to forgo the ejectment of settlers claiming under Nicolls's patents providing they paid their quitrents. This concession was calculated to allay the anxiety of many small owners who held warrants, but no proprietary titles, to lands. With a popular following, the Dockwra-Sonmans faction could aspire to make its weight felt in the assembly.

In West Jersey similar factions appeared, striving for the governor's favor and for power in the assembly. The West Jersey Society joined forces with the Scots proprietors of East Jersey in support of high-priced lands. It also allied itself with the strongly organized Quaker bloc that controlled the Council of Proprietors under Samuel Jennings and Thomas Gardiner, Jr. The Quakers themselves needed aid in safeguarding their right to vote and sit in the assembly and in extending these privileges to office-holding and sitting on juries. They were still suspect in official circles because of their refusal to bear arms, to support the crown's defense measures, and to take oaths, especially that of allegiance.*

---

* Despite Cornbury's instructions, not until 1729 were Quakers permitted to substitute an affirmation for the oath. Even in that year Governor Montgom-

The West Jersey Anglican faction was led by Colonel Daniel Coxe, son and heir of the former chief proprietor, and the old, anti-Quaker coterie that included Jeremiah Basse, Thomas Revell, and Hugh Huddy. This small but powerful faction strove to gain control of the Council of Proprietors and—through its East Jersey ally, the Nicolls patentee group—to thwart the land monopolists. They sought the support of Cornbury and Ingoldsby.

Cornbury, however, chose to build up a party of his own. Known as the "Cornbury Ring," it had repercussions in the colony for several decades. Ambitious both for power and money but unable to control the lower house, the governor made use of his patronage and the provincial council. The latter, intended to represent all factions, was soon filled by placemen. Young Peter Sonmans was appointed a councilor, then a justice of the supreme court. He was indeed a scoundrel, engaged in mulcting the Sonmans inheritance, then, as the proprietors' agent, in pocketing quitrents. Though finally indicted for embezzlement, he did great harm. Roger Mompesson, an able London lawyer and a favorite of Cornbury, was appointed chief justice of New York and New Jersey. Robert Quary, the ex-officio councilor, fitted neatly into the group. Like the energetic scheming Colonel Coxe, he disliked the Quakers and had fallen out with Lewis Morris. Others in the ring were the ever greedy Ingoldsby; Judge William Pinhorne of New York, related to Ingoldsby and Mompesson by marriage; Basse, the province secretary; Peter Fauconnier, province treasurer and venal land speculator; and Alexander Griffith, long-time attorney general. Coxe and Revell led the hue and cry against the West Jersey Quakers.

The ring pushed first to disenfranchise the Quakers, a move that, if successful, would allow them to dominate the assembly. Once in power, through chicanery and legislation they could stack the East Jersey Board and the West Jersey Council and force these groups to vote large dividends of land to avaricious men. The possibility of loot for the governor and his friends was

---

erie requested its disallowance by the crown. The measure was saved through the persuasiveness of New Jersey's colonial agent, the influential Quaker Richard Partridge.

enormous. The ring also scented opportunities of raiding the public purse. Though they were not entirely successful, harm enough was wrought as the game of wits unfolded in the assembly.

At the first meeting in November 1703, the Scotch faction and its allies tried to railroad through the famed "long bill," a proposal that among a number of things would authorize the proprietors to sell at auction the lands of those in arrears of quitrents—a lethal blow aimed at the Nicolls patentees. While the long bill was pending, Cornbury pressed for a revenue measure; but because the assembly's tender fell short of his expectations, he first prorogued, then dissolved it. He could now afford to wait, since New York had granted him seven years' support and other boons. From East Jersey came an unexpected windfall—the patentees' faction conceived the notion of collecting a purse "for the good of the country." This fund, the nefarious "blind tax," estimated at from £500 to £1,500, found its way to the governor.

The Cornbury Ring was solidifying. Coxe and Quary promised to protect the Nicolls patentees, to aid the Anglicans against the Quakers, and to support Cornbury's militia bill, which the Scotch faction, out of deference to the Quakers, had refused to do. In new elections, however, the land-grabbing faction again failed to win a majority. Cornbury then brazenly refused to confirm three Quakers in their seats on the ground that they lacked the property qualification. Temporarily in control, the ring forced through a militia bill that included a fine of £1 on all who would not serve, a blow to the Quakers. Next, the easy-land men, hoping to gain popularity, broadened the franchise by substituting the ownership of a freehold for the 100-acre requirement. This and other tampering was later disallowed by the crown. In 1705, however, the franchise was lowered to £50 sterling for voting and £500 sterling in personal property for membership in the house. Though the inhabitants gained, the motivation—to seat more antiproprietary men—was purely political.

Cornbury's reward was a revenue measure of £2,000, which he accepted reluctantly because of its short duration of two years.

But he had thwarted the Quaker boast that the royal governor "would be kept poor enough." A tax of £10 per 100 acres was laid on all lands, including the proprietors' unimproved lands, itself a violation of the royal instructions. The per capita levy of 6s. on every freeman was soon unpopular, because it fell heavily on the small farmer. The Scotch proprietors' group protested the tax on unimproved lands, and it was later disallowed, but by then Cornbury had spent the receipts. Since the appropriation failed to designate specific expenditures, the governor helped himself to £830 and distributed lesser amounts to his favorites.

In May 1705, when the Board of Trade ordered the reinstatement of the three Quaker members, the land monopolists regained a majority. The lower house voted to confirm all proprietary land titles, then it refused to produce a revenue measure. Cornbury retaliated by proroguing the assembly, and there was no further meeting for two years. In England, meanwhile, the Whigs gained control, and Cornbury was no longer untouchable. The Board of Trade, now at liberty to crack down, ordered him to restore Lewis Morris, with whom he had quarreled, to the council; to transmit the assembly proceedings, which he had neglected to do; to cease appointing "contemptible persons" to office; and to return to the East Jersey proprietors their records that he had seized, a power play with obvious implications.

In August 1705, when Peter Sonmans appeared with a commission to be receiver general of the East Jersey Board, Cornbury confirmed it over the Board's protest that it was improper because it depended on Sonmans's claim of $5\frac{1}{4}$ of the original twenty-four shares. On appeal, the queen in council ruled that since Peter's father was an alien, his lands reverted to the crown. Cornbury, at the time engaged with Sonmans in land peculations, did not remove him but stalled for time. The West Jersey Council was easier to handle. Cornbury simply denied its authority to function until its officers, who were Quakers, took the oath of allegiance, an illegal demand. The members of the ring then helped themselves to lands, perhaps upward of half a million acres. Sonmans, as East Jersey receiver general, and Basse, as province secretary, certified the grants. Havoc was also played with the East Jersey proprietors' lands. The New Britian tract in Essex, 170,000 acres, and the Ramapo tract in the northern Passaic–Bergen County area, 42,500 acres, were sold to speculators, some of whom, including the province treasurer, Fauconnier, were members of the ring. Sonmans was so reckless in his land-grabbing that he seized New York lands along the disputed area.

By the time the assembly reconvened in April 1707, opposition to Cornbury had hardened. Samuel Jennings, the Quaker veteran, was speaker, and he was joined by the imperious Lewis Morris, now a member, in a fierce battle with the ring. The Quaker faction and the Scotch proprietary party were joined by the representatives of the heavily taxed small landowners. The governor had the temerity to request a support bill of twenty-one years' duration. He also threatened to disqualify Quakers from membership, but the house ignored him.

Refusing to consider a revenue measure, the house launched an investigation of the "blind tax." While the struggle went on, Lewis Morris drew up on behalf of the assembly a list of grievances which Jennings, as spokesman, presented to the governor in person. Jennings's "triumph" consisted in reading the list item by item, pausing frequently to stare the governor out of countenance, a confrontation that prompted Cornbury to declare that "Jennings had the impudence to face the Devil." When the governor accused the assembly of "hawking after Imaginary Grievances," Morris told him that the queen's instructions had no validity unless she allowed colonial represent-atives in Parliament; that the assembly would be governed only by its own laws; and that if the governor refused to assent to them, they would vote no financial support whatever. This was strong talk!

At the October session, when the assembly unanimously refused to bring in a support bill until the governor acted upon its grievances, Cornbury prorogued it. Morris then dispatched to London a complete resumé of Cornbury's acts and behavior, even to his dressing daily in female apparel. Unknown to Morris, the crown had decided to replace its governor. New York was as eager to be rid of him as New Jersey, for there also he was distrusted and ridiculed.

John Lovelace, Baron of Hurley, arrived in December 1707 as Cornbury's replacement. In keeping with the Whig policy of colonial appointments, Lovelace was a military man, ranking as a colonel. The fourth assembly convened in March 1708 with a majority determined to break up the ring. Secretary Basse was indicted for perjury and Sonmans for his arbitrary actions on the bench. Mompesson, scenting his vulnerability, resigned as chief justice. When Governor Lovelace, exhibiting a friendly attitude, requested a support measure, the house ruled that whoever he nominated as treasurer, in place of the removed Fauconnier, must be satisfactory to it. In its insistence in formally confirming the new appointee, Miles Forster, the house had gained a new right—that of participating in the selection of the province treasurer. The house's awareness continued. Its revenue bill provided a one year's supply only, and it set forth the amount of the salary of each provincial officer. The house made it clear that it trusted the governor, but not the carry-over council.

In May 1709 the accommodating Lovelace died and was succeeded temporarily by Ingoldsby, the lieutenant governor. Elated, the ring moved swiftly. Ingoldsby immediately confirmed the huge New Britain patent and licensed countless Indian purchases. Patronage was the order of the day, with 198 offices,[*] large and small, going to ninety favorite henchmen. Mompesson returned as chief justice, with Coxe, Sonmans, and Huddy as associates. Morris was again suspended from the council, and the presidency was given to Pinhorne, Ingoldsby's father-in-law.

Meanwhile the War of the Spanish Succession had repercussions in America.[†] With the Deerfield massacre in Massachusetts, the crown and all New England felt that the time had come for reprisals against the French. It was decided to send an expedition against Canada made up of a British fleet and 3,000 colonials, New Jersey's share of the responsibility being to supply

---

[*] A few paid small salaries, but the large majority entitled the incumbent to small fees pertaining to the office.

[†] 1701-1713. In England and America it was known as Queen Anne's War.

and finance a cadre of 200 men. The assembly's response was indifferent. The Quakers, who despised Ingoldsby, were opposed in principle, while Lewis Morris challenged the legality of Ingoldsby's commission because the crown had neglected to renew it. The assembly proposed a minimal measure: it would furnish volunteers only and support them by issuing £3,000 in bills of credit.* This measure was unexpectedly defeated, whereupon Ingoldsby dissolved the assembly. Francis Nicholson, the expeditionary commander, highly irritated, forced Ingoldsby to reconvene it. Though a militia bill was passed, the house, following Morris's independent line, boldly designated itself as "the general assembly." Moreover, it appointed two special treasurers, one from each division, to account for all expenditures under the act and three commissioners, all members, to purchase all military supplies. Since the house also stipulated that all unspent monies must be reappropriated, there was no way for Ingoldsby to get his hands on the appropriation, so he again dissolved the assembly. The ambitious expedition against Quebec never materialized, because New York and New Jersey refused to cooperate. As a result, the crown suffered a loss of prestige in the colonies.

Through seven fateful years, from 1703 to 1710, New Jersey had experienced its initial contact with royal government. The crown had failed to provide, as optimistically anticipated, statesmen capable of healing the wounds and resolving the problems inherited from the proprietary period. To cope with the enlarged powers of the executive, the assembly soon learned that it must practice both vigilance and ingenuity. With the formation of the Cornbury Ring, all factions of the lower house accepted this necessity. Thus strange bedfellows—Anglicans and Quakers, Nicolls patentees and Scotch proprietary followers—acted from time to time in unison.

The strategy of the house, now and in the future, was to withhold financial support until the governor agreed to concessions. For example, it voted support bills for one year only, and its appropriations were for specific allocations, not a general

---

* This was fiat money, dependent solely upon the credit of the colony.

grant to the sovereign. It forced the treasurer to submit his accounts and actual vouchers to the house, thus curbing the governor's access to public funds. It also exerted strict control over special appropriations and asserted a right to participate in the appointment of the province treasurer. The avenues to embezzlement were thus closed. The representatives were also determined to thwart the governor's efforts to manipulate elections and to stack the house through preemptory disqualifications, a gross invasion of its privileges. And in case of extremity, it would refuse to meet at all. Radical men like Morris and Jennings had the temerity to question the royal prerogative itself, with the former insisting that royal commissions and instructions did not have the force of law unless confirmed by the assembly. The crown as yet did not see fit to challenge such claims; it simply ignored them. Since crown and Parliament were now involved in European power struggles that were to last a generation, colonial legislatures were enabled, during years of neglect, to build up a substantial equity in self-government.

In 1710, after an unhappy transition, New Jersey entered a long period of royal government during which she shared practices and experiences common to all royal colonies. For the most part provincial government in the colonies was limited in scope and conservative. So long as his property was protected, the ordinary citizen did not expect government to solve his problems. By the same token he relied on his own initiative and resources to cope with community problems. Few laws were adopted by the assemblies that interfered with town or county governance, and neither the assembly nor the governor interfered to any noticeable degree. Since virtual representation was not practiced in America, the assemblymen, as residents of their constituencies, truly represented the interests of their districts.

As in other colonial legislatures, the New Jersey assembly devoted its time and energies to a scant handful of provincial issues. With the possible exception of the perennial land problem, these were revenues, appropriations, currency, and defense. Appropriations, especially for the support of the government, were debated in nearly every assembly, and the means of supplying the costs of government kept the question of taxation uppermost. The governor had his instructions from the crown to consider in his dealings with the assembly. Until 1763, when Parliament became deeply involved in colonial matters, the governor relied on the colonial secretary and the Board of Trade for guidance, with the final decisions made by the Privy Council.

Closely tied to revenue and appropriations was the problem of the currency. New Jersey had no currency of her own, and what specie existed was drained away for goods either from England or, customarily, from New York City or Philadelphia. To maintain a viable currency New Jersey, like other colonies, depended upon the emission of paper money, some fiat, but mainly bills of credit that represented loans to the individual secured upon his real property. Such loans were retired through amortization. Paper money was popular, for the inhabitants believed not only that plentiful supplies of paper money were essential to their prosperity, but also that by means of this magic device they could dispense with all but a minimum of taxation. The assembly made the felicitous discovery that by using the interest from the land office loans for the support of government, it had solved the revenue problem. The crown from time to time tried to put on the brakes, but after all Whitehall was 3,000 miles away, and the crown's authorities were surprisingly indifferent, even at times negligent. Since the creditor influence in New Jersey was weak and her foreign trade of feeble proportions, opposition in the colony was not as pronounced as in the great commercial colonies. New Jersey thrived during this period of salutary neglect; and on balance the local entrepreneurs, whether in trade or in land, did share in the general prosperity that was attributed in part to paper money. With the economic depression that followed the French and Indian War, new demands of the crown, along with Parliamentary interference, brought into sharper focus the issues of revenue, appropriations, and paper money.

By 1710, the assembly had achieved a sense of awareness vis-à-vis the royal governor, whoever he was. It was learning also that by controlling the purse it could bring him to book. During the period from 1710 to 1756 the assembly hit upon a number of practices and devices by which it could thwart the governor's wishes, whether his personal ambitions or his instructions from the crown. Many, but not all, were practiced in other royal colonies. The New Jersey assembly succeeded in bringing such dealings to a fine art, and in so doing it consolidated, refined, and advanced the degree of self-government.

Richard Ingoldsby's commission as lieutenant governor of New York and New Jersey was revoked in October 1709, but his successor, Robert Hunter, did not take office until June 1710. Hunter was the ablest representative of the crown since Governor Richard Nicolls. A brilliant soldier under Marlborough and with influential friends in England, he was highly esteemed in official circles. Joseph Addison, Secretary of State for the Southern Department and one of Hunter's admirers, initiated the proposal to send him to America. Hunter was a man of distinguished appearance and attainments; and happily enough, he possessed a modest fortune.

As New Jersey's governor, Hunter steered a middle course, keeping tight rein on the council, making impartial appointments, and offering to refer the inevitable land disputes to the courts. The reactionary council immediately showed its colors by stifling important measures that originated in the house, especially one that would permit Quakers to hold office. But the council dare not oppose the support bill. It petulantly attempted to reduce the house members' modest stipend for attendance, only to suffer threats to enter all provincial salaries in the house journal and to reduce the salaries of the highly disliked Attorney General Griffith and Secretary Basse. The house also took the precaution of limiting the governor's salary to the period during which he held office. Councilor Daniel Coxe, like Governor Ingoldsby before him, charged that the Scotch-Quaker–dominated house was conspiring to reduce the governor and other provincial officers to abject dependency.

The assembly then launched a full-scale attack upon the Cornbury Ring. It demanded the removal of councilors Pinhorne, Mompesson, Sonmans, and Richard Townley, and of Secretary Basse. The governor, however, saw fit to withhold the house's indictment of Cornbury, since at home a Tory administration was temporarily in power. In the spring of 1711, in view of the council's actions, Hunter abandoned his studied neutrality and embraced the Scotch-Quaker party. He courageously recommended to the crown the removal of councilors Pinhorne, Coxe, Sonmans, and William Hall. With his Whig friends out of office, Hunter feared that his proposals would fail, and pending the outcome, he refrained from calling an assembly. However, the Privy Council accepted his recommendations. Though not successful in its attempt to have Hunter recalled, the Anglican coterie rallied enough support in high church circles to believe that eventually it would have the Quakers disenfranchised.

It was not until 1713 that Hunter felt free to convene the assembly. With a Scotch-Quaker majority, long-delayed reforms were undertaken. The assembly proceeded to confirm the governor's schedule of legal fees, asserting as a right that such fees were not binding unless enacted into law. It adopted a measure, objected to by speculators like Sonmans and Coxe, providing that deeds and other conveyances be recorded in county court books open to all. The bills of 1709, which were fiat money, were retired and exchanged for 1711 notes (also fiat) to circulate as legal tender; this provision was welcome in a community where specie was lacking. This mild easy-money legislation in time led to greater deviation from hard-money policy. Support bills were passed, one granting salary appropriations for two years and another designed to care for the province debt by making use of the surplus remaining from the 1711 military appropriation. The Privy Council, wishing to protect the governor's salary, did not disallow the act. By this time the crown authorities recognized that colonial assemblies, regardless of the prerogative, were determined to control revenue appropriations.

Governor Hunter's difficulties were eased considerably with the death of Queen Anne in 1714. She was succeeded by a cousin—George I, formerly Elector of Hanover—and the Tories, in power for four years, were ousted. Too many were suspected of being Jacobites, as indeed were a number of officials in New Jersey and other colonies. The Whigs were to maintain their hegemony for fifty years. With the death of Henry Compton, the powerful bishop of London, the project of creating an American bishopric was dropped, to the chagrin of men like the Reverend

Portrait of Robert Hunter, royal governor (1710–1719), attributed to
Sir Godfrey Kneller. *Courtesy of The New York-Historical Society.*

John Talbot of Burlington and the Reverend William Vesey of New York. The established church and Parliament slowly modified their attitude toward the nonconformists, and with the end of the war against France even the harshness toward the Quakers diminished.

With the Whig return to power, Secretary Joseph Addison of the Southern Department and Paul Docminique of the London proprietors, both strong supporters of Hunter, were appointed to the Board of Trade. The new secretary of state, Lord Charles Townshend, was also friendly. At the time the governor's enemies in New Jersey—Coxe, Sonmans, and Basse—were planning to destroy him. Actually Colonel Coxe had journeyed to London to prevent the renewal of Hunter's commission but had failed. By 1715 Hunter felt more secure. He notified the Board of Trade that he had dismissed the hated attorney general, Alexander Griffith, and had replaced him with Thomas Gordon of the Scotch party; and he took occasion to excoriate "that noisy old fool, Coxe" and Talbot, "who incorporated the Jacobites in the Jerseys in the name of a church." When Hunter learned that Cornbury had opposed his recommissioning, he submitted the assembly's charges that he had suppressed five years before.

With the backing of the Board of Trade, Hunter made a clean sweep of the council, ridding the government of the Cornbury Ring. Secretary Basse was replaced by an easy-going Englishman who appointed a deputy, while the office of surveyor general went to James Alexander, the capable Scot, a Hunter protegé. The governor's outlook was dimmed, however, when the astute electioneer Coxe and his south Jersey henchmen spread rumors that Hunter would be replaced and produced a majority in the spring elections of 1715. Claiming that the voters had been deceived, Hunter dissolved the assembly, only to witness a second, then a third Coxe victory!

Elected speaker, Coxe determined to punish the governor. The house disqualified Captain Thomas Farmar as a nonresident, thus increasing Coxe's slim majority. Nevertheless Coxe's star was waning, for his tactics had antagonized fair-minded men. Foreseeing the desertion of several members, Coxe and his cronies resolved to avoid certain defeat by absenting themselves from the house, thus assuring the failure of a quorum. The governor ordered a round-up of enough members to produce a quorum, then the pro-Hunter majority expelled Coxe for contempt and elected as speaker John Kinsey, an able lawyer and scion of an old West Jersey Quaker family. Eight other truants were also expelled, and the New Yorker, Farmar, was restored to his seat. Again Coxe journeyed to England to appeal, but to no avail. Although Hunter was worried by the threats of the Anglican clique and by the rumor that he would be assassinated, his friends in the colony and in England reassured him. Coxe never recovered politically. His land peculations in West Jersey came to an end when James Alexander was chosen receiver general of the West Jersey Council of Proprietors and Lewis Morris, named its agent by the West Jersey Society, was elected president. Coxe, Basse, and their faction in the council had for years been helping themselves to the West Jersey proprietors' lands, just as Sonmans and his clique has been mulcting the lands of the East Jersey proprietors.

The chief business of the important seventh assembly, meeting from 1717 to 1721, was to solve the fiscal problem. By now £2,000 in bills of credit were outstanding, and no revenue act had been voted for a year. Stirred up by Coxe, the inhabitants had fomented an antagonism to taxation that the representatives felt they could not assuage. Of all men, it was Jeremiah Basse, now a member from Cape May, who proposed the solution. He advocated that new bills be issued to replace those oustanding and that the new issue, if adopted, be retired systematically by means of an annual sinking fund. The house, relieved, immediately voted £4,000 in paper bills. Its members were pleased with themselves for delivering their constituents from the burden of "groaning taxes."

Hunter's last assembly met in Perth Amboy early in 1719. The house, believing that Hunter would soon be recalled and wishing to assure the voters of its concern for economy, voted the governor his salary for one year only; reduced the chief justice's salary because he resided in New York; cut the secretary's salary because he lived in England; and rejected the Board of Trade's recommendation that it appoint a colonial agent. Then it censured its treasurer, Thomas Gordon, for carelessness that was surely its own and salved its conscience by appointing two provincial treasurers, one for each division. With the skill of an experienced politician Basse put an end to some of this nonsense, whereupon he was rewarded with the attorney generalship!

In the spring of 1719 Hunter received a well-merited leave of six months, and Lewis Morris, as council president, took over the reins of government. Hunter decided not to return and arranged to change places with William Burnet, comptroller general of customs. Robert Hunter had made an able governor because of his excellent judgment. In England he was respected even during the period of Tory control because he diplomatically refrained from embarrassing the friends of Lord Cornbury. In New Jersey he refused to be badgered by the ring or by the Anglican clique. Nor was he cowed by the antics of an ever hypercritical and parsimonious assembly. He deliberately sided with the Scotch proprietary party, despite the fact that they were land monopolists, simply because there was no other organized party he could turn to. Dependence on the Quakers would have made him more vulnerable to his enemies, while a close alliance with the Nicolls patentees would have needlessly stacked the opposition. The influence of the wealthy Scotch proprietary party was not only a foil against the ring, but it gave Hunter leverage against the well-organized West Jersey faction led by Coxe. Hunter gave the assembly considerable head at times, but the only real loss to the royal prerogative was in assenting to the house's insistence in confirming the schedule of court fees. The assembly had made this a privilege of its own. Hunter defeated Coxe's efforts to prevent the assembly from meeting, and he held within bounds the assembly's proclivity for easy-money legislation. Despite all his difficulties, concludes New Jersey historian Donald Kemmerer, "he left New Jersey in the most peaceful condition it had known for decades."

Governor William Burnet was an ambitious man who had lost his inheritance through the failure of the ill-starred South Sea Company. Son of the renowned Bishop Gilbert Burnet, he was well educated, though sent down from Cambridge for idleness. Later he accumulated a noteworthy library and indulged in curious literary endeavors such as the study of the Book of Revelations. His actions were often hot-headed, though by nature he inclined toward candor. As governor of New York he fell under the influence of powerful councilors like Cadwallader Colden, Lewis Morris, James Alexander, and William Provoost, his second wife's uncle. These men warned him, as Hunter did also, that he must cultivate his assemblies since they controlled the purse. Unfortunately Burnet did not follow this advice. In New Jersey he fell out with the Scotch proprietors' leader, the unctuous Dr. Johnstone, whom he regarded as shady, and with George Willocks, whose Jacobite leanings offended him. He did not call an election but reconvened the seventh assembly. To show the governor who was boss, the Scotch-Quaker majority followed the tactic of nonattendance. Undaunted, Burnet ordered the minority to elect a speaker and proceed to business. The others soon put in an appearance.

The governor needlessly irritated the house by his strict constructionism. He insisted upon returning to the pound sterling qualifications for voting and for house membership.* The house balked, resolving that its laws were binding unless disallowed or repealed. The governor then demanded a support act extending through the life of the sovereign, as was the practice in Parliament. After a struggle, interspersed with day-to-day adjournments, Burnet announced that unless he received a five-year grant, he would not sign any act. The assembly defiantly produced a two-year support act. The council mischievously muddied the waters by presuming to amend this money bill, favoring the governor's wishes, and to curry favor with the electorate it proposed to reduce taxes. When the house refused to yield, Burnet dissolved the assembly.

Lacking support from apathetic crown authorities, Burnet finally took his brother Gilbert's advice "to manage softly." Treated more tactfully, the assembly passed a five-year support bill, then to assuage the proprietary interest it reduced the assessments on improved lands. The assembly's attitude was

---

* The assembly in Lovelace's administration had substituted provincial currency, worth two-thirds sterling, for both.

affected, too, by the governor's pleasingly objective view of a pet project, a loan office bill.

Since 1709 New Jersey had been experimenting with paper money. The people doted on it because of its convenience, because of the lack of specie, and because it represented a safeguard against deflation. First adopted as a wartime emergency measure, the advantages of having paper money in circulation were soon recognized. Since the issue of 1711 provided for retiring bills of credit through sinking fund provisions, the inhabitants dreaded the return of tight money, a fear to which the house was quick to respond. With a hue and cry raised by debtors, the house limited the interest rate in 1719 to 8 percent and in 1722 to 6 percent, and it permitted taxes to be paid in wheat at less than the market price. Creditors were alarmed, but their voice carried little weight in the lower house.

The loan office act of 1723 set up a government-operated land bank that would make loans to private citizens who put up their lands as security. A total of £40,000 legal money would be issued, £4,000 of which would be used to expunge the province debt. The remainder would be lent to applicants in amounts of from £12 6s. to £100, secured by mortgages on land and houses at interest of 5 percent.* The borrower would amortize his loan through a twelve-year period. As the annual payments of principal and interest were made, the government would destroy annually a fraction of the bills, and in twelve years the entire loan would be retired. The counties were required to stand by their quotas, which were based on wealth and population. Since the bill was a revenue measure, a nonsuspending clause was not included.† The assembly assured Governor Burnet that the plan

---

* Technically loan office certificates. The earlier bills of credit (so-called) were fiat. Both were paper money, and both were popularly known as bills of credit.

† A royal governor's instructions required colonial laws of a dubious nature to include a suspensory clause that would subject them to later review and disallowance, thus giving the crown a hand in legislation. Common illustrations were laws issuing bills of credit, laws affecting the prerogative, laws affecting external trade, and laws repealing previous laws. The assemblies tried to avoid

was workable, and the latter, who assented reluctantly, received £1,000 for "incidentals." To appease the Board of Trade the assembly thoughtfully appointed New Jersey's first colonial agent, Peter Le Heupe. On Burnet's plea, the crown did not disallow the loan office act.

In retrospect, the loan office act did help the small man for whom it was intended. In Burlington County, for example, the average loan was only £35. Few loans were forfeited, and after two years New Jersey bills were readily accepted in New York and Philadelphia. And as Jerseymen were sending more and more produce to these commercial cities, they preferred payment in Jersey bills. As legal tender they could be used to pay taxes and creditors. Since for several decades to come there was a steady rise in exports and employment, rampant inflation, feared by some, did not develop. The creditor class, having little direct dealings with London merchants, was neither large nor strong enough to oppose successfully the introduction of paper money.

In 1725 a significant corollary of the easy-money policy was adopted. The assembly, as perhaps it always intended, voted to use the unneeded interest money accumulating from the loans to pay the costs of government rather than retire the bills in advance of schedule. The assembly was thus weakening the sinking fund requirement. As the number of loans increased, the voters were convinced that their interest payments to the provincial treasury were assessments enough and regarded any increases of taxes as unwarranted. Anticipating Burnet's objections, the assembly voted him a support act of five years and £500 for "incidentals." The Board of Trade protested but as usual did nothing. Its contention that New Jersey bills would lead to credit deterioration in comparison with other colonies proved in error. Nor was there any outcry from New York or Pennsylvania, since New Jersey did succeed in maintaining some semblance of sinking fund orderliness.

The result of the paper money policy was that New Jersey's tax structure hardly changed during the royal period. The loan office arrangements took care of most of the increase in government expenditures, principally the payment of salaries and the maintenance of the assembly. Traditionally taxes were laid on goods, chattels, and land. By 1704 the land tax was £10 per 100 acres, and after 1710 there was a small per capita tax of 6s. on all freemen whose real or personal property did not exceed that amount. For purposes of taxation, various kinds of livestock were assigned values. During Governor Hunter's time, when regular appropriations for the support of the government were initiated, a tax of £10 was laid on each imported slave, though planters intending to settle could bring in their slaves free. Hunter explained that the impost on slaves was recommended because the Board of Trade wished to encourage the importation of white servants.

There were minor taxes, but only the tax on hard liquor produced any substantial revenue.* From time to time the assembly levied import and export duties. For example, export duties were laid on pipe and hogshead staves, to promote the manufacture of casks and other finished wood products, and on wheat, to encourage the farmer to grind and bolt his grain before exporting his crop. Interestingly, because of the need to compete in the Philadelphia market the western division was permitted to ship wheat and timber free of duty.

In 1718 the taxes for the support of government were apportioned among the several counties, the ratios (but not the amounts) holding for several decades. In 1726 the census revealed a population of 32,442, including 2,581 blacks, mainly slaves. Monmouth County, with the largest population, paid the highest tax, £250. The figures for the others were as follows: Essex, with 4,230 inhabitants, paid £180; Burlington with 4,216 paid £270; Hunterdon with 3,377 paid £70; Middlesex with 4,000 paid £158; Salem with 3,977 paid £195; Gloucester with 2,229 paid £117; Bergen with 2,673 paid £111; Somerset with 2,271 paid £52; and Cape May with 669 paid only £42. By 1745 Hunterdon, the fastest-growing county, advanced to 9,150 in population and was first in rank, followed by Monmouth, Essex, and Middlesex. By then Morris, a new county west of Essex with

---

* Financial affairs, 1703–1738, are discussed in detail in Edwin P. Tanner, *The Province of New Jersey, 1664–1738* (New York, 1908), 502–558.

4,400 inhabitants, was developing rapidly.* County and township taxes, principally for jail maintenance, roads, and care of the poor were not onerous and, as in the other colonies, were levied by the justices of the peace and administered by elected overseers.

Since sinking fund interest was used in maintaining the cost of government, it was increasingly difficult to muster any backing for new taxes. Actually, though the system was refined in later years, the trend was downward. Thus under Governor Burnet the per capita tax was reduced from 6s. to 4s., and occupied lands were assessed at £5 per 100 acres instead of £7. To satisfy the proprietary interest, unimproved land for the most part was assessed at only £4 per 100 acres. Taxes were paid in gold, silver, paper currency, or (more often) in wheat. The latter was valued at 5d. per bushel, less than the going New York-Philadelphia market rate.

With the death of George I in 1727 Governor Burnet was notified of his transfer to Massachusetts. He summoned a new assembly, the memorable ninth, to prepare for Governor Montgomerie's coming. Old Dr. Johnstone was reelected speaker, but it was John Kinsey, Jr., the able Quaker attorney,† who guided the assembly to new heights from 1727 to 1733. He sponsored a triennial act, contending that Parliament itself had adopted a septennial act.‡ Burnet at first opposed the measure as a violation of the prerogative, but the assembly was adamant. (The act, however, was later disallowed.) The principal business before

---

* For population figures see Evarts B. Greene and Virginia D. Harrington, *American Population Before the Federal Census of 1790* (New York, 1932), 109–111.

† Kinsey, born in Burlington, moved to Pennsylvania in 1733 where he had a brilliant career as assemblyman and speaker, attorney general, and chief justice. His influence in New Jersey politics continued until his death, appropriately while visiting Burlington in 1750. In 1732 he sponsored the first compilation of New Jersey laws.

‡ Such an act would guarantee frequent elections and force the governor to convene the assembly at regular intervals. Not until the adoption of the State Constitution of 1776 did New Jersey achieve this boon, with Article 3 calling for annual elections.

the assembly was the adoption of a support bill. When Burnet informed the assembly that the Board of Trade would no longer permit the use of loan office interest money as revenue, the legislature, to appease him, extended the period of support and voted him £600 for "incidentals." The bill was also honeyed with the provision that henceforth unappropriated interest money would be allocated by the assembly *and* the governor. Burnet advised the board that no taxes would ever be voted as long as there was unspent money on the treasurer's books and that, had he not assented to the supply act, no support whatever would be forthcoming.

John Kinsey then pushed through a fee reduction bill that was later disallowed as a violation of the prerogative. The Board of Trade charged Governor Burnet with accepting presents for agreeing to such measures. Finally the indefatigable Kinsey sponsored a proposal that New Jersey be permitted a governor of her own. The measure would have carried except for Burnet's known opposition. With so many acts up for his approval, this one was dropped for the time, but the seed had been planted. This session of the ninth assembly concluded late in 1728. Though several important measures were to be disallowed, the province had the benefit of them for four years. The idea of having a separate governor for New Jersey had taken root, and the assembly had amplified the means of dealing with recalcitrant governors.

Whereas Burnet had served for eight years, his successor John Montgomerie was in office only for two. The new governor, who did not arrive until late in 1729, was a minor courtier, wealthy and affable, and anxious to represent the king in style. Despite good advice from Hunter and Burnet he immediately fell out with the powerful Colden-Morris New York clique. Like Burnet he did not call for new elections but chose to reconvene the ninth assembly. He was soon writing home of the "impracticable Schemes" of "unmanageable Quakers" and of their utter disregard for the prerogative. He requested that the triennial act and the act permitting Quakers to substitute the affirmation for the oath be not acted upon lest he lose his bargaining position. In 1731 the board did disallow the triennial act. The house meantime again resolved to petition for a separate governor, and, failing to check this maneuver, Montgomerie dissolved the assembly without assenting to a single law. When the tenth assembly met in May 1730 with John Kinsey as speaker, Montgomerie was more circumspect, for the board had ignored his recommendations. He actually signed a support bill that permitted the use of loan office interest for support. The board, loaded with the Duke of Newcastle's indifferent placemen, neglected to follow up its former prohibition.

By 1730 New Jersey was facing economic difficulties. The loan office act had generated a prosperity that was destined to wane as the sinking fund provisions took effect. Deflation was setting in, with the usual complaints about tight money and rising prices. Again bills were introduced to ease the plight of debtors and to reduce interest rates. In May, a loan office bill was introduced which called for a paper money emission of £20,000, with an extension of the term of refunding from twelve to sixteen years and the re-lending after eight years of the principal of all monies sunk. The new measure included the by now sacred provision permitting interest receipts to be used for support purposes. The governor, in pursuance of a recent instruction, insisted that the bill contain a suspending clause. Owing to the persuasiveness of New Jersey's new agent, Richard Partridge, the Privy Council approved the act.

Montgomerie died unexpectedly on July 1, 1731, and senior councilor Lewis Morris was again acting governor. Morris endeavored to capitalize on his position by urging the Duke of Newcastle to appoint a separate governor. The duke ignored the hint and bestowed the New York–New Jersey post on William Cosby, a pretentious man with a bad reputation as governor of Malta.* Matters went badly with him when he quarreled with Morris and Alexander, both of whom boycotted the council meetings. Cosby met the assembly only once, in 1734. It endeavored to win him over to supporting its cause for a separate governor by voting him a bonus of £200. Then it repassed the

---

* Cosby's career in New York was dominated by his role in the famous Zenger case.

disallowed triennial act that, to its chagrin, Cosby vetoed. Next the assembly insisted upon confirming a new fees schedule promulgated by the governor, on the ground that unless it approved, the schedule was invalid. Though the Privy Council rejected this act, the assembly believed that by its expression of intent its views were made known in the provincial courts.

Like his predecessor, Cosby desired a generous support act. The assembly dallied, producing first another paper money bill for £40,000, even though the act of 1730 had just taken effect. Adopted overwhelmingly, it was confirmed later through the ministrations of agent Partridge. The assembly obligingly voted support through 1738 to be derived from the accumulated interest surplus, and as a concession it permitted the governor to sign the warrants for expenditures. Cosby received a bonus of £200, while Partridge and Richard Smith, a leading member who had gone to London to assist Partridge, were awarded £1,000 for their efforts. The Board of Trade all but acknowledged the hopelessness of forbidding the use of interest money for government support; indeed the money was always spent before such appropriations could be disallowed, and in any case, if they were, the only sufferers would be the governor and the other provincial officials. For a period of sixteen years, until 1751, the inhabitants of New Jersey would pay minimal taxes.

Governor Cosby died in March 1736. Assured of support for five years, he had not bothered to convene more than one assembly. Those meeting subsequently were determined that there would be no further support acts of five years' duration. Since 1730, through bribery and other means, the assembly had not only been able to force the royal governor to do its bidding, but it was able to soften, almost at will, the force of the royal prerogative. It was fortunate indeed for the American colonies that the long-time secretary of state, the Duke of Newcastle, used his high office to stack the Board of Trade and the other crown agencies with weak, lazy, and ill-informed favorites. After ridding itself of the Cornbury Ring, the New Jersey assembly had come into its own—the most singular accomplishment of the Union Period, 1703–1738.

7

ROYAL GOVERNMENT,
1738–1757

The man who succeeded Governor Cosby was to be New Jersey's most controversial leader during the royal period. Lewis Morris entered public life as a very young man in 1692 and was active for fifty-five years. He held every important office in New Jersey: assemblyman, councilor, acting governor, and governor, as well as being chief justice of New York. Highly independent, he fought on both sides of numerous issues. Fundamentally he was an eighteenth-century aristocrat who had little patience with the vagaries of the populace. He was honest and, by his lights, honorable. Morris was talented in another respect; more perceptively than others he could pinpoint essential defects in the colony's governance and in its relationships with the crown. For the most part his suggestions fell on barren ground, causing him much annoyance and confirming his belief in the incompetence of those he dealt with, whether assemblymen, governors, or crown officials. Lewis Morris loved power, but the limitations of power irked him. He was destined to be an irascible, not a great governor.

Single-handed, Morris prevailed upon the crown to grant New Jersey its own governor. He went to London in 1735 with the avowed intention of ridding New York and New Jersey of Governor Cosby, but despite his wire-pulling the crown stood by its weak proconsul. He failed also to recover the chief justiceship of New York, from which he had been removed for his part in the famous Zenger libel suit.* In England Morris made several powerful friends whom he all but alienated by his stubbornness. Sir Charles Wager, Lord High Admiral, was one. Thanks to Cosby's premature death, and to Wager's persistence in his behalf, Morris was appointed as the first royal governor of New Jersey alone in January 1738. Unfortunately he was by then sixty-eight years of age, and until his death eight years later he became more and more intractable.

Morris strove unremittingly to impose his will on the assembly and employed every weapon within his control, including the sanctity of the governor's instructions and frequent appeals to the crown and the prerogative. To combat him, the lower house used every stratagem in the book and invented new ones. These fierce internecine struggles took place against a background of unrest and rioting induced by a resurgence of the land problem and the pressing demands of the crown for military assistance. After Morris's death, his conflict with the assembly still unresolved, the province finally regained a modicum of domestic tranquility.

On his appointment Morris made two innovations, both commendable and sanctioned by English practice. Justices would henceforth be appointed "during good behavior," instead of "during the king's pleasure." The good-behavior clause, adopted in Britain during King William's reign, was intended to safeguard justices from arbitrary removal.† In the colonies it would prevent a governor from removing a justice whom he disliked, as Cosby had removed Morris himself in New York. Secondly, just as George I had ceased to attend meetings of the Privy Council,

---

* In November 1734 John Peter Zenger, printer of an anti-Cosby paper, the *New York Weekly*, financed by Morris, James Alexander, and other influential New Yorkers, was arrested for libel. Disqualified by Chief Justice James DeLancey, Alexander turned to Andrew Hamilton, the Philadelphia lawyer, to act as defendant. In August 1735 Hamilton won his case, arguing that citizens have a natural right to protest against the abuse of power. This verdict has been traditionally regarded as the landmark of freedom of the press in the colonies. More recent research has revealed the limitations of the verdict; see Leonard W. Levy, ed., *Freedom of the Press from Zenger to Jefferson* (New York, 1966), Introduction and Part I, 1–74, for documents and comments.

† In 1752 the crown instructed all governors to grant commissions "during pleasure" only, a position that was amplified in 1761.

so Morris announced that he would no longer sit with or preside over the provincial council. The upper house gained in stature, for its senior councilor, like the speaker of the house, would sign all bills. The governor lost little since he retained the veto. Now the general assembly truly consisted of governor, council, and lower house.

The eleventh assembly met at Perth Amboy in the autumn of 1738. It had not met for five years, and there had been no election for eight, a situation Kinsey's triennial bill would have prevented. Governor Morris began by lecturing the assembly, as he would for eight years. When dissatisfied with the performance of a provincial officer, he admonished, the legislators should not reduce his salary, but rather complain to the governor. Moreover, the house should not endeavor through gifts to bribe a governor to accept laws that he could not approve. The assembly's duty was to enact laws for the good of the province and to supply funds for the support of the government. Unfortunately Morris began to cavil about his own salary. He was also irritated when, with a balance of £1,800 in interest accumulations in the treasury, the house insisted upon using it as revenue to support the government. The expenditure of such funds, Morris stated, must be determined by the governor, council, and lower house. Rather than accept the support act, Morris dissolved the assembly. On appeal, the Board of Trade refused to disallow the act. Highly chagrined, Morris advised the board that the house regarded itself as the equal of the House of Commons and that it would take an act of Parliament to make it recognize its duty. The lower house, which had distributed all revenues in the treasurer's hands since the Lovelace administration, had every intention of continuing to do so.

Morris called for new elections, but despite his efforts at manipulation the assembly of 1740 staunchly opposed him. His attitude became more conciliatory, as he had been instructed to obtain an appropriation for the crown's expedition against the Spanish in the West Indies.* This adventure of 1741 was to prove

---

* England was at war with Spain, 1739–1744 (War of Jenkins' Ear), and with France, 1744–1748 (King George's War).

a fiasco, as hundreds of men perished through disease before Cartagena. The house, led by the Quaker members, procrastinated as long as possible, then brought in a bill for £2,000, to be doled out from interest fund money by "trustees" appointed by the assembly. Morris angrily accepted the measure, then adjourned the house. When it reconvened, he told the members that by ignoring the council in appointing trustees, they were acting illegally. Not impressed, the assemblymen went home, leaving only the speaker and two members to care for adjournment. Morris again appealed to the Board of Trade, but in vain. On this occasion he urged the crown to take over the loan office system in all the colonies and use the interest accumulations to pay the salaries of officials. Only in this way could it control the dangerously large issues of paper money and enable its governors to rule without dependence on the assemblies. Like his earlier proposals, this recommendation was ignored.

The twelfth assembly, which met at Burlington in 1742, was led by Richard Smith, now spokesman for the Quaker party, and two other strong men, Benjamin Smith and Thomas Farmar. They introduced a fee bill, already disallowed three times, by incorporating it into the support bill. When Morris objected, the representatives unanimously adopted a separate fee bill. The governor warned that New Jersey would be charged with attempting to make itself "independent of Great Britain." Although there was a balance of £5,000 in the treasury, the house insisted upon adopting a new paper money bill calling for the emission of £40,000 in bills of credit. To sweeten the bill the house included the required suspending clause and a poorly concealed bribe of £500 for the governor. Morris scolded the house, accepted a support act for one year only, then dissolved the assembly. The house was resolved never again to adopt a support bill, even for a year, unless the governor would agree to sign some popular measure. The Board of Trade accepted Morris's strictures with faint praise.

Though Morris appealed to the electorate in a rash of broadsides, which no former governor had ever attempted to do, the voters had little liking for his solicitude about the royal prerogative. The newly elected assembly of 1742, the thirteenth, revealed no change of attitude. Morris took the offensive, announcing that only the two branches of the legislature acting jointly could dispose of the accumulated interest monies. Rejecting his contention, the house voted paper money and fee bills, seeking to compel the governor to sign them in exchange for a support bill. The council laid the money bill on the table, whereupon the house proceeded to halve the salary of Chief Justice Robert Hunter Morris, the governor's son and a leading councilor. An attempt to reduce the governor's salary failed. After the house accepted a suspensory clause with the fee bill, the governor signed it. Morris was losing; by now he was regarded as an old scold who really did not have the interest of the colony at heart. The assembly distrusted him and was determined to punish him.

The tug of war continued. In June 1744, upon news that war between England and France was imminent, the council brought in a needed militia bill, to which the house gave only six votes. In response the house adopted a paper money bill for £40,000, to which it attached a rider for the purchase of arms. Since Morris, now seventy-four and suffering from gallstones, could not do battle, the council temporarily took up the fight. After angry exchanges, the house passed a bill eliminating the councilors' fees and spitefully halving the salaries of the governor and the chief justice. The council had insisted that the paper money act was not needed, pointing out that money for arms was available in the treasury and that many in Parliament now regarded paper money issues as detrimental to the colonies and to the well-being of the British merchants. Unfortunately, it became known that Morris had instructed Agent Partridge not to oppose a bill in Parliament forbidding colonial bills of credit to pass as legal tender.

The assemblies of 1745 and 1746 reveal the quarrel with the governor at its bitterest. When Morris sent an insulting message, the house replied that though its members were indeed "plowmen," they were not "idiots." Morris threatened to veto all legislation until he obtained a support act and a militia act. The house finally gave him both, noting sarcastically that since it was their third meeting in ten months, the members must accustom themselves to dissolutions rather than to passing laws.

Meanwhile, when Governor William Shirley of Massachusetts proposed to capture the French stronghold of Louisburg with the aid of the other colonies, the New Jersey assembly evaded the issue, cool as always to foreign adventures and their costs. On the governor's appeal, it did appropriate £2,000, to be drawn from the interest funds and to be expended only upon the authority of its own trustees. The governor complained bitterly, but in the interest of imperial cooperation he accepted the measure. Despite his threats, the assembly again surmised correctly that the crown could not afford to disallow its tender of aid.

With the Indians on the warpath in New York and a land riot under way in New Jersey, Morris pleaded once more for a stronger militia act. The house repeated that it would give him his law only if he accepted the measures it regarded as important. Vindicated by the voters in the elections of February 1746, the house forced the governor to consider its key bills. A second land riot revealed an increasingly dangerous internal situation. Unfortunately word arrived from England that the fee act of 1743 was to be disallowed, on the governor's recommendation! The house offered a penurious support bill, providing that Morris first accepted its other measures. This stance was so galling to the old governor's pride that he avenged himself by signing only the militia act, then prorogued the assembly. Reconvening, the house resolved to adjourn from day to day until the governor capitulated. On May 21, 1746, in the midst of the struggle, Morris died. His personal shortcomings—impatience and short temper—had canceled out his undoubted talents.

His successor, Jonathan Belcher, was to hold the governorship from 1747 until his death in 1757. His appointment was typical, the result of wire-pulling. Like Morris, he was a colonial; reared in Boston and Harvard-educated, Belcher entered politics as a member of the Boston élite and was several times elected to the Massachusetts council. On the death of Massachusetts Governor William Burnet, with whom he had quarreled, Belcher managed to secure the post for himself, to the surprise of even his friends. He was governor from 1729 to 1741, upholding the very policies that he had objected to in Burnet. He lost out in the end to his astute rival, William Shirley, because of his opposition to the popular easy-money measures of the assembly. Learning of Morris's serious illness, he sought the aid of his brother-in-law (New Jersey's agent, Partridge) in gaining the post. He persuaded the Duke of Newcastle that his undoubted acceptance by the New Jersey Quaker party would restore tranquility. His experience was also a factor in his appointment.

In New Jersey, Belcher anticipated the steady salary which he needed and, above all, a peaceable tenure. A trimmer by nature, he was prepared to compromise, a situation that the assembly readily took into account. In Massachusetts he had experienced the necessity of getting along with popularly elected assemblies. To the relief of the New Jersey proprietors, especially Richard Hunter Morris and James Alexander, Belcher did not disturb the old council, which had feared that a New England man might have little sympathy with the proprietors' monopolistic land policy.

In truth, Governor Belcher inherited a difficult situation. Robert Hunter Morris was a power in the council, which with Alexander he all but controlled. Alexander, a Scottish exile befriended first by Governor Hunter and then by Lewis Morris, had served variously as surveyor general of New Jersey and New York and as a councilor of both. With influential political connections through his New York marriage, he had forged ahead in New York as an able attorney and successful businessman, worth by the seventeen-forties an enormous £150,000. With Robert Hunter Morris he later researched and wrote the famous Elizabethtown Bill in Chancery in defense of proprietary rights. The younger Morris, too, was able but lacked Alexander's detached logic. Through his father's influence, he had been named a councilor and chief justice of New Jersey. Both men were powers on the proprietary boards.

Governor Belcher fell heir to New Jersey's ancient curse, her land problem. The East Jersey Board, because of the machinations of the Cornbury Ring, had been mulcted by the predatory manipulations of men like Sonmans and Fauconnier. In 1714, knowing Governor Hunter's wish that land disputes be settled by the courts, the East Jersey Board had initiated a test case that turned on the validity of the proprietors' titles to Elizabethtown lands. One Edward Vaughan held a proprietors' title, while Joseph Woodruff defended his "Clinker Lot" * survey, a title issued by the Elizabethtown associates on lands outside the original bounds of the town. In 1718 the verdict went in favor of the proprietors, prompting a number holding similar titles to purchase proprietary titles. In 1725 the board was reorganized with Lewis Morris as president, and it was greatly strengthened by the legal talents of Alexander. Under energetic leadership, it began to reassert its rights. In 1731, with fresh encroachments by the Elizabethtown associates, the board decided on a number of ejectment suits. The test case, Lithegow vs. Robinson, again involved a Clinker Lot right. The board's counsel, Alexander and Joseph Murray, was opposed by equally skilled legal talent, John Kinsey, Jr. and Richard Smith, with Chief Justice Robert Lettice Hooper on the bench. After three years of litigation the Elizabethtown patentees were upheld by the jury.

With this victory the associates took the offensive, becoming in fact a large land company in rivalry with the proprietors' board. They collected dues, guaranteed old titles, and voted to lay out 100-acre tracts in disputed lands under the guise of Second and Third Lot Rights based upon the original Nicolls patent and first settlers' agreements. Claiming that the surveys underlying these distributions were laid out by stealth at night, the proprietors responded by sending their agent, John Vail, to gather evidence for new ejectment suits. But the associates, with a steady income, were able to employ counsel and to contest the proprietors' claims in involved litigation. Nevertheless, the board persevered in its suits as its only remedy. On Alexander's advice, it decided to resume the all but abandoned practice of collecting quitrents.

---

* Holders of original Elizabethtown titles were known as "First Lot Right Men," as opposed to the later "Clinker Lot Right Men." Donald L. Kemmerer suggests that "clinker" denotes "a crafty fellow," in this case one who profited from the proprietors' difficulties by claiming title to remote land.

Through this tactic, it hoped to hold a club over the associates. The countless suits that followed brought favorable decisions but little income; thus in 1737 the board decided to dissolve its land monopoly by issuing dividends to shareholders until all its holdings were distributed. The time had come to cash in on its monopoly. Henceforth it would be the responsibility of the individual owner to defend his title to the lands allocated him.

The West Jersey Council of Proprietors, too, was subject to stresses and strains but experienced little of the popular violence that beset the East Jersey Board. Rather, its troubles grew out of the attempts of rival factions to gain control. The stakes, huge areas of undivided land, were high indeed. The West Jersey Society, monopolists who favored holding out for high prices, had succeeded in postponing additional land dividends. But, fearing that its lands would be gobbled up by the Cornbury Ring, it healed its breach with the council, and its agent, Lewis Morris, was elected the council's president.

In 1712, the astute Colonel Daniel Coxe, with the aid of Secretary Basse, manipulated matters so that he was elected president of the council, with Daniel Leeds appointed co-sur-veyor. These three, augmented by Peter Sonmans as the presumed heir of his father's West Jersey share, the venal Peter Fretwell, and other land jobbers, proceeded to mulct the council of enormous holdings. A fourth dividend under their ministrations led to the distribution of 200,000 acres. The agents of William Penn, also an original proprietor, became alarmed and intervened to restore order. The frauds of Leeds were exposed, but he was protected in the courts by "that vile fellow" Attorney General Alexander Griffith.

In 1715, when Governor Hunter overcame Coxe, Lewis Morris again became president of the council through the influence of the West Jersey Society, with James Alexander as surveyor general. When Coxe was finally eliminated, the council in 1736 was able to consider a fifth dividend of all undistributed holdings below the Falls of the Delaware. By then many new faces had appeared on the West Jersey Council.

Troublesome as these internal disputes were, the boards of both divisions had to deal with another serious problem, that of the squatter. Not only had this lawless element settled as small farmers in the area of the Oranges northwest of Newark, but ignoring the consequences they had moved westward into southern Morris and Hunterdon counties. Soon they were poaching freely on northern West Jersey lands. In 1735 Lewis Morris as the society's agent discovered that a hundred of them had plumped down on the society's 15,000-acre tract in Hunterdon. Morris forced them to sign leases, which they resented. Others called "black faces" vowed to assassinate Colonel Coxe when earlier he had threatened to dispossess them. The East Jersey Board appealed to the West Jersey Council for cooperation on the ground that both the associates and the squatters were encroaching on West Jersey lands as well as their own.

When Morris became governor in 1738, the situation in East Jersey was tense. Dozens of settlers with titles from the Elizabethtown associates stood to lose their lands, purchased in good faith, if the courts ruled against the associates. Others, claiming under titles issued by swindlers like Sonmans, were likewise alarmed. Underlying the entire situation was the bitter feeling that the rich were intent upon exploiting the poor. Through councilors appointed by Governor Morris, the East Jersey Board was able to kill any objectionable legislation, and it was widely held that the council members were influencing the ejectment cases in the courts. Despite the fact that the associates were represented in the lower house, they could not cope with the veto tactics of the upper chamber.

The proprietors decided finally to initiate a test case against the associates to settle the question of land titles once for all. If they could get it into the court of chancery, where the governor acted as presiding judge, the outcome would be predictable. Alexander and his colleague Murray began the preparation of the Elizabethtown Bill in Chancery. The associates sought to counter this maneuver by petitioning the king in council to appoint a royal commission to rule upon the dispute. Though their emissaries did get a petition before the Privy Council in 1744, no action was taken.

Meanwhile the East Jersey Board continued to harass the

Lewis Morris, royal governor
(1738–1746). *Courtesy of the New
York Public Library Picture Collection.*

Colonel Daniel Coxe. *Courtesy of
the New York Public Library Picture Collection.*

so-called Clinker Lot Right Men in the courts. Alexander began ejectment suits against those in the Van Giesen and Horseneck districts, now the site of the Oranges. The settlers, who had little to show for their lands, were forced to become tenants or leave, and by 1745 the proprietors boasted that they had cleared the land from thirty miles away to within three or four miles of Elizabethtown. Morris and Alexander were optimistic over the success of their tactics.

The Elizabethtown associates continued to sell small parcels as the need for land grew. As early as 1735 they had the temerity to offer lands in Somerset County, twenty miles from the town. A selling point was that such lands contained fine stands of timber, and since the inevitable lawsuit was subject to appreciable delay, the occupier could reap a good profit; by now East Jersey's timber, principally oak, hickory, and walnut, was in demand in New York. Many such interlopers were successful, since proprietary records were frequently lost or faulty, and there were conflicting claims under the titles issued by speculators.*

In 1745 Alexander filed the Bill in Chancery that had long been in preparation. Sixty defendants were given sixty days to answer their subpoenas. The board meanwhile continued its ejectment suits, giving rise to violence. When several claimants were jailed in Newark for cutting timber in the Van Giesen purchase, a mob freed them; and when an attempt was made to arrest members of the mob, a second riot ensued, with hand-to-hand fighting with the militia. Earlier Governor Morris had demanded a strong militia bill to quell the rioters, but the house had temporized. Samuel Nevill, defeated as speaker because he was a proprietor, was threatened with assassination for defending the proposed militia bill.

When Governor Morris died, he was succeeded in an acting capacity by John Hamilton, senior councilor, who was also

---

* In 1775 James Kinsey, the able New Jersey attorney and delegate to the Continental Congress, wrote as follows regarding early New Jersey land titles: "A person reading these Transactions can hardly suppose the Partys to have been in their senses when they executed some of the Deeds." Cf. Richard P. McCormick, "The West Jersey Estate of Sir Robert Barker," *Proceedings of the New Jersey Historical Society*, LXIV (1946), 138.

president of the East Jersey Board. He too called for a measure aimed at the rioters, threatening to appeal to Parliament to restore order, but the house rejected his plea. During the summer of 1748, when Somerset County jail was broken into by another mob, Hamilton ordered the sheriff to arrest all the rioters. At the same time, Robert Hunter Morris directed John Ferdinand Paris, the proprietors' agent in London, to urge the crown to send troops to restore law and order. Paris was a prominent London lawyer first used by Lewis Morris in 1735 in finding his way about London, then retained by the board to care for its interests there. Paris resented Richard Partridge, the colonial agent, and the two were usually at odds.

In the 1747 session of the assembly Acting Governor Hamilton again threatened action. The rioters in effect were encouraged when the house steadfastly refused to act, their attitude being that the more disturbance, the greater the possibility that the king would intervene in behalf of the downtrodden. In June Hamilton died, only to be succeeded by another ineffectual old man, John Reading. Riots came thick and fast, with jailbreaks and violence in Perth Amboy. Judge Samuel Nevill, in charge of the trial of twenty rioters, charged the grand jury of Middlesex County to indict them for high treason but got nowhere. Reading and his council again demanded the passage of an antiriot act. While the matter was pending, Governor Jonathan Belcher arrived.

The new governor promised the council that he would restore law and order. Although he told a delegation of rioters that he meant to uphold the king's authority, he left the impression that he would consider concessions. The Quakers, in sympathy with the rioters, controlled the lower house, and to them Governor Belcher felt indebted. Though opposed to the rioting, they had long been attached to the associates politically. Partridge, Belcher's sponsor in London, was allied with John Kinsey, the former speaker, Richard Smith, the governor's chief advisor, and Charles Read, an influential Burlington council aspirant. It was Kinsey, now chief justice of Pennsylvania, who was preparing the associates' "Answer" to the proprietors' Bill in Chancery.

Boundary problems, too, occupied the proprietors intermittently during the Union Period. Dormant since 1688, the date of the Barclay-Coxe agreement fixing the line between East and West Jersey, the matter was reviewed in Governor Hunter's time. The old Keith Line of 1687 ran only from Little Egg Harbor to the south branch of the Raritan. Trouble among the settlers in the disputed area prompted James Logan, Penn's agent, to attempt a settlement. An act was passed in 1719 directing that the line run from Little Egg Harbor to the northernmost branch of the Delaware be "straight and direct." This region was unsettled in Keith's day. Under the act the proprietors of each division were instructed to compensate any injured parties. But Colonel Coxe, then president of the West Jersey Council, refused to take action, and little was accomplished. Finally in 1743 the East Jersey Board took the initiative and ran the Lawrence Line, named for the chief surveyor. It was never annulled, and though attempts were made in 1769 and 1775 to have it shifted eastward by the West Jersey proprietors, the dispute was not finally settled until after the American Revolution.

A second dispute, just as irritating, that cropped up from time to time involved the New Jersey–New York boundary. The quarrel was aggravated by the rival claims of speculators and settlers and by the encroachments of squatters, but not until 1762 did the New Jersey assembly take action. After prolonged negotiations with New York, both colonies agreed to accept the Fishkill tributary as the main branch of the Delaware. Then New York severed negotiations because of a disagreement over the location of the eastern terminus. Not until 1767 were serious negotiations resumed, and not until 1773 was the boundary finally approved by the Privy Council. Its royal commission in 1769 ruled that the northern station should be 40°21′19″ instead of the old 41°40′. New Jersey, as a result, lost several hundred thousand acres. In all the boundary negotiations of the later period, the ambitions of interested parties—proprietors, large landowners, and speculators—were paramount. Admittedly the interests of settlers, caught up in the manipulation of monopolists, political and otherwise, were rendered secondary.*

---

* Larry R. Gerlach, "Revolution or Independence? New Jersey, 1760-1776"

Belcher's first assembly, the sixteenth, met in November 1747 and received his requests for legislation to end rioting and for a revenue measure. Salaries were now three years in arrears. As one could anticipate, the house brought in a support bill, coupled with a loan office bill and a fee bill. The council warned the governor that civil strife was imminent and introduced a strong measure to curb rioting. The assembly was in a dilemma—to declare rioting treasonable would antagonize many voters, but not to act would encourage violence and constrain the governor to call for English troops. Belcher appealed to the influential Kinsey of Pennsylvania to intervene. As a consequence, the house produced a mild measure to suppress riots but without the funds to implement it, and it insisted upon amnesty for all who petitioned by October 1, 1748. Then it voted its pet loan office and fee bills.

It was now up to Belcher, who had learned in Massachusetts that to antagonize was not to rule, to gain the crown's assent for the latter measures. He worked through his brother-in-law, Partridge, warning him that Robert Hunter Morris would oppose the assembly's measures because it had refused to honor his father's claim to salary arrears. Belcher then informed the Duke of Bedford, secretary of state for the southern department, who dealt with the colonies, that without the loan office act there would be no funds forthcoming for the support of the government. At Robert Hunter Morris's behest, John Ferdinand Paris worked in London to have the assembly's acts disallowed, and his arguments prevailed. The Board of Trade accused Belcher of not being frank. It disallowed the loan office act on the ground that Parliament again was considering a bill to outlaw colonial paper money, and it delayed confirming the fee act because the assembly was dilatory in dealing with rioters. With the loan office act in abeyance, the house, anticipating that it might be driven to impose taxes, passed a county quota bill. The council, convinced that a tax measure would impose a levy on unimproved proprietary lands, rejected it.

The assembly met again in the fall of 1748 with the fate of its

(unpublished Ph.D. dissertation, Rutgers University, 1968), gives the best account of the later phases of these boundary disputes, pp. 93–106.

favorite acts as yet undecided. Since few rioters came forward seeking amnesty, it was clear that they were being influenced by a newly found demagogue, Amos Roberts. James Alexander demanded that his machinations be stopped and that the council insist upon a measure leading to the conviction of lawless men. As the squatters continued to plunder valuable timber on proprietary lands, the Board of Proprietors petitioned the legislature to take action. When the sheriff of Essex County, William Chetwood, arrested Roberts for treason, a mob freed him from Newark jail. Belcher, stirred to action, appealed again to the assembly, charging that such acts were "in a sort of open Rebellion against the King." Alexander and others testified that "like hungry locusts" the lawbreakers had devoured all the timber on the Passaic behind Newark and Elizabethtown and were extending their activities westward. So blatant were their acts that even the associates disowned them. The outlaws now reverenced Roberts as a king, it was stated; he had formed them into an organized band, with collectors to levy taxes, courts to decide disputes, and a militia of their own. The rioters were boasting that, if necessary, they would raze Perth Amboy, the proprietors' town, to the ground.

Still the assembly procrastinated, refusing to vote funds to quell the disturbances. Robert Hunter Morris openly attacked the governor for his lack of leadership. When the assembly, persuaded by a rioter member, John Low, voted to do nothing, Morris and the council resolved to petition the Privy Council. They also sent a strong letter to the Duke of Bedford, charging that the governor was in sympathy with the rioters. By now thoroughly discomfited, Belcher called an election; no change resulted, however, as the "Capmen and Mobmen" defeated the "Wigmen and Gentlemen." Almost desperate, Belcher told the assembly that it must vote funds for the maintenance of law and order, or he would request the crown to intercede. The house had the governor over a barrel and knew it. It piously resolved that the colony was too poor to provide jail protection and that the Essex County offenders should be given a longer reprieve under the pardons act. In sum, the governor was *persona non grata* with the assembly, and even the council had lost confidence in him. In his appeals to the crown Belcher did nothing but complain of the assembly's refusal to cooperate.

The governor's status in London was weakening. The miracle is that he was retained until his death six years later. The Duke of Bedford was more interested in colonial affairs than was his predecessor, Newcastle, while Lord Halifax, the Board of Trade's head from 1748 to 1761, had established himself virtually as the colonial secretary. Breaking precedent, the board recommended that Robert Hunter Morris's man fill a council vacancy instead of the governor's nominee, Charles Read. Thomas Penn, the Pennsylvania proprietor, who was worried about the encroachments of New Jersey squatters on his lands, lent his influence to Paris's efforts to have Belcher removed. In the summer of 1749 the board discussed the feasibility of sending a new governor accompanied by troops or of reuniting New Jersey and New York. When Morris learned of the board's deliberations, he wrote to Paris to delay any decision until he reached London. Always ambitious for a governorship, there was the possibility of obtaining a lieutenant governorship or even the hard-pressed Belcher's post. He intended also to present the proprietors' side of the land problem to the English authorities. The assembly sent a petition to the Privy Council setting forth its views of the rioting and other pertinent matters. Alarmed, Governor Belcher wrote not only to the board but also to Lord Chancellor Hardwicke, his patron. He asserted that the disturbances would not be laid to rest by reuniting New Jersey and New York, or even by sending troops, and that the land disputes must be settled by some unbiased commission or court. Richard Smith, long a councilor, wrote that appropriating money to safeguard the jails was impracticable "because of the general Outcry or dislike of those called Proprietors."

Robert Hunter Morris remained in England a long time. The board was impressed by his presentation and, indeed, used much of it in its report to the Privy Council. It criticized Belcher for not acting to suppress rioting at the start. Nevertheless, the board came to the conclusion that order could not be restored so long as the royal governor was utterly dependent upon the assembly. Belcher's low point was in 1750, when his nominees for vacant council seats, able men, were set aside for Morris's henchmen. But, as usual, Morris pressed too hard. Belcher's persuasive letters, especially those to Hardwicke, were given more heed. The latter did not impugn Belcher's integrity but wrote him candidly that his chief failure was his inability to uphold the king's laws. Petitions from Essex, Middlesex, and Somerset counties also served as a corrective to the extreme allegations of Morris and Paris. The board made its recommendations in the summer of 1751. From the assembly's point of view they were unexpectedly lenient, as that body was simply instructed to restore tranquility. The board also recommended that a royal commission be appointed to study the nature of the disorders.

It was common knowledge that Belcher was in poor shape financially, for no salary had been paid him for fifteen months and he had been forced to sell some of his New England property to keep himself solvent. When in February 1751 the assembly refused him a salary grant, he lectured it for its disrespect for the king's representative, then dissolved it. In May elections were held for a new house, the eighteenth assembly. There were many new faces, and the membership was slightly more conservative. Charles Read, a good friend of the governor, was elected speaker. Happily for Belcher, a two-year support bill was enacted. Read was responsible also for the passage of an oft-defeated tax bill. Attached was a "declaratory" clause implying that the proprietors' lands would not be the principal target of the contemplated tax levy. Though the council was appeased, James Alexander complained that the proprietors would be taxed for all the lands they claimed, while the squatters would take shelter behind the proprietors' declarations. In consequence the council attempted to amend the bill, leading the house to send the measure directly to the governor for signature while accusing the council of trying to wreck the harmony it was striving for. Belcher refused to sign the bill without the assent of the council. He wrote Partridge that certain councilors, however, were determined not to accept any proposal that would subject "their vast Estates in Lands to taxation."

The assembly was confronted with a dilemma, for by January 1752, when it reconvened, the provincial debt had risen to an enormous £8,000, and the treasury was empty. The people had paid no taxes to speak of for sixteen years and little during the twelve before that. Deciding upon concessions, the house voted to assess squatters for the land they occupied, and other matters irritating to the council were resolved. In sum, the council had prevented excessive levies on proprietary lands, the house had stopped the council from amending a revenue bill, and Governor Belcher finally got his salary and arrears.

By 1752 the rioting had tapered off. Many of the leaders had vanished when it appeared likely that the crown would crack down, and some were sufficiently discouraged to actually leave the province. The Answer to the Bill in Chancery was filed, and both sides agreed to a test case, Winchell vs. Tomkins, that was to be argued before the supreme court with Justice Samuel Nevill presiding. Then the proprietors, who had fought every postponement, began to lose interest. There were many rumors, all conjectural. One had it that Belcher was endeavoring to have the case argued in the court of chancery, where he would preside and (presumably) favor the associates. Another was that the proprietors were waiting for the return of Robert Hunter Morris; a third was that they could expect no help from England. Morris himself was against the proposal to reunite New Jersey with New York, and some feared that the trial itself would lead to more rioting. When the proprietors desisted, the crown postponed the appointment of a royal commission, while the choice of Robert Hunter Morris as lieutenant governor of Pennsylvania removed him from the scene in 1754. Both proprietary boards quietly continued with the dissolution of their holdings.*

Governor Belcher's remarkable powers of survival enabled him to hang on for five more years, none of them happier than the preceding five. He held his own in the council despite the fact that the crown had refused to appoint his nominees; unexpectedly, it was the council and not the governor that led in upholding the royal authority and in pushing measures to preserve law and order. In London, Agent Partridge was practically

---

* The vexed Elizabethtown Bill in Chancery was never heard of in any court during the colonial period.

superseded by Paris, the council's man. For ten years Morris and Alexander had denied Belcher the easy, quiet life he had promised himself in New Jersey. The assembly had sized him up for what he was and at little cost had obtained a fee act and a paper money act, which was later disallowed, however. During the period of the land riots, Belcher had been made to dance to the assembly's tune. The house's triumph lay in not being forced to abandon the Elizabethtown associates or to punish the rioters, and it had escaped with but a mild rebuke from the crown. In 1752, after nearly a half-century of royal government, the lower house controlled the power of the purse and, through it, the governor. It had, brazenly, even attempted to get a revenue bill adopted without referring it to the council.

8

NEW JERSEY AND THE EMPIRE

New Jersey was not alone among the colonies in finding her assembly compelled against its will to absorb some bitter lessons regarding its status in the British Empire during the decade following 1763. As England became involved in a life or death struggle with France,* the crown deliberately reassessed its position vis-à-vis the American colonies. The French constituted an aggressive and formidable foe in North America; to retain her hold on the continent, Britain needed aid from her colonies, and she was determined to have it no matter what the consequences.

The New Jersey assembly had never taken kindly to England's imperial designs. In the past Britain's expeditions to Canada and the West Indies had been aborted or had failed completely. To the members of the assembly who had very reluctantly voted assistance, such schemes seemed not only remote but without any useful purpose. New Jersey had made a great case of her poverty, lack of money, and lack of trade; when these arguments failed, she managed to take care of imperial levies without taxing her citizens, and this felicitous practice had become a way of life. The colony's outlook was thoroughly provincial and inner-directed. Thus unfitted to cope with the rising challenge of imperial relationships that confronted her in the mid-eighteenth century, inglorious years lay ahead before this small royal colony manifested maturity in her attitudes toward the mother country.

---

* The Seven Years War, 1756–1763, known in America as the French and Indian War.

From 1749 to 1763 the assembly had made no progress in obtaining new paper money emissions, since the crown had disallowed one act after another. Yet bills in Parliament to outlaw colonial bills of credit were never, as such, adopted. In refusing further issues of paper money in New England, the Board of Trade in 1751 did permit issues of non-legal-tender paper money for the purpose of meeting provincial charges and wartime expenditures, but support issues were required to be funded in two years and wartime issues in five. This policy in time extended to other colonies. In New Jersey, Councilor Richard Smith, the foremost advocate of paper money, died in 1750. Robert Hunter Morris, who controlled the council, was as ever opposed to such measures, but in 1754 he left the province for Pennsylvania.

When the assembly met in the spring of 1754, Governor Belcher insisted that it remedy the desperate financial situation. More to pave the way for a gigantic loan office act than to please Belcher, the assembly, being informed that there was £20,000 in paper money outstanding, £15,300 of unpaid wartime bills of credit, and £4,600 in unsunk loan office notes, enacted a measure to retire the bills of credit at the rate of £1,500 per annum and another to oblige delinquents to pay up their loan office arrears. The council, representing a creditor interest, strongly opposed the assembly's £60,000 loan office bill; nevertheless, the latter sent it to London with a strong petition, hoping that agent Richard Partridge could manage its allowance.

Meanwhile, hostilities with France broke out in America. The French erected Fort Venango in northwest Pennsylvania, alarming traders and speculators in Pennsylvania, New York, and Virginia. The colonial governors were instructed to obtain measures for a concerted defense. New Jersey's assigned quota was 120 men and £500. Governor Dinwiddie of Virginia warned the French of trespass, sent Captain William Trent to erect a fort at the present site of Pittsburgh, key to the Ohio Valley, and appealed to neighboring colonies for assistance. When Belcher presented Dinwiddie's request to the assembly, he was met with the usual stock arguments, but the house offered to reconsider if its loan office act was allowed. When Belcher made so bold as to

Jonathan Belcher, royal governor (1747–1757). *Courtesy of the New York Public Library Picture Collection.*

suggest a tax, the assembly found it convenient to adjourn. When it reconvened in June 1754, the house was in a bad humor. It had learned that the Privy Council would agree to the loan office act, but only on two conditions: that the bills not be legal tender and that henceforth interest receipts be appropriated by warrants signed by the governor in council. Since these proposals were unacceptable, the house ignored Belcher's requests for aid to Virginia and refused to send delegates to the intercolonial conference at Albany. Belcher berated the assembly for its failure to recognize a common danger, then dismissed it. New Jersey's provincialism stood exposed.

When Belcher in October again warned a newly elected assembly of French encroachments, the house, somewhat impressed, voted assistance to repel the French in the Ohio Valley, but conditioned its tender on the crown's allowance of a new loan office act of £70,000—£60,000 for ordinary purposes and £10,000 for use against the French. The first £10,000 in interest money would retire the £10,000 granted the king for military purposes; the next accumulation would repay earlier war debts; and all later monies would be reserved as a fund to assist colonies in danger. However, the assembly insisted that all bills be legal tender; otherwise borrowers would refuse to take up loans. The house was convinced of its cleverness, as all interest money was assigned to the king's use. Belcher, writing the Board of Trade, commented that the act was dangerous in that it would probably depreciate the value of New Jersey's bills. Yet he requested an immediate decision, warning that the assembly would do nothing until the crown acted.

In October 1754, with General Braddock named commander-in-chief of the British forces, plans were made to take Forts Duquesne, Niagara, and Beauséjour and to fortify Crown Point. The crown anticipated aid from the colonies. Braddock arrived in Virginia in February 1755, while Governor Shirley of Massachusetts undertook to strengthen Crown Point. The same month, the New Jersey assembly voted a meager £500 in aid, to be expended in provisioning the king's troops should they march through the colony. It refused to strengthen the militia law, informing Belcher that he might order New Jersey militiamen to

New York only if her frontiers were attacked. The assembly was still awaiting the fate of its £70,000 loan office act. In April, with Braddock and Shirley both demanding assistance, Belcher told the assembly that it should delay no longer. It voted reluctantly to supply 500 men to assist Braddock, placing the regiment in charge of Colonel Peter Schuyler. Avoiding the recommended conscription, the assembly offered thirty-shilling bounties for volunteers and voted £15,000 in legal-tender bills, valid for five years, to cover military expense. In signing the act the governor diplomatically overlooked the absence of the customary suspending clause required by the crown.

In July 1755 Belcher convened a special session to inform the assembly of Braddock's defeat and of the approach of a French fleet, transporting an army, which had slipped through the English blockade of the St. Lawrence. He pleaded for additional aid. The assembly had meanwhile learned that its loan office act had been rejected, and it therefore refused to adopt a strong militia act or even a measure forbidding trade with the enemy. In view of the existing danger, it did move an appropriation of £70,000 in bills of credit to support New Jersey's troops but added the unacceptable proviso that the issue be valid for six instead of the permissible five years. When Belcher protested, the house cut the amount in half, arguing the poverty of the colony. In the fall, with hostile Indians attacking at Easton and on the upper Delaware, Belcher ordered militiamen to the frontier. Again the assembly postponed action, fortified by similar attitudes in the New York and Pennsylvania assemblies. By December 1755 the New Jersey situation was all but desperate. As petitions poured in from threatened frontier communities, the assembly was finally constrained to appropriate £10,000 in bills of credit of five years' duration to build blockhouses and provide troops. Though the assembly had ignored the governor and the crown, it dared not turn its back on its constituents. By now the Moravian town of Gnadenhutten, across the Delaware in Pennsylvania, had been burned.

With defense funds exhausted, Belcher in May 1756 demanded still another appropriation. The assembly offered £15,000 in bills, provided "a reasonable time" was allowed to sink them, but Belcher refused to violate his instructions and offered only to forward the assembly's petition to the crown. With another spate of Indian depredations, the house swallowed its pride and voted £17,500 on the five-year basis. In August the Earl of Loudoun, Braddock's successor, reached America with fresh troops. But the French commander Montcalm, who had arrived in Canada several months previously, immediately took the Oswego forts, giving the French undisputed control of the Great Lakes. This victory unleashed the Indians, causing further attacks, including the murder of the Swartout family in New Jersey's frontier Sussex County.

Loudoun demanded aid from the colonial assemblies but received little, except from beleaguered New York. Early in January 1757 he met with the New England commissioners and obtained satisfactory understandings with their colonies. He then held an equally successful conference with the southern governors in Philadelphia. New York also readily complied, but New Jersey balked at furnishing 1,000 men. Despite Belcher's pleas, the house offered only an additional 500, coupling this measure with an appropriation of £10,000 in bills of credit. By now, the valiant Schuyler and half his men had been captured at Oswego. At Belcher's behest, General Loudoun addressed the New Jersey assembly and impatiently awaited its decision. The house unanimously rejected the request for 1,000 men, charging Belcher to explain to Loudoun that the colony was so burdened that nothing could be done unless paper money of more than five years' duration could be issued. Unless afforded relief, the province must cease all aid by summer. In a nutshell, New Jersey was the only colony that had refused to honor her assigned quota; this dubious distinction made her unpopular not only with the British military establishment but with the crown itself.

In the face of three disallowances, the assembly readied a new loan office act. It adopted a £60,000 proposal, with the interest appropriated for the prosecution of the war "in such a Manner as the Legislature may apply it." An additional £29,000 in bills of credit for the immediate use of the king was voted, to be retired gradually out of the interest payments. Belcher pigeonholed the entire measure. With the news in the summer of 1757 that Fort

William Henry (near Lake George, New York) had capitulated and that a large portion of New Jersey's troops had been taken, the old governor, now stricken with palsy and beset with worry, died on August 31. Belcher had never failed in his duty of urging the assembly, against its will, to vote essential war measures, and to his credit he refused to yield to its importunities with regard to paper money issues.

Senior Councilor Reading, an aged man, became acting governor pending the arrival of a new executive. Not relishing his post, he deferred to the assembly, an advantage the house seized upon. In October 1758 Reading acquiesced in an issue of £30,000 in bills, to be retired between 1768 and 1773, a five-year period to be sure, but not the legal 1758–1763. Meanwhile, with William Pitt as prime minister, the crown decided to reimburse the colonial assemblies for their war appropriations. In March 1758 the New Jersey assembly voted an additional £50,000 in bills, callable from 1774–1778! This amount, added to the £30,000 previously voted, gave a staggering total of £80,000, almost the equivalent of the last loan office measure still pending in London. The house then voted to bring the New Jersey regiment up to a strength of 1,000 men and offered volunteers a bounty of £12, hoping to avoid the draft of men that General James Abercromby, Loudoun's successor, demanded. The regiment bore the sobriquet "Jersey Blues" after their colorful uniforms. To obviate the necessity of quartering royal troops in private homes, the assembly also voted to build barracks capable of caring for 1,500 men in five towns. Those at Trenton are the only ones still standing today. Their construction had solved what promised to be a sensitive local problem.

Meanwhile the war went on. In 1758 Abercromby was repulsed at Ticonderoga with great losses, including heavy casualties among the New Jersey troops. The tide was turning, however. General Jeffery Amherst took Louisburg, the first major British victory; Colonel John Bradstreet destroyed Fort Frontenac; and General John Forbes took Fort Duquesne. On Abercromby's removal, Amherst was appointed commander-in-chief. Meanwhile, in June 1758 Governor Belcher's successor arrived—the well-connected Oxford graduate Francis Bernard, who had won a reputation as an able lawyer in London. Bernard served for only two years, but he brought a new energy to a colony that had been saddled for twenty years with old executives and councilors, many of whom were approaching senility. Of an analytical cast of mind, he strove to reconcile rigid attitudes in London with the prevailing provincialism in the assembly. Well coached by New Jersey's colonial agent, Partridge, he appealed to the Board of Trade to modify his instructions regarding paper money issues. The board did agree to drop the irritating suspending clause, though it reiterated its provisos that the bills must be sunk in five years and could not be legal tender. This was a mild concession, but Bernard's activity was noticed favorably by the assembly.

Before meeting with the assembly in June 1758, Bernard attempted to deal with the problem of Indian depredations, for in May and June more than forty persons had been killed. He increased the frontier guard to 150 men and proposed to General Forbes and to Governor William Denny of Pennsylvania that meetings be held with the Indian chiefs. The assembly agreed to meet the governor halfway. Two militia companies (150 men), a blockhouse, and fifty police dogs were provided. To supply the necessary funds the assembly proposed an issue of £10,000 in legal-tender bills, to be sunk in 1766 through taxes. Although Bernard objected to the provisions making the bills legal tender and to the six-year sinking fund clause, he was forced by the exigencies of the situation to give his assent. In explaining his predicament to those at home, he wrote that he dared not veto the appropriation, though it was "hard doctrine that I should disobey His Majesty in order to serve more effectually." The assembly had also voted £1,600 to expedite the governor's efforts to secure a treaty of peace with the Indians, the funds to be raised in part by lotteries. Happily the negotiations were successful. Since only a small sum was paid the Minisink and their allies to compensate them for the seizure of their lands, the bulk of the appropriation was used to purchase 3,000 acres of land in Burlington County to establish an Indian reservation. Bernard was elated, the assembly grateful, and the Board of Trade relieved. The assembly (though only by a single vote) gave

Bernard £500 "for extraordinary expenses," which the governor, blessed with a numerous family, deigned to accept.

The legislature then reverted to its favorite activity of endeavoring to increase the paper money supply. Even the governor conspired to have the regulations liberalized. He requested that he be permitted to assent to an issue of £40,000, to be retired in 1764 and 1766, these bills to pass as legal tender. He reasoned that the money was sorely needed for the campaigns of 1759 and that the colony was indeed laboring under financial strain. After lengthy consideration the Board of Trade acquiesced on condition that the money be used to support a regiment of 1,000 men and 200 frontier guards. The time for sinking the bills was extended to six years, and the question of legal tender was not raised. The board insisted however that the money expended must be paid on warrants signed by the governor in council and checked by the royal auditor general. Thus Governor Bernard was successful in part, but only because such concessions had already been made to New York and Pennsylvania. Meanwhile the assembly voted an additional issue of £50,000 in legal-tender bills to be retired during the years 1764–1767. In assenting to these measures the governor was again constrained to make explanations to the crown, and to water down objections he named himself paymaster of the regiment while agreeing to commissioners appointed by the house. Though he told the assembly that this was "not a proper time to rectify these abuses," he made it clear that when conditions were more settled he would not be a party to such measures. Nevertheless the assembly had won a victory, prompting Bernard to support a suggestion in London that Parliament provide for the salaries of colonial governors, the sooner the better in his judgment.

England was now moving toward victory in America. The French were forced to abandon Ticonderoga and Crown Point; Oswego and Niagara fell; and, finally, Wolfe defeated Montcalm at Quebec, leaving only Montreal to be invested. Since Bernard was in high repute in England, in a shift of governors he applied for and was granted the Massachusetts post. He had played an important role in pacifying the Indians about Easton; he had extracted men and supplies from the assembly; and he had kept paper money emissions within bounds without stirring up the legislature or antagonizing the people. And, importantly, he had instilled in the assembly some sense of responsibility in imperial matters.

Thomas Boone, whose home was in South Carolina, served briefly as governor beginning in July 1760. A friendly man, he merely reminded the assembly that monies voted by the crown should be signed by the governor in council, otherwise he would be in violation of his instructions. The house, unimpressed, continued in its customary course, pausing long enough to vote him £500 for "extraordinary expenses" during wartime. The governor signed the appropriation act. Soon after, when he obtained the governorship of South Carolina, he tarried only long enough to greet his successor, Josiah Hardy, brother of a former New York governor. Hardy, too, had a term of little more than eighteen months, but unlike Boone he was dismissed, not transferred. The crown had decided to make an example of a governor who violated his instructions, and Hardy was made the scapegoat in an effort to stiffen royal policy. He had failed to raise sufficient troops and had neglected to insist that the assembly sink its paper money according to schedule. The crown concluded that New Jersey was setting a bad example for the neighboring colonies. It was the matter of judicial tenure, however, that led to Hardy's eventual undoing. No question of principle was involved in New Jersey, since Hardy's dismissal had nothing to do with the issue being raised in New York, Pennsylvania, and other colonies—an issue that later led to the charge in the Declaration of Independence that George III had made judges "dependent on his will alone." Hardy had in fact violated his instructions in recommissioning judges with the "good-behavior tenure" that they had enjoyed before the accession of George III instead of the required tenure "at the king's pleasure." *

New Jersey's last colonial governor was William Franklin, the able natural son of Benjamin Franklin. He remained until the

---

* Jerome J. Nadelhaft, "Politics and the Judicial Tenure Fight in Colonial New Jersey," *William and Mary Quarterly*, XXVIII (1971), 46–63.

outbreak of the Revolution. After distinguishing himself at Ticonderoga, young Franklin was named a captain in the militia and then was appointed comptroller of the colonial post office under his father. While the senior Franklin was in London, William studied at Middle Temple and became a lawyer. Though a Whig, he was named governor of New Jersey in February 1763 at the age of thirty-three, after a searching examination by Lord Halifax because of his youth. Perhaps the ministry was hoping to win the father to the Tory cause; in any event, the younger Franklin ultimately did become a Tory. Operating a considerable farm near Burlington, the new governor became intensely interested in New Jersey's agriculture and in her economic well-being.

Franklin's administration was directly affected by the new British colonial policy. The Seven Years War was over and with it the period of salutary neglect. The colonial assemblies were now called upon to defend the privileges they had won, first from the royal governors and then from the crown. The British government, in turn, saddled with a huge national debt and a doubling of expenditures, sought to make the colonies bear a larger share of this burden.* To secure peace in America vis-à-vis Canada and the Indian tribes, the ministry, headed by George Grenville, ruled that 7,500 troops must be maintained in America. A western boundary, the Proclamation Line, was delineated, beyond which the colonists, temporarily, must not settle. This act alarmed colonial land speculators and expansionists. Then the Sugar Act of 1764 cut the duty on molasses and other West Indies products in the effort to stamp out smuggling that had arisen under the much higher duties imposed by the Molasses Act of 1733. In a further attempt to curtail smuggling, violations would be tried in admiralty courts instead of the more permissive colonial courts.

The northern colonies were particularly affected by the restrictions on the West Indies trade. This commerce had

---

* By 1766 the national debt was about £140 million and the annual debt charge between £4 and £5 million. Britain's annual budget was about £10 million. See also Gerlach, "Revolution or Independence," 240.

enabled them to secure bills of credit by which they could obtain the manufactured goods they bought from Britain. Unlike the southern colonies, they could not pay in staples like tobacco and rice. To make payments in specie they traded with the French and Spanish West Indies as well as the English islands. New England sent dried fish and timber, while the middle colonies shipped flour, meat, and staves. New Jersey, with little direct foreign commerce, found in this trade, which was conducted through New York City and Philadelphia, an outlet for her forest products. The northern colonies obtained from the West Indies specie and molasses. The latter was distilled into rum in exchange for slaves sold principally in the West Indies and the southern colonies. From the West Indies, too, the northern colonies obtained sugar and fruits for direct shipment to England. The strict enforcement of new duties threatened the trade of the middle and New England colonies and with it the importation of manufactures and luxury goods from Britain. The drying up of bills of exchange and credit in London aggravated the economic recession to which the cessation of war had contributed substantially.

Concurrently Parliament in 1764 forbade the issue of paper money as legal tender in all the colonies. This action was in part a response to the complaints of British merchants who rebelled against accepting depreciated legal-tender bills in payment of colonial debts. While admitting that the bills of the middle colonies had not depreciated badly, the Board of Trade reported to Parliament that the broad prohibition was necessary both for the trade of the kingdom and the economic security of the colonies. The adoption of the Currency Act of 1764 had deleterious effects in New Jersey.

For years New Jersey had depended on her paper money emissions to ease her economic situation. Between 1754 and 1764 this small province had authorized the issuing of £347,000 in paper money, a total exceeding that of any other mainland colony. Prices rose during this period, but no more than in New York and Philadelphia. Indeed New Jersey bills usually passed at a premium in the two cities with which New Jersey transacted most of her business. Until the end of the French and Indian

War, New Jersey refused to impose new taxes, despite the warnings of Governor Bernard. When Parliament reimbursed the colony for a third of her war expenditures, New Jersey actually reduced her taxes. By 1765, with her heavy debt and her inefficient tax collections, New Jersey had mounted the largest indebtedness of all the colonies—a total of £300,000, out of which £50,000 represented arrears of taxes and loan installments. From £12,500 to £15,000 per annum was earmarked for the next eighteen years for retiring bills of credit outstanding. The Currency Act had cut off the usual avenue of relief, more paper money.

When the assembly met at Burlington in May 1765, there were evidences of depression. Debtors demanding relief sought measures to restrain lawyers from collecting debts and to prevent shopkeepers from giving credit of more than £6 to any one person, and, predictably, they pressed for another loan office issue. Since the prices of wheat, flour, and other produce had fallen sharply, bounties were offered for the raising of hemp, flax, and even silk. A kind of bankruptcy law was adopted to aid debtors with families, and surplus funds from military appropriations were used for the support of the government. The assembly refused to grant the governor a higher salary or a house-rent allowance. Yet, on the rumor of a delayed Parliamentary reimbursement for wartime expenditures, the assembly again lowered taxes.

In the spring of 1765, intent upon raising more money in support of the American military establishment, Parliament passed the Stamp Act, effective in November. Among other provisions, all legal documents, newspapers, almanacs, and licenses must carry stamps. In its preparation the legal-minded chief minister, George Grenville, had consulted the colonial agents, seeking suggestions for a less objectionable kind of tax. Benjamin Franklin recommended setting up a general loan office in America, an idea advanced by Lewis Morris in 1740. Though it would take power from the assemblies, he thought the colonists would prefer a loan to a tax, and the plan would provide the colonists with their much-needed currency. But Grenville went his own way, and the Stamp Act became law.

In America the measure was discussed and attacked all through the summer. The level-headed Massachusetts Governor Bernard thought it inexpedient. Joseph Galloway and John Dickinson of Pennsylvania, who later opposed the break with England, attacked the law. Everywhere it was recognized that if the proceeds were used to pay military expenses, the assemblies would be deprived of the means of controlling royal officials, particularly the governors. In June 1765 the Massachusetts assembly invited delegates from all the colonial assemblies to attend a protest meeting in New York in October. Robert Ogden, speaker of the New Jersey house, advised against precipitate action, arguing that a well-reasoned petition would carry more weight, but he had little influence. In August a Boston mob hanged in effigy Andrew Oliver, the stamp collector designate.

The press succeeded in arousing public animosity. In the middle colonies, for example, More's *Country Almanac* of New York carried a reprint of the law,* as did the *Constitutional Courant* (printed on James Parker's press in Woodbridge), which also circulated in New York City. The *Pennsylvania Journal* carried the story that William Coxe, the collector assigned to New Jersey, was unable to rent a house since no one would insure it against violence. Coxe was implored by friends to resign, even if he must forfeit his £3,000 bond. To Governor Franklin's dismay he resigned on September 3, despite assurances that General Thomas Gage, the British commander-in-chief, would provide troops if necessary to enforce the collections. The New Jersey council warned the governor against haste, predicting that the appearance of troops would provoke disturbances, and it suggested that the stamps themselves be held in New York. Franklin wrote the Board of Trade that no one would give bond for the position of collector, "the Office being now, by one Means or other, become very obnoxious to the people."

In September the New Jersey lawyers joined the fray. They met at the court in Perth Amboy, with Chief Justice Frederick

---

* Thomas More (Moore) was a Philadelphian; his almanac was printed and sold in New York by James Parker.

Smythe presiding. After discussion they adopted a compromise position similar to that followed in other colonies: not to buy the stamps, while simultaneously strongly opposing riotous behavior. George Washington, independently, was advocating the same policy in Virginia as the best way of bringing about repeal.

A number in New Jersey, including the highly respected lawyer Richard Stockton, urged Speaker Robert Ogden to send a delegation of assembly members to the Stamp Act Congress. Since it was too late to reconvene the assembly, Ogden called an unofficial meeting at Sproul's Tavern in Perth Amboy. Twelve members gathered and designated Ogden, Hendrick Fisher of Somerset County, and Joseph Borden of Burlington County as delegates.* Franklin, apprehensive of stirring up the people, did not intervene. On October 7, the delegates from nine colonies convened in New York. Though Virginia, North Carolina, and Georgia were not represented, because of manipulation, it was known that their assemblies favored this meeting inspired by James Otis of Boston. Following the twelve-day meeting, the congress approved a declaration of colonial rights and grievances and addressed petitions to the king and both houses of Parliament. The leading argument of the congress was that the Stamp Act was not consistent with the British constitution, because all colonial appropriations were gifts to the king freely granted through their assemblies. Only two men—Robert Ogden of New Jersey and Timothy Ruggles of Massachusetts—withheld approval, the former because he favored separate protests from the several colonial assemblies and from influential individuals. For his stand Ogden was burned in effigy in New Jersey. But when the merchants of Boston, New York, and Philadelphia entered into nonimportation agreements as a means of bringing pressure for the repeal of the Stamp Act, New Jersey, with her rural outlook and her essentially domestic trade, did not participate.

Since public sentiment was opposed, no stamps were made

---

* This meeting in September and subsequent events connected with the Stamp Act repeal mark the entrance of Richard Stockton and John Hart, as well as Fisher and Borden, into the arena of protest and intercolonial cooperation.

available in New Jersey on November 1, 1765, the date of distribution. Just a week before, while swearing allegiance at a gathering ostensibly to celebrate the accession of George III, the inhabitants of Elizabethtown declared that the Stamp Act violated their liberties and resolved to prevent its execution in every lawful manner. They also agreed to hold in contempt any person accepting employment to administer the act. When William Coxe was called before the council and asked why no stamps were available, he replied that their sale would cause violence and injury to their purveyor. The council decided, wisely, to leave the stamps aboard ship in New York Harbor, and Governor Franklin himself disclaimed any authority to appoint a successor to Coxe.

Speaker Ogden advised the governor to call the assembly, and it met in Burlington on November 26. Ogden resigned, asking only the privilege of entering in the minutes his reasons for not signing the resolutions of the Stamp Act Congress. The house then accepted the reports of the other delegates, Fisher and Borden, approved their conduct, and passed resolutions based on those of the congress. In addition the house stated that the Concessions of 1664 prohibited taxation without the assent of the assembly and that the assembly had never acquiesced in the crown's contention that the governor's commissions and instructions had superseded this instrument. Thus, in violating their privileges and liberties, one of which was the right of self-taxation, the crown had broken its word. Moreover, if taxed by the assembly and by Parliament, the colony would be beholden to two taxing bodies. The Stamp Act, in its judgment, was unconstitutional; however, the house advised the inhabitants not to engage in violence lest they endanger efforts being made to have the act repealed.

Meanwhile, loosely organized associations known as the Sons of Liberty put in an appearance. The name was borrowed from an expression used in the House of Commons by an opponent of the Stamp Act, Isaac Barré, in referring to the tax-resisting colonists as "sons of liberty." When the Woodbridge "Sons" called upon William Coxe to confirm his resignation as collector and Coxe obliged, toasts were drunk to the confusion of any appointee refusing to resign the office of "stamp master." In February 1766 the Woodbridge association declared the Stamp Act unconstitutional and voted to oppose it with their lives and fortunes if called upon. Similar demonstrations took place in Elizabethtown, Piscataway, and Freehold and in Hunterdon and Sussex counties, most of them sponsored by the Sons of Liberty. Little protest was evident, however, in the Quaker communities of the western division.* The lawyers and the press continued their opposition, with the former, despite the pressure from the Sons of Liberty, adhering to their stated policy of nonparticipation. The bar did agree, however, that if by April 1 there was no repeal, the lawyers would resume their business without stamps.

Fortunately for all, the Grenville ministry fell in July 1765. Pitt immediately espoused repeal, even complimenting the Americans on their resistance. Moreover, the nonimportation agreements adopted by the American merchants were beginning to hurt, presaging a decline in the export of manufactures and widespread unemployment. Petitions poured in from London, Leeds, Bristol, Glasgow, and elsewhere as depression set in. Late in February 1766, Pitt carried repeal, assuaging opponents by attaching the Declaratory Act upholding the right of Parliament to make laws binding upon the colonies "in all cases whatsoever." In New Jersey and elsewhere there was rejoicing. The assembly complimented the crown for relieving their uneasiness and promised to vote funds when requisitioned "in the Antient and Accustom'd manner." The united colonials had successfully defied Parliament.

Since financial aid from the colonies was still essential, Pitt drew a distinction between indirect or external taxes and direct or internal taxes. Thus if the Stamp Act, a direct tax, was unconstitutional, import duties were not. Pitt, now elevated to the House of Lords, was the real head of the Grafton-Chatham ministry that took office in July 1766, but with Pitt temporarily

---

* Gerlach, "Revolution or Independence," 284–291, presents the best discussion of the activities of the New Jersey "Sons." Moderate in tone and middle-class, their protests were most vigorous in East Jersey owing to the influence of the New York City "Sons."

ill the brilliant Charles Townshend, chancellor of the exchequer, assumed leadership. When in January 1767 Grenville, now the opposition leader, moved that America should support her own military establishment, Townshend surprisingly supported the resolution. In truth, the House of Commons was becoming irritated with the attitude of some of the colonies: to wit, New York's refusal to vote military supplies and Massachusetts's petty attitude toward Governor Bernard. The fine distinction between internal and external taxation was ignored. Townshend agreed that henceforth governors and judges would be paid by the crown, thus rendering them independent of the assemblies, and that the colonists must provide the funds. Paying lip service to Pitt's philosophy of external taxation, Parliament levied import duties on tea, glass, paper, and lead paints, the collection of which would be made by officials appointed by the crown. It was estimated that these taxes would yield £40,000 annually. Townshend died in September, before his measures were put into effect.

This new legislation created an uproar in America. John Dickinson in his "Letters from a Farmer in Pennsylvania" argued that Parliament had no right to impose taxes for revenue, only duties to encourage and regulate trade. Benjamin Franklin thought that this was splitting hairs; either Parliament had the right or did not have the right to make colonial laws, and he thought it did not. Late in December 1767 the Massachusetts assembly petitioned against the Townshend Acts, and in February it adopted a letter for circulation to all the colonies proposing joint protests. The author, Sam Adams, argued that though Parliament theoretically was the supreme law-making body, it could not levy taxes on the colonists because this violated a right guaranteed by the British constitution. Moreover, no people were free if their governors and their judges were appointed and paid by the crown.

Lord Hills Will, Viscount Hillsborough, who became colonial secretary in January 1768, ordered Governor Bernard to secure the recall of the Massachusetts circular letter and directed the other governors to dissolve their assemblies if they replied to it. Virginia, incensed by Hillsborough's order, defiantly sent out a circular letter of her own. In April 1768 the New Jersey assembly sent a petition to the king modeled on that of Massachusetts.* The New York merchants then led the way in the adoption of a second nonimportation agreement. By the end of 1769 its effects were felt in England, and her merchants began to bring pressure on Parliament to repeal the Townshend Acts. In truth, the ·yield from the duties hardly paid the cost of collecting them.

Frederick Lord North, who became prime minister early in 1770, was willing to sponsor repeal, but not under pressure. He proposed to abolish all duties but one on the ground that they taxed British manufactures, an error. He retained the duty on tea, as proof that Parliament had the right to tax the colonies. Many hard-pressed colonial merchants accepted this action as surrender and abandoned the nonimportation agreements, but the majority of the colonists were not happy with what seemed to be an abdication of principle.

The Quartering Act was another source of irritation. In 1765 Parliament passed a law instructing the colonial assemblies to furnish certain supplies to royal troops quartered in barracks. In 1766 the New Jersey assembly complied, though, as Governor Franklin pointed out, it did not provide all the items specified. The assembly refused to do more, adding that the Quartering Act was as much a levy as the Stamp Act. Actually the New Jersey act was faulty and niggardly, and the house had insisted upon appointing its own commissioners to administer it. In 1768 Governor Franklin informed the house that its first Quartering Act, that of 1766, had been disallowed because of its inadequacy and because purchases were made by its commissioners instead of by the governor in council. The council tried to persuade the house to grant the governor and council the power of appointing the commissioners, with Franklin volunteering to choose men nominated by the house. The latter refused on the ground that this was a money bill, not to be amended in council. Other colonies—New York, Virginia, and South Carolina—also procrastinated.

---

* Without Franklin's knowledge. New Jersey was ahead of New York and Pennsylvania.

Happily for Franklin, the house altered its act by providing that the appropriation be spent by the governor in council. The assembly's barracks masters had proved extravagant, if not fraudulent. Franklin's accounts were to be sedulously examined by the house, but the governor and council, for the first time since Cornbury's administration, were permitted to administer a revenue act. When the law came up for renewal in 1771, Franklin was able to demonstrate that expenditures had been reduced by a third. Unfortunately, the assembly was in bad humor because its latest loan office act had been disallowed, and by a vote of eighteen to three it summarily cut off the barracks supplies.

Franklin was now in a quandary. His pleas were rejected on the ground that the colony was poverty-ridden; his patience was exhausted, and he prorogued the assembly. He wrote Secretary Hillsborough of his dilemma, meanwhile using short proroga-tions until instructions were received from the crown. Hillsbor-ough was informed that indefinite prorogations were impractical, since soon there would be no funds for the salaries of public officials, and that to dissolve the assembly would result only in an increased popular majority. Franklin was sure that the assembly would give in if the crown allowed a loan office act, the interest funds from which could be used to maintain royal troops. His alternative suggestion was to have the king and Parliament suspend the assembly's privileges, a radical step. Hillsborough was angered at the assembly's contempt for the authority of Parliament, but he ordered Franklin to continue his prorogations until the crown reached a decision. With other colonies to deal with, he wrote General Gage that in New Jersey he had a choice of enforcing the authority of Parliament or withdrawing troops stationed there, if it could be done without the appearance of surrendering to the assembly.

The assembly met again in November 1771. The governor did not mention a barracks bill, which he knew the majority would oppose. Several weeks later, on ascertaining that the house wanted several measures approved, he proposed the bill. He reasoned persuasively that the British commander should be reimbursed for his personal outlays for supplies and also in-

William Franklin, royal governor (1763–1776). *Courtesy of the New York Public Library Picture Collection.*

formed the house that the royal troops in New Jersey had been ordered to East Florida and would not be replaced. His proposal was beaten by the narrow margin of ten to nine. Without a loan office act, it was argued, only new taxes could produce the funds. In the end the house gave in, but to save face it voted only £318 instead of the £418 requested to reimburse the British commander.

The governor had won a difficult struggle. Two years later, in passing a barracks appropriation of £300 to care for the expenses of the few remaining troops, the house actually commended him for his economical handling of funds, and in 1774 it allowed him £1,400, if needed, to supply the king's troops. When Hillsborough's successor, the Earl of Dartmouth (William Legge), complimented Franklin on the assembly's "zeal for the King's Service, & respect for the supreme authority of Parliament," the prudent governor dared not publicize it.

All the while the assembly, pressed by the populace, strove for ways and means to emit more paper money. New Jersey was not alone in this quest. Since the end of the French War, all governmental expenses had been met out of accumulated interest from the loan office acts. With no new issue sanctioned, the surplus was drying up, and annual retirements steadily reduced the supply of bills in circulation. In England colonial agents led by Benjamin Franklin worked unceasingly for the repeal of the restrictive Currency Act. In January 1767 they persuaded one group of London merchants to petition the Board of Trade in favor of new emissions of money and their use of the bills as legal tender except for sterling debts. If the board agreed, American merchants would be enabled in the absence of specie to import British manufactures, and at the same time the British merchants would be protected from having to accept depreciated currency at par. The New Jersey assembly was pleased when it learned that Benjamin Franklin had praised the colony's paper money record before the Board of Trade.

In New Jersey petitions poured in to the assembly from the counties complaining of the scarcity of money. Governor Franklin wrote his father that in his opinion the American assemblies would be willing to make permanent allocations for provincial salaries if they were permitted to use the remainder for other public services. In other words, the younger Franklin thought that to solve the currency problem the assemblies were willing to grant the governors this degree of independence. The crown for its part needed only to promise that the governors must convene an assembly when the speaker and a majority requested it.

Because of the clamor of debtors begging relief, the New Jersey assembly of April 1769 dutifully enacted another loan office act, which the Privy Council disallowed immediately. It indicated, however, that it would approve a £100,000 loan office measure if such a large amount could be justified and if the bills were not made legal tender, the cause of disallowing the act of 1769. Even Governor Franklin was discouraged, pointing out that both New York and Maryland had notes in circulation that were legal tender at their treasury offices. He was more disturbed in 1770 when New York managed to gain approval for an issue of £120,000 acceptable as legal tender at the colonial treasury. At this time of nonimportation agreements the crown was particularly interested in placating the New York merchants. The New Jersey assembly blamed the crown rather than the governor for the disallowance; thus Franklin received his salary, though he experienced difficulty in persuading the assembly not to cut off the appropriation for the maintenance of the royal troops. New Jersey did obtain allowance for her loan office act just before the outbreak of the War of Independence but was forced to swallow the proviso that the notes not be legal tender even at the loan office.

Other difficulties arose during the early seventies. In 1771 Secretary Hillsborough insisted that colonial agents be appointed by vote of both houses of their respective assemblies. The elder Franklin, who now represented New Jersey as well as several other colonies, complained that the crown through its governors would now control such appointments. His son, however, assured him that the assemblies could take care of themselves simply by omitting the agent's salary from the support bill. Benjamin Franklin was so concerned over Hillsborough's instruction that he seriously considered resigning as a colonial agent.

In August 1772, at the opening of the twenty-second assembly,

Governor Franklin requested it to increase the salaries of provincial officials, warning that the crown, otherwise, was ready to place them on the civil list. By this time, of the several royal colonies, only New Jersey and New Hampshire officials were entirely dependent upon the assemblies for their salaries; in New Jersey only the chief justice, Frederick Smythe, had been placed on the civil list. He was to be the only one, though others (including Franklin himself) petitioned unsuccessfully for similar stakes. The New Jersey assembly, somewhat smugly, stated that it did not care whether the crown paid the colonial officers or not; but on second thought, it took the precaution of raising some salaries.

On March 5, 1770, four colonials were killed in a scuffle with British soldiers in Boston. Sam Adams and Dr. Joseph Warren seized upon the incident as propaganda against the iniquities of British rule. Though Captain Preston and the soldiers, defended by no less than John Adams and Josiah Quincy, were acquitted of the charge of murder, the name "Boston Massacre" stuck. On December 16, 1773, after a long period of calm, Boston merchants allied with Sam Adams and his radicals to prevent the unloading of East India Company tea destined to be vended by the company's agents. When Governor Thomas Hutchinson refused to let the ships and their cargoes return to England, Adams and his supporters led a band of fifty men disguised as Mohawk Indians aboard the ships, and they proceeded to dump 342 cases of tea into the bay. Neither the Boston Massacre nor the famed Boston Tea Party, however, attracted much attention in New Jersey. A local incident created more of a sensation.

On the night of July 21, 1768 the Perth Amboy home of Stephen Skinner, provincial treasurer, was robbed of £6,570 belonging to the colony. When the assembly met in October, it resolved to censure Skinner. Franklin and the council defended him from the imputation of wrongdoing in a struggle lasting until 1774. The assembly went further, insisting not only that Skinner be dismissed, but that it name his replacement. The house was irked when Franklin, to show his trust, appointed Skinner a member of the council. Governor Franklin and the council yielded to the house's unanimous resolution that its own nominee be appointed; then it passed an act, in March 1774, requiring the treasurer to give bond. By now hostility to Franklin was mounting.

In New Jersey, as in many colonies, few events had taken place that could be regarded as heralding revolution. There were no dire warnings of impending conflict. Though New Jersey may have sensed vaguely that the colonies were entitled to certain adjustments long overdue, rebellion against the mother country was as remote as the Revolution itself was unexpected. Franklin, governor since 1763, was able, wise, and persevering. He was thoroughly familiar with the penchants of the lower house—its dedication to paper money, its avoidance of taxes, and its sensitivity to interference by the governor and his council. Through patience and good will, Franklin had judiciously solved several thorny problems, particularly those dealing with the enforcement of the Stamp Act and with the quartering of royal troops.* The people neither hated nor loved him, but they respected him as governor. More than once he had demonstrated his intense concern for the economic well-being of the colony, and he could never be accused of trying to enhance his reputation in attempting to exploit his accomplishments. It was not the governor who placed New Jersey on the road to Revolution.

---

* He was also an astute parliamentary tactician, calling the assembly infrequently—on one occasion not for eighteen months, giving validity to John Kinsey's earlier arguments in favor of a triennial act. Actually only four assemblies were convened between 1754 and 1776. It is thought that only about one-third of the eligible white males voted in the elections.

9

NEW JERSEY ON THE EVE OF THE REVOLUTION: THE ECONOMIC AND SOCIAL PATTERN

The population of New Jersey at the advent of the Revolution was approaching 130,000, in a total colonial population of more than 2,500,000. She was one of the smaller colonies, exceeding in population only Rhode Island, New Hampshire, Georgia, and Delaware. New Jersey was not to be compared with the leaders: in New England, Massachusetts was first with 291,000; in the middle colonies, Pennsylvania boasted 270,000; and in the South, Virginia outstripped all the colonies with 500,000. New Jersey's population had grown steadily since the beginning of the century. In addition to natural increase there was a modest immigration from neighboring New York, Pennsylvania, and Delaware, and smaller increments from New England, Britain, Ulster, Germany, and Switzerland. Governor Cornbury attributed the immigration from New York to New Jersey's fertile lands and low taxes. Despite some exodus to the west there was a sharp increase after 1763. From 1760 to 1770 the population rose from approximately 94,000 to 117,500.

The distribution of New Jersey's population is reflected in the creation of new counties: Somerset in 1688, Hunterdon in 1713, Morris in 1739, Cumberland in 1748, and Sussex in 1753.* Only

---

* Until 1770 Cumberland was represented in the assembly by Salem, and Morris and Sussex by Hunterdon. When representation was finally granted, the size of the lower house increased from 24 to 30.

Old house on Essex Street, Hackensack. *Photographed by George W. Walsh, 1905. Courtesy of The New York-Historical Society.*

Cumberland was in south Jersey. By 1772 Hunterdon with 15,500 was the most populous county, overtaking Burlington with 13,000, Monmouth with 12,500, and Essex and Middlesex with about 11,500 each. Morris had grown to 11,500. Except for Burlington, facing the Delaware, the southern counties lagged.

Since New Jersey remained essentially rural, her towns had not increased greatly in size—there were simply more of them. Elizabethtown led with about 1,200 in 1776, while the two capitals, Perth Amboy and Burlington, had about 500 each. Salem was practically static. The newer towns were Trenton and New Brunswick, at the heads of navigation of the Delaware and the Raritan, with about 150 families each. Both were situated on the New York-Philadelphia highway. Other towns of note were Hackensack, Freehold, Morristown, Bordentown, Princeton, and Gloucester. There were many new villages located at crossroads or at stream bridges where local business or local government was carried on. New Jersey had no great commercial cities; in fact her hinterland was completely controlled by the two giants, New York and Philadelphia, each of which, with more than 20,000 inhabitants, now exceeded Boston's 17,000.

In proprietary New Jersey the concentration of population had been in the Hackensack, Passaic, and Raritan valleys and in the fertile portions of Monmouth as far south as Freehold. Later the settlers fanned out to the west and the south. Some cultivated the rich limestone valleys of Morris County, west of Essex and Somerset, exporting their grain and livestock to New York. Others settled the fertile lands of northern Middlesex and Sussex. The opening of still other areas in Morris and further west and south brought a new flow of emigrants that lasted from 1730 until the Revolution.*

Agriculture and the raising of livestock were the chief occupations of Jerseymen. As in all the northern colonies, husbandry was the principal means of making a livelihood and supporting a family. The land provided practically all the necessities; rarely

---

* For a good survey of New Jersey's population before 1776, see Stella Sutherland, *Population Distribution in Colonial America* (New York, 1936; reprinted, 1966), 97–119.

did the farmer need to buy anything to wear, eat, or drink. The exceptions were salt and nails and, for those above the subsistence level, sugar, tea, coffee, and rum. The farmer was his own craftsman, building his house and barn and fashioning his own utensils, furniture, and farm equipment. His womenfolk produced tallow, soap, and the necessary apparel. Along the stream banks sawmills, then flour mills, put in an appearance.

New Jersey, New York, and Pennsylvania were known in the mid-eighteenth century as "the bread colonies," with New Jersey for a time in the lead. Wheat was her most bountiful crop, followed by corn and hay and such lesser grains as rye, oats, barley, and buckwheat. Hunterdon, which in 1755 included Mercer County, was alleged to be "the most plentiful wheat country for bigness in America." The colony's principal fiber crops were hemp for cordage and flax for cloth. Animal husbandry flourished on a large scale. Cattle had many uses—power, meat, dairy products, and leather. Just before the War of Independence New Jersey was foremost among the colonies in sheep raising, with 144,000 head. Hog raising was universal, and Jersey hams, bacon, and salt pork found their way, with other produce, as far as the West Indies.

Colonial agriculture, except for that carried on by the Pennsylvania Dutch wherever they emigrated, was severely criticized. Jared Eliot, Yale-educated minister of Killingworth (Chester), Connecticut, and the best-known commentator on American agriculture, complained—as did Peter Kalm before him—that colonial agriculture was rudimentary and highly exploitive. Charles Read, one of the few who was experimenting in south Jersey, agreed in a letter to Eliot, stating that the Jersey farmers refused "to leave the beaten road of their Ancestors" and were "Averse to running any Risque at all." Few in New Jersey were abreast of the revolution in agriculture that had begun in England about 1750, although Governor Franklin was interested in raising fiber crops, on which bounties were offered, on his 600-acre farm outside Burlington, and the future war governor, William Livingston, experimented with crops on his large farm outside Elizabethtown. The *New American Magazine* and the almanacs published by Isaac Collins and Shepherd Kollack printed notes on agriculture that reached the few New Jersey agronomists. In 1775 the most widely read work on agriculture, *American Husbandry*, published anonymously in England though believed to have been written by Arthur Young, observed that "the American Planters and farmers are in general the greatest slovens in Christendom." The author charged them with neglecting the use of manure, crop rotation, root crops, and legumes so necessary to restore "the butchered soil." The industrious Germans were the exception. As in Pennsylvania, they ferreted out the limestone soils, nurtured the ground with manure, planted cover crops, recognized the value of fallow, and practiced the rudiments of crop rotation. Their only chagrin was their failure to produce a satisfactory grape for wine-making.

Lacking large towns and a densely populated hinterland, New Jersey had no cadre of skilled craftsmen. There was little specialization such as the stocking-making of the Pennsylvania Dutch and no guilds like the Carpenters Company of Philadelphia. One can cite only isolated instances like the leather-making of Newark, the glass-making of the Salem County Wistars, or the distilling of applejack in the north.

The rise of Trenton as an important commercial and industrial center was a singular development of the mid-century. Founded in 1709 and located at the Falls of the Delaware, by 1740 it emerged as a transshipment and processing town, superseding Burlington in economic importance. As Hunterdon and Sussex achieved agricultural preeminence, thousands of tons of wheat and other grains, lumber and other forest products, and livestock reached Trenton on flatboats, rafts, and long, narrow-beamed Durham boats. Here also the main wagon roads converged on the ferry. Craftsmen were attracted to Trenton as sawmills and flour mills were erected for processing lumber and grains. Soon there was a paper mill, a tannery, a pottery, and a sturgeon-packing and -pickling operation. These products, consolidated and reduced in bulk, resumed their journey to Philadelphia. Trenton's prosperity rose from its unique geographical situation.

Transportation by land had improved greatly. The main roads ran from Elizabethtown and Perth Amboy to New Brunswick and hence to Trenton. Here most of the traffic crossed the Delaware, with a remnant proceeding to Burlington and the towns further south. The ninety-mile trip from New York to Philadelphia was cut to two or three days. Travel by stage rose in popularity, aided by the changing of horses, regular service, and improved inns. By 1770 Burlington had lost its primacy in the Delaware River trade. Only its historic role as the alternate capital vested it with more than local importance.

Governor Franklin wrote glowingly of the spread of the iron industry westward. Bog iron was plentiful throughout the province; in fact it was New Jersey's principal mineral resource. The oldest extraction took place at the Morris family mine at Tinton Manor in Monmouth before 1700. Years later there was mining throughout the Highlands, at Charlottesburg, Hibernia, Ringwood, Mount Hope, Andover, Long Pond, Morristown, and Bloomingdale. Forges and furnaces were plentiful, and pig iron and bars were shipped to New York. Soon there were steel furnaces, plating mills, and slitting mills for nail-making. In 1750, after long agitation, Parliament passed an act admitting pig and bar iron to Britain free of duty but forbidding the erection of additional slitting mills, rolling mills, and steel furnaces. Copper, too, was mined in small amounts, especially in the Piedmont at New Brunswick, Belleville, Rocky Hill, and Bound Brook, as well as at the famous Schuyler mines near Newark, the oldest and by far the most productive.

The iron industry developed later in south Jersey, but it became equally important. It was largely the work of one man, Charles Read of Burlington, an entrepreneur and long-time politician and office-holder. As deputy secretary of the province for many years, one of Read's duties was to make an accounting of all mining activity. Aided by the knowledge he had gained, Read discovered on several of his holdings in interior Burlington County large quantities of bog iron on cedar swamplands. When assays showed a metallic ore content averaging 45 percent, he determined to develop an industry, and around 1765 he selected four sites, Taunton, Etna, Batsto, and Atsion, all east of Medford near the Gloucester County line. On obtaining Governor Franklin's consent to dam the streams, forges and furnaces were erected. Where necessary indentured servants and even a few slaves were brought in. The largest ore-gathering area was at Batsto, where free labor was plentiful, and the greatest conversion to bar was at Atsion. Read's operations were successful, but in time he sold his interests to various partners, having overextended himself in a variety of other activities. During the War of Independence the south Jersey iron industry was an important source of cannonballs for the American army, and at Batsto much-needed salt was also panned. Activity continued throughout the first half of the nineteenth century, with the manufacture of a variety of ironware for domestic uses.

During the eighteenth century New Jersey was commercially dependent upon New York and Philadelphia. Despite all efforts to develop flourishing ports, her export trade never amounted to much. Governor Bellomont's attorney general had written in 1698 that New Jersey had only four or five sail engaged in foreign trade, and Governor Belcher a half-century later noted that this figure had risen to but twenty. Shipments to Europe and the West Indies during the 1760s amounted to only £30,000 per annum in value, while in 1763 Philadelphia's exports were worth £708,000 and New York's £526,000. One observer, Robert Rogers, commented in 1765 that New Jersey, "though well cultivated and thickly seated," lacked foreign trade and was "kept under." In 1770 in *The American Traveller* Alexander Cluny wrote more fully that the people "having no considerable foreign trade of their own, exchange their commodities at those two places [New York and Philadelphia] for foreign goods, and consequently leave a profit there, otherwise they might have for themselves." Governor Franklin noted the absence of foreign trade and pointed out that manufacturing, discouraged by the crown, was practically nonexistent. Thus the colony lacked the credit balances with which to purchase imports from England such as woolens, hats, and cutlery as well as the commodities of the West Indies.

New Jersey's trade, then, was small in comparison with that of the other colonies. Though she was well endowed with agricultural, mineral, and forest resources, the bulk of her overseas exports found their way to England and the West Indies by way of New York and Philadelphia. No bar iron, for example, left East Jersey for Britain in the year 1771. Perth Amboy did ship to England 45,000 feet of oak boards and 18,000 staves, but New York sent 474,000 staves alone. Likewise, though Burlington exported 45,000 feet of pine boards and planks, Philadelphia shipped 590,000 staves and 300,000 feet of board, much of it originating in New Jersey. With the exception of 5,000 pounds of copper through Perth Amboy, incidentally the largest copper shipment from the colonies, New Jersey's additional exports—a little flour, corn, beeswax, tallow, and dried fish—were meager. In consequence her imports were negligible. In 1771 nothing of note entered Perth Amboy, the official port in the north, and only small quantities of sugar, rum, cocoa, and salt entered the south Jersey ports of Cohansey, Salem, and Burlington. While New Jersey was importing 235 hundredweight of brown sugar, 1,650 gallons of rum, and 2,200 bushels of salt, Philadelphia received 7,000 hundredweight of sugar, 521,000 gallons of rum, and 40,000 bushels of salt.*

In 1776 New Jersey's population was, if anything, more diversified than in 1702.† Slightly less than half were now English in origin. The Indians had all but disappeared, but the Negro population, principally slaves, had increased to a total of one-twelfth of the whole. Three-fifths of the people resided in the northern half of the province above a line connecting Trenton with the ocean.

The older East Jersey towns sheltered little coteries of wealthy and even cultured men. The substantial New England Congregational element was now Presbyterian, while the number of affluent Anglicans had grown steadily. Perth Amboy, the northern capital, was neatly laid out, with its central square, its marketplace, and its appealing Anglican church, Trinity. It supported a wealthy clique, known as "the Group," composed of

---

* See also Roger T. Trindell, "The Ports of Salem and Greenwich in the Eighteenth Century," *New Jersey History*, LXXXVI (1968), 199–214.

† U.S. census figures for 1790 are pertinent: English 47%; Dutch, 16.6%; German, 9.2%; Scotch, 7.7%; Scotch-Irish, 6.3%; Swedes, 3.9%; French, 2.4%; others, 6%. Negroes not included.

merchants, landowners, and royal officials. Among the Group was a majority of the provincial council and two-thirds of the Board of Proprietors. This élite class was conservative and aristocratic, completely divorced from contact with the lower orders. Black house servants were a status symbol. These men were connected by ties of business and marriage with the influential families of New York City—for example, James Parker, board president, was related by marriage to his predecessor, the renowned James Alexander; while Cortlandt Skinner, vice president and former speaker of the assembly and attorney general, was Parker's brother-in-law. The Group stood for law and order, and its members were referred to in Governor Franklin's reports to the crown as "the Friends of the Government." Perth Amboy's gentry was to suffer severely for its loyalty.

Other East Jersey towns had pretensions of glory. The largest, Elizabethtown, "a very pretty place," with its Presbyterian and Anglican churches and its well-spaced houses and gardens, harbored a small upper class whose fortunes were accumulated through dealings in land and lucrative law practices. The Daytons, the Ogdens, Elias Boudinot, and William Livingston were among its members. As in Perth Amboy, a number were natives of and still active in New York City. Newark, second in population, though boasting a number of fine houses and an academy, was less favored by the opulent. Morristown, hardly a dozen miles to the west, with access to a rich agricultural and iron-working hinterland, also nurtured a budding aristocracy. A number of landowners, many with New York connections, maintained estates nearby. Peter Kemble, long-time council member, was connected with the Schuyler, Van Cortlandt, and DeLancey families. His lands were worked by slaves, and his adjacent properties were leased to tenants. Kemble led a gentleman's life and was renowned for his library and his hospitality. At nearby Basking Ridge lived William Alexander, son of James, who styled himself Lord Stirling. He modeled his estate upon that of an English nobleman, complete with deer parks, and he traversed the countryside in a coach of six ornamented with his alleged coat of arms. Overextended and almost bankrupt at the outbreak of the Revolution, surprisingly he joined the American army and served faithfully under General Washington, whom he greatly admired. Outside prosperous New Brunswick, also, large estates appeared along the Raritan, while the village of Princeton attracted persons of substance as a "seat of learning and politeness."

At the time of the War of Independence, the tradition of the New Jersey landed gentry was well established. A number of Philadelphia and New York estate owners resided there. Among them existed a modicum of sophistication. For example, William Bayard, a New York merchant, led an idyllic life on his farm and orchards at Hoboken, while Arent Schuyler, his neighbor, worked his lands with fifty slaves. Another neighbor, Archibald Kennedy, Sr., receiver general and customs collector of New York, had the misfortune of putting together an estate made up of parcels of land claimed by contentious freeholders of Bergen, a situation that led to his harassment until his death in 1763. His son, at odds with the natives because of his loyalism, sold all, including farms, deer parks, orchards, greenhouses, and stables, and became a captain in the British Navy. Many estate owners, though not all, were forced to leave because of loyalist sympathies.

The ironmasters of Morris, Bergen, and Sussex constituted a tight coterie. Prosperous before the Revolution, they were even more so during the war. They owned the best lands, handled most of the currency in circulation, and maintained the largest domestic establishments. Their houses were furnished with luxuries, and they sported elegant equipages. Their workers, by contrast, were a migratory lot of woodchoppers, colliers, teamsters, miners, and forgemen, many living from hand to mouth. Their tenants, too, lived in shabby dwellings. To a man, the ironmasters believed in class superiority. John Jacob Faesch, a Swiss entrepreneur who was skeptical of religion, supported the church on the ground that "religion was a good thing to keep the lower classes in subordination." Unlike many of their wealthy compeers to the east, these men were economic realists, entirely willing to cast their lot with the patriot cause.

The social ties of New Jersey with her neighbors were so close as to be almost unique among the colonies. They dated from the founding of the colony and flourished during the whole colonial period. Long-standing commercial and other economic relationships prompted close personal associations, with many intermarriages. The leading merchants of Newark, Elizabethtown, Perth Amboy, and New Brunswick dealt directly with their New York counterparts, while in West Jersey the large factors and wholesalers allied with the scions of the great Philadelphia mercantile houses. Philadelphia's hinterland also extended up the Delaware, bringing its entrepreneurs into intimate contact with the river élite.

In like manner New York and Philadelphia capitalists were active in New Jersey as landowners and land speculators. This relationship also led to intermarriage among the leading families of three provinces. For example, the Kembles, Skinners, Alexanders, and Rutherfurds of East Jersey intermarried with New York's leading families, and similarly a number of West Jersey families were connected by blood with the Coxes, Logans, and Pembertons of Philadelphia. During the later period a number, especially businessmen and lawyers, enjoyed illustrious careers in several provinces. A few of the outstanding Jerseymen in this category were James Alexander, John Kinsey, Jr., and his son James, Samuel Smith, and William Livingston. Since for many decades New Jersey's legal profession was greatly undermanned, the ablest lawyers of New York and Philadelphia were seen frequently in the New Jersey courts. Reciprocally, during the later period, the foremost New Jersey lawyers enjoyed important practices in the two cities. Among them were James Kinsey, David Ogden, Cortlandt Skinner, Richard Stockton, Elias Boudinot, and Charles Read.

New Jersey was also closely affiliated with her neighbors through religious and educational ties. Presbyterian, Anglican, Baptist, Lutheran, and Quaker leaders met frequently in Philadelphia and New York. During the prewar period, for example, John Witherspoon of Princeton was an important figure in the Presbyterian Synod,* just as the Reverend Thomas Bradbury

---

* Largely through the influence of Witherspoon, the Philadelphia and New York Synods were united in 1758.

Chandler of Elizabethtown was a leader in the Anglican councils in New York City. Jerseymen were drawn into the stormy religious and educational conflicts that raged in the neighboring institutions of higher learning—King's College and the College of Philadelphia. New Jersey Freemasons, since there was no Grand Lodge in New Jersey, looked to New York for direction. Neighborly bonds were cemented by overlapping memberships on the governing boards of King's College, Queen's College, the College of New Jersey, and the College of Philadelphia. Of equal importance was the association of future leaders who attended these institutions as students. All of these bonds contributed to a common interest as the three neighboring colonies entered the mainstream of the movement for independence.*

In northern New Jersey the Dutch, like the vast majority of Jerseymen, were farmers. Continually augmented by immigrants from New York, they were ensconced in the upper Hackensack, Passaic, and Raritan Valleys, with the greatest concentrations in Bergen and Somerset counties. Dutch farmers moving westward eventually occupied rich lands in Morris County also. Thrifty and hard-working, they clung tenaciously to the land. An endogamous group, they adhered to the Dutch tongue and the Dutch Reformed Church, intermarried, and bequeathed their acres to their heirs. Taking to slaveholding, they maintained somewhat larger farms than their English neighbors. With little interest in politics, these prosperous agrarians were content to reap, sell, and save, "being spectators to their own wealth."

The Germans and the Scotch-Irish were latecomers, reaching New Jersey during the first third of the eighteenth century. Many of the Germans crossed over from Pennsylvania, where they were well established. Always seeking fertile lands, they filtered through Easton into Hunterdon, Morris, and Sussex. They came first as tenants and servants but soon owned the lands they had earmarked. With generations of experience behind them in the Palatinate and elsewhere on the Continent, the Germans were expert farmers concerned with the quality of the

---

* For a detailed account of these intercolonial relationships, see Gerlach, "Revolution or Independence," 38–44.

soil and its suitability for crops, pasture, and orchards. Their farms were distinguished by their neat appearance, great barns, and substantial houses. By 1775 it was estimated that 12,000 Germans had settled in New Jersey. Those coming directly from the Continent tended to settle in Essex County, but their most important settlements were in the northwest, at Amwell, New Germantown, Rockaway, and Bedminster.

The Scotch-Irish flooded into Pennsylvania from Ulster between 1709 and 1715 via Newcastle and Philadelphia and settled to the west of the Pennsylvania Dutch. A number of these poor folk, however, oppressed in Ulster, found their way directly to New Jersey. They took to the hills in Somerset and Morris and spread westward into Hunterdon, western Morris, and Sussex, where they were met by others infiltrating from Pennsylvania. They were Presbyterian and Calvinist to the core, independent to a man, and blessed with few scruples about squatting on vacant lands.

Like other colonies, New Jersey exhibited both frontier conditions and islands of poverty. On the northern frontier, conditions became more rugged as one moved through Hunterdon into Sussex. Here were the new breeds—Germans, Swiss, Scotch-Irish—and here also were migrants from the eastern counties who were struggling to obtain a foothold. Though endowed with pockets of arable land, timber, iron ore, potash, and other forest products, the northern frontier was harsh; for the ambitious, however, it was challenging. The Scotch-Irish, independent and touchy, suffered from a narrow provincialism which prompted one visiting New England lady to score them as ignorant and envious, qualities she attributed to the lack of common schooling.

New Jersey's rural poor eked out a subsistence living on marginal lands, and a large number were squatters. Many lived in one-room shacks and slept on beds of leaves. They were grossly ignorant and without the benefit of church or clergy. Pitched on lands they did not own, they were blessed with children, "of which," noted one contemporary, "they have commonly more than they know what to do with." These defenseless folk were used by scheming men during the bitter land struggles that characterized the whole history of the eastern division.

Class lines in New Jersey were flexible. As elsewhere in the colonies wealth was esteemed, but despite her coteries of wealthy men New Jersey was essentially middle-class. Governor Belcher in 1748 characterized the province as "the best country I have seen for middling fortunes, and for people who have to live by the sweat of their brows." This generalization held for decades. In 1776, 90 percent of the people fell into this category. The great mass of the farmers, the majority of the town folk, and the Dutch and Germans could be counted among this industrious middle class.

South Jersey, like the north, had its affluent and its poor, yet even more than in the north the bulk of the inhabitants were of the middling class and engaged in farming. The earliest settlers were Quakers, with a sprinkling of Anglicans in Burlington and groups of Swedes and Dutch further south. As in the north there were some large estates, especially in Burlington and Hunterdon, a number of which were owned by wealthy Philadelphia Quakers whose forebears had originated in West Jersey.

The Quakers were farmers for the most part. Unlike their wealthy compeers in Philadelphia they were not, as Dr. Alexander Hamilton noted in 1744 and the Reverend Andrew Burnaby in 1760, completely absorbed with the price of flour. If dissatisfied with the Quaker discipline, they tended to drift into the Anglican Church. By 1745 the Quakers had lost their historic majority in the West Jersey counties. In the whole of New Jersey in 1746, there were only 10,000 in a population of 61,000. Burlington County with 3,200, Gloucester with 1,500, and Salem with 1,100 were still regarded as Quaker bastions, though there were non-Quaker majorities in each. A few Quakers still resided in the north in the Shrewsbury-Middletown district. The Quakers exerted an influence out of proportion to their numbers not only because they were farmers with like interests, but because as members of the Society of Friends they formed a closely knit group.

Since 1701 the number of Quaker meetings had increased

slowly but steadily as the settlers fanned out. By 1776, there were meetings at Bordentown and Trenton as well as along the ocean as far north as Tuckerton. North of the Falls of the Delaware the meeting followed the settler into Hunterdon, Morris, and Sussex, and these remote posts were visited by influential public Friends like John Woolman. Haddonfield and Mount Holly had achieved an importance comparable to that of Burlington and Salem. The relative strength of the Quaker districts is reflected in the assessments laid by the Yearly Meeting in 1758: Philadelphia, £32 10s.; Chester, £25; Burlington, £17; Gloucester and Salem, £11; Bucks, £10; and Shrewsbury and Woodbridge, £4.

The Quakers were not given to pretentiousness, except for a few who set store on their Philadelphia mercantilist connections. Even the most affluent lived, by design, unostentatiously. Quaker married Quaker, and family holdings were maintained intact through the years. Arriving early in West Jersey, they chose the best lands. The larger farms were worked with the help of indentured servants, then of slaves. In later years, because of the Society's disapproval of slavery, the indentured servant resumed prominence. The Reverend Nicholas Collin in 1771 described the Quaker farmer as hard-working, prosperous, and respectful of his neighbor and of authority. He added that the Quakers were not impressed with those who made a show of wealth or of high public office. The older Friends, he noted, lived comfortably, but with little interest in glamorous houses, elegant furniture, or other trappings of the rich.

The Swedes and Finns on the west bank of the Delaware were a static group, numbering in 1776 hardly 500. By then the younger Swedes were deserting the Lutheran Church, taking English spouses, and abandoning their native tongue. A number of the more affluent families joined the Anglican Church, and many of the lesser folk were attracted to the Moravian sect by its evangelical missionaries who arrived from Pennsylvania during the forties. The War of Independence brought bewilderment and devastation from which these simple people never recovered. The link with the old country was severed finally when the Swedish crown in 1789 invited all ministers and teachers to return. In the end the Swedish parishes became Episcopalian, and the process of Americanization was complete. Today one must search for traces of the West Jersey Swedes, such as a few names on gravestones at Swedesboro and Repaupo. The ancient churches —Trinity (Old Swedes) at Swedesboro and the smaller St. George's at Georgetown—are vestiges of the Swedish presence.

There were islands of poverty in West Jersey, such as the areas worked by cedar choppers—a group who lived in huts along the edge of the pine barren and were engaged in "mining" the logs preserved for hundreds of years in the amber-colored "ooze." Other woodsmen felled and hauled the oak, gum, and red cedar that was in demand in Philadelphia for construction, shipbuilding, and export. At Batsto, Atsion, and the other ore compounds lived groups of laborers engaged in digging the bog iron deposits. The largest concentration of the poor lived along the marshy, infertile river banks of the Delaware from Raccoon Creek to Oldman's Creek. Here a mixed group subsisted. Writing in 1775, the Reverend Nicholas Collin stressed "the wild nature of the country and the poverty of the people." Emotional instability was prevalent, and these inhabitants were characterized by petty avarice, fraud that was taken for cleverness, and acts of violence. "Everything," wrote Collin, "is cold and ugly." Here as elsewhere, the War of Independence afforded a pretext for outbreaks of personal vengeance.

The status of the indentured servant and the slave in New Jersey was well below that of the average freeman. Until the War of Independence, servants were regarded as lawless by those who believed that society must be protected from them. Judging by the number who simply ran away during the confused period that began in 1776, many must have been maltreated. With 10,000 Negroes in 1776, principally slaves, New Jersey had a higher slave population than any colony north of Maryland, with the exception of New York. The majority were found in north Jersey, though for a period they were freely used on the larger farms in the south.

In proprietary East Jersey laws were passed at an early date to uphold the master's right in his servant. Since on the whole labor was in demand, the servant was highly valued. In 1668 the first East Jersey assembly adopted a law, reenacted in 1675, requiring a captured runaway to serve double the time of his unlawful absence. In 1682 and 1683, under the Twenty Four Proprietors, the servant code was enlarged, with more severe penalties for runaways and with penalties for those assisting runaways. Steps were taken simultaneously to assure servants some rights and to protect them from abuse. Cruelty, especially, was punishable. The servant must be given essential food and clothing. If the master destroyed his servant's eye or his tooth, the servant was freed. No servant could be compelled to serve more than four years or, if an apprentice, beyond the age of twenty-one, and no servant could be taken out of the colony without his consent. The "custom of the country" was spelled out: at the expiration of his term the master was obligated to provide the servant with two suits of apparel, an ax, a hoe, and seven bushels of seed corn. Those who had been promised land must receive it.

In West Jersey, where servants were fewer, "the custom of the country" was similar: ten bushels of seed corn, two horses, and an ax. In 1692, the first year of Andrew Hamilton's governorship, a law was adopted directing all inhabitants to report "suspicious" persons to the constable, on the ground that they might be runaway servants. The West Jersey courts were solicitous regarding the welfare of its numerous apprentices. As in East Jersey, they could not be bound after twenty-one years of age, especially if they were orphans. The influential Yearly Meeting of Friends kept a watchful eye on Quaker masters. In 1687, as a precaution, it urged English Friends not to bind out Quaker children coming to America to non-Quakers.

Slavery in New Jersey was almost as old as white bond servitude. Dutch sea captains who called at New Amsterdam offered slaves for sale, as they did elsewhere in the Dutch possessions. At the time, the Dutch enjoyed commercial hegemony in the Caribbean. About 1672 the English joined in exporting slaves from Gambia or the African Gold Coast. Slavery itself was an ancient institution in the Dark Continent, and because those taken prisoner in the countless tribal wars were enslaved, the supply was inexhaustible. The petty native kings on the coast between the Senegal and the Congo had no difficulty in purchasing prisoners from the interior tribes and selling them to the European "slavers."

Negro slavery, introduced by the Dutch, was a success in the British West Indies because the black adapted himself more easily to the rigors of the climate than the white servant. Recognizing African custom, the planter permitted the slave to live in plantation villages, and to protect his high financial investment he took pains to preserve the institution of the family, so valued by the black, and to provide adequate living conditions. At the same time, the authorities took essential steps to police the slave population. A rudimentary slave code, the first in the English colonies, took shape in Barbados in 1654. The later mainland codes, including that of New Jersey, followed those of the West Indies. The earliest laws, applicable to both servants and slaves, were principally concerned with runaways, and punishments were stipulated for those engaged in kidnapping or in any way abetting them, as well as for the escapees themselves. The planter enjoyed a large measure of liberty in meting out punishment for thieving, disobedience, and similar misdemeanors—frequently a whipping or worse. For a time the clergy were forbidden to baptize slaves in the mistaken notion that once baptized, the slave became free.*

Little is known of the Negroes in New Amsterdam save that there were few. Some were slaves, others were indentured servants, and some at least were freemen. With the English conquest, the Duke's Laws (borrowing from the Massachusetts law) recognized life servitude. Slaves were taken from New York to New Jersey at an early date, large landowners like Lewis Morris, Sr., William Sandford, and Isaac Kingsland—emigrants from Barbados—being familiar with the advantages of slave labor.† Ownership of slaves was not confined to the wealthy,

---

* Carl and Roberta Bridenbaugh, *No Peace Beyond the Line: The English in the Caribbean, 1624–1690* (New York, 1972), especially Chs. 8 and 11, presents the most recent account of African slavery and its introduction into the British West Indies.

† For example, John Berry brought his family, two servants and thirty-two slaves; Samuel Moore, his eight children and two slaves; and Michael Smith, three servants and sixteen slaves.

however; a number were brought to New Jersey as Dutch farmers entered in force from New York. Their labor was valued, since by the end of the seventeenth century few indentured servants were arriving from Britain.

By contrast with the eastern part of the province, there were few slaves in proprietary West Jersey. When the Quaker founder, George Fox, made his notable missionary trip to America in 1671, he was frowned upon in Barbados for preaching to Negroes. Two years later several Quakers there were presented to the grand jury for permitting blacks to attend a Quaker meeting. The heavy fines imposed prompted a number of them like Lewis Morris, Sr. to migrate to the mainland. With this background the early Quakers took no interest in owning slaves.

The number of slaves in New Jersey increased slowly until Governor Hunter's time and then accelerated, especially in the eastern division. From 1698 to 1717 few slaves entered directly from the West Indies, however, and from 1718 to 1727 only 115 did so; the great majority of Jersey's slaves entered from New York. A New Jersey population estimate of 1715 lists 21,000 whites and 1,500 Negroes, principally slaves, and the census of 1726 records 2,580 blacks in a population of 32,442, with only 409 in West Jersey. The largest numbers were in Bergen and Monmouth counties. By 1745 the total population had risen to 61,000, with 4,600 slaves. For the first time Burlington and Hunterdon counties reveal appreciable numbers. By 1775 there were nearly 10,000 slaves in a population of 125,000.

Indifferent attempts were made to limit the entry of slaves. With the imposition of an import duty of £10 in 1714, Governor Hunter explained that its object was to encourage the entry of white servants, "to better people the colony." Persons migrating to New Jersey and intending to settle permanently were exempt from paying the duty. The law had no effect. Except for the unsuccessful attempts to curb the slave trade during Governor Morris's administration, the subject was not revived until 1761. The following year an act was adopted levying a duty on slaves, but the Board of Trade disallowed it for technical reasons. It was not until 1769 that an act was passed levying a duty of £15 proclamation money on each slave, a measure not restrictive enough to interfere with the lucrative trade.

During the early period, when slaves were few, the mainland colonies followed the example of the West Indies, and the laws lumped together white servants, Indian servants, and Negro slaves. In 1683 in East Jersey all three were protected from physical abuse, and masters were required to provide sufficient food and clothing. In West Jersey an act of 1692 forbade the selling of rum and other strong drink to Indians and Negroes. The basic code of the royal period was adopted in 1714 and applied to Negroes, Indians, and mulatto slaves. Gradually tightened, and armed with stiffer penalties, it remained in force until the Revolution, regulating the conduct of those in servitude. As in all colonial codes, slaves were forbidden to purchase alcoholic beverages or other wares without their master's consent; they could not be abroad without the master's pass; and those guilty of striking a white man, ravishing a white woman, or stealing would be whipped publicly. Informers received rewards for reporting the slave or anyone illegally aiding him. Since the assumption was that "it is found by experience that free Negroes are an idle, slothful people, and prove very often a charge to the place where they are," the code provided that anyone manumitting a slave must enter a bond of £200 and pay the sum of £20 a year during the freedman's lifetime. No freed slave was permitted to hold land in fee simple. Other acts spelled out the penalties for crimes and misdemeanors committed by slaves; among the more common punishments were forty stripes of the lash, the maximum permitted, for those guilty of stealing hogs or chickens. Increasingly large fines were imposed on those furnishing a slave with a gun or a pistol. With the outbreak of the War of Independence, stronger measures were taken in some localities in the belief that the slave (and the white servant too) would run away in a time of confusion. The Shrewsbury Committee of Safety in 1775, for example, confiscated all arms in the possession of Negroes, whether free or not, and restricted severely the movement of all slaves.

Like other slaveholding colonies, New Jersey was subject to the ever-latent fear of slave insurrection. Such apprehensions accounted for the harshness of the punishments and for the fact that erring slaves were sometimes convicted and punished with questionable speed. In several instances where a slave was to be executed for a heinous crime, others nearby were summoned to witness the proceedings, for salutary effect. The boiling point of public hysteria was low in northern New Jersey, especially in view of the slave revolts of 1712 and 1741 in New York City. Although these disorders sent out shock waves, in fact there were no slave insurrections in New Jersey in colonial times.

Counteracting these prejudiced attitudes toward the Negro were the humanitarian influences of the Great Awakening and the renewed concern for the plight of the Negro on the part of the Quakers. Renowned Presbyterian preachers like Samuel Davies of Virginia, future Princeton president, helped in the softening process. In *The Duty of Christians to Propagate Their Religion Among the Heathens, Earnestly Recommended to the Masters of Negroe Slaves in Virginia* . . . , published in 1758, Davies denied that "the Christianizing of Negroes makes them proud and saucy, and tempts them to imagine themselves upon an Equality with White People." Davies boldly asserted that Negroes were ignorant "as to Divine Things" not through a lack of capacity but because of lack of instruction by their masters. His views spread, especially in the strongly Presbyterian middle colonies.

From the time of George Fox, Quakers had persisted in asserting that the Negro was a human being and should be treated as such. While in Barbados in 1671, Fox urged that they be given the equivalent of freedom dues. But it was not until the 1740s, when slaves were becoming numerous in Pennsylvania and West Jersey, that Quaker concern revived. It dates from 1743, when John Woolman of Mount Holly recognized in himself a deep aversion to slavery; his convictions were confirmed during a trip through Virginia and Maryland three years later. His views on slavery were published in 1754 in a pamphlet, *Some Considerations on the Keeping of Negroes: Recommended to the Professors of Christianity.* Since the slave, Woolman argued, lacked a voice of his own, his case was being neglected to the extent that slavery itself was taken for granted. He urged a revolutionary consideration: that slavery entailed misery for both the slave *and* the owner, a conviction later shared by Thomas Jefferson. In his rewritten *Considerations . . . , Second Part . . .* published in 1762, he not only dwelt upon the inhumanity of the slave trade, but pointed up the obstacles in achieving abolition. The slaves, poorly fed and clothed and condemned to servile labor, were regarded as "a Sort of People below us in Nature," whereas they should be accepted as human beings, as "our Kinsfolk." He clearly recognized that the whole matter was complicated by ancient beliefs. The Negro was of a different color, hence suited for slavery, but the white child, though "born of Parents of the Meanest Sort," was never regarded as a candidate for a lifetime of servitude. "The Ideas of Negroes and Slaves," he wrote prophetically, are so "interwoven in the Mind." Though this was Woolman's last tract on the subject, he preached his antislavery sentiments until his death eight years later. His work was taken up by others, particularly the prolific Anthony Benezet of the Philadelphia Meeting. David Cooper, the Burlington Quaker, in 1772 repeated Woolman's thought that the idea of slavery was rooted in absurdity and that much of it was selfishly reasoned. "The low contempt with which they are generally treated by whites," he wrote, "leads children from the first dawn of reason to consider people with a black skin on a footing with domestic animals, form'd to serve and obey." *

The French and Indian War posed difficult problems for the Society of Friends, whose leaders were dedicated to the ideal of peace. Distress over the naked violence on the Pennsylvania frontier led to a reconsideration of their position vis-à-vis a number of vexing problems, one of which was the increasing practice of keeping slaves. In 1758 the Yearly Meeting recorded the hope that Friends would desist from holding slaves and that they would consider eventually setting their slaves at liberty. For the moment it was ruled that any Friend buying or selling slaves

* See also Winthrop D. Jordan, *White Over Black: American Attitudes Toward the Negro, 1550–1812* (Chapel Hill, 1968), 271–276 and *passim*. Woolman's two antislavery tracts, together with a third, *A Word of Remembrance and Caution to the Rich . . .* , are printed in Phillips P. Moulton, *The Journal and Major Essays of John Woolman* (New York, 1971).

should be debarred from Meeting. From 1758 to 1777 Friends were frequently urged "to do the thing that was right" in reference to the keeping of slaves. Ultimately, writes historian Winthrop D. Jordan, the Friends became "a quiet voice of conscience to the nation."

The antislavery activity of John Woolman and the Yearly Meeting had repercussions in New Jersey. Instigated by the Quakers of Burlington County, petitions reached the assembly in 1768 praying that the importation of slaves be prohibited and that the laws governing the manumission of slaves be reformed. New antiimportation bills were introduced in 1773, without success. A year later, petitions were received from Salem, Perth Amboy, and Essex County, but because of the tense political situation that was developing, they went unheeded. As a consequence, laws prohibiting the importation and the manumitting of slaves were not adopted until after the Revolution.*

By 1776 the Indian had all but disappeared in New Jersey. In 1725 the Unalachtigos, the Lenape subtribe in the south, had migrated to the Juniata Valley of Pennsylvania on their way, ultimately, to western New York. After the Easton Treaty of 1758, the Unami, the centrally located subtribe dwelling south of Sourland Mountain west of Hopewell, migrated to the Wyoming Valley of Pennsylvania under their noted chief Tedyuscung. Remnants remained, together with the Minisink and Pomptons, Minsi bands living in the remote northwest. The frontier Indians were unhappy because later settlers, especially the land speculators, were none too scrupulous in compensating them for their lands. Drink and disease took a heavy toll, and to add to the Indians' difficulties their food supply was whittled down by the ravages of the white hunters and the settlers dammed their streams, interrupting travel by canoe. Old antagonisms reawakened when, during the French and Indian War, many frontier settlers who were fearful of raids from Pennsylvania extended their hatred to all Indians, good and bad.

As with the Negro, the Indian had supporters working

---

* On this topic, see Arthur Zilversmit, *The First Emancipation: The Abolition of Slavery in the North* (Chicago, 1967).

patiently in his behalf. The humanitarian impulses engendered by the Great Awakening stimulated interest in the plight of the Indian, especially among the Presbyterians. A group of New York and New Jersey ministers as early as 1740 appealed for aid from the leading Scottish philanthropic agency, the Society for the Propagation of Christian Knowledge. Funds were made available for the support of two missionaries to the Indians, Azariah Horton on Long Island and David Brainerd in the Delaware River district near Easton. Brainerd, a Yale-educated minister, labored first on the Delaware then settled at Crosswicks, southeast of Trenton, where he established an Indian reservation with a church and a school. Worn out and beset with privation, he died of tuberculosis two years later, in 1747. The Society then appointed his brother John to continue the work. Because of the hostility of Robert Hunter Morris and other landowners toward the settlement, Brainerd and his supporters were forced to seek another location. Aided by the Society and a newly established Quaker organization entitled the Association for Helping the Indians, Brainerd persevered in his work until 1755. The outbreak of the French and Indian War interrupted plans to purchase a tract of 2,000 acres on the edge of the Great Pine Barren.

In 1756 aid for the Indian came from an unexpected source. The New Jersey assembly, concerned with native unrest on the frontier, began a study of the Indian problem. Meetings were held at Burlington and Crosswicks beginning in January 1756, and as a result the assembly, led by Richard Smith, Samuel Smith, and Charles Read of the Quaker party, adopted the noteworthy act of March 1757. Under its provisions the Indians, except those in the northwest, would be given compensation for their land claims. The cost would be modest, since many had already left the province, and it would be defrayed partly from the defense fund and partly by means of public lotteries. An effort to compel the proprietary boards to foot the bill failed.

A conference at Burlington in 1758 dealt with the northwest Indians, the Minisink and the Pomptons. The difficulties involved were complicated by the absence of any deeds. In June Governor Bernard arrived, and in view of the dangerous situation on the frontier he turned immediately to the Indian problem. Learning that representatives of Pennsylvania were about to meet with the Indians at Easton, he determined that New Jersey should take part. Meanwhile, he cautioned the frontier settlers of Sussex to refrain from harassing the Indians until the results were known. Despite difficulties created by several Pennsylvania delegates, the governor and his associates were able to direct the conference to a successful conclusion. In addition, with funds provided by the assembly the Minisink and the Pomptons were compensated for the illegal seizure of their lands and satisfied in regard to other sources of irritation. In all Bernard spent only £1,500, leaving enough to purchase a tract of 3,000 acres in the pine barrens south of Medford to establish a new reservation for the remaining Indians of New Jersey.

John Brainerd was summoned from Newark, where he was then living, to become superintendent. At Brotherton, as the reservation was aptly called, houses and a church were erected. In time, more than 100 out of a total estimated by Bernard as no larger than 300 New Jersey Indians were gathered there. Brainerd carried on for ten years as the number of dwellers gradually diminished. Conditions after 1768 had deteriorated, so that when the Lenape at Lake Oneida in New York long after the Revolution invited the Brotherton Indians to join them, the latter decided to accept. The reservation lands were sold, the receipts being used to help them migrate.

Meanwhile, concern for Indian welfare continued. When untoward incidents occurred, cool heads were able to prevail; for example, when Indians fleeing from Pennsylvania sought refuge in south Jersey in 1764, Charles Read counseled that they not be molested unless they disturbed the peace. He appealed not only to humane kindness but to the example set by the earliest Quaker settlers. Again in 1765 when Read, a justice on circuit in Sussex, was faced with the murder of an Indian, he insisted, following an ancient precedent, that another Indian be present at the trial. When the white settler was executed, the slain man's widow was given £40 in compensation and her husband's rifle. On balance—save for a few frontier incidents—New Jersey deserves high credit for her humane treatment of the Indians.

In conclusion, New Jersey in 1776 was a land of opportunity for a man of industry and thrift. There was work for all, relatively easy access to land ownership, and no inflexible class barriers for the ambitious settler. Despite the fact that 10 percent of the wealthiest owned a third of the land and that nearly 30 percent of the families were landless, class relationships were relatively harmonious. Life was not quite as idyllic as it was portrayed by numerous travelers; their outlook was often colored by the hospitality of affluent hosts who, with few exceptions, gave little thought to the plight of the poor, the indentured servant, the Indian, or the slave. The colony was essentially rural, with farming the leading occupation but with a substantial interest in the exploitation of mineral and forest resources. New Jersey manufactured few finished products, engaged in little overseas commerce, and had few direct links with the mother country. Her middle-class farmers were not greatly absorbed in political matters, despite the noisy factionalism engendered in the assembly. As citizens, they were concerned at most with the local tax rates, and they were unanimous in their belief in the efficacy of an easy-money policy. The average Jerseyman was highly moral, a member of a church or a sect, and ambitious for the well-being of his family and the future of his children. During the years from 1702 to 1776, however, new forces—moral, spiritual, and political—were impinging upon the New Jersey community, and their influence must now be assessed.

10

NEW JERSEY ON THE EVE
OF THE REVOLUTION:
THE LIFE OF THE SPIRIT
AND THE MIND

The life of the spirit flourished in New Jersey until the outbreak of the War of Independence. Not only were the inhabitants receptive to the new sects and the Great Awakening that swept through the colonies in the 1740s, but the older denominations had experienced a steady growth. In 1775 there were nearly two hundred congregations in the colony. The Presbyterians led with fifty, followed by the Quakers with forty, the Dutch Reformed and the Baptists with thirty each, and the Anglicans with twenty. Scattered among these were a few Swedish Lutheran, German Lutheran, and Moravian Pietist congregations, but the Methodists had barely appeared. Eighteenth-century New Jersey, with its diverse populace, was a fertile ground for the missionary. Since the stronger churches, the Presbyterian and the Dutch Reformed, strove to achieve an educated ministry and an educated laity and since the Quakers and the Anglicans also believed strongly in schooling, it is no surprise that the churches led in kindling the life of the mind as well as that of the spirit. Church-sponsored academies came into being, while the Presbyterians and the Dutch Reformed succeeded in founding institutions of higher learning.

The Presbyterian church grew more rapidly than any other, aided by its Congregational undergirding in the old East Jersey towns; under the aegis of the Philadelphia Synod its influence spread throughout New Jersey, especially in Morris, Hunterdon, and Sussex. The Scotch-Irish migrations to Pennsylvania and New Jersey from 1718 to 1730 accelerated this growth. These ardent believers, wedded to a highly centralized form of church government, had little patience with the loosely exercised authority of the New England Congregational churches. In 1721 a predictable struggle broke out at the synod when it was proposed that the synod's acts should be binding on all churches. Jonathan Dickinson, the Elizabethtown minister and leader of the Congregationalist faction, protested vigorously, but it was a losing battle. When in 1729 it was moved that all ministers subscribe to the Westminster Confession of Faith, Dickinson and his supporters barely succeeded in watering down the resolution. In 1736, with a greatly increased Scotch-Irish representation, it was voted overwhelmingly that the Confession be accepted "without the least variation or alteration." Rather than withdraw, the Congregationalists chose to continue the debate, and it was waged in one form or another until the adoption of the tenuous Plan of Union in 1801. At the root of the whole controversy was the accident of history which had given the Scots a highly centralized form of government and denied it to the English Calvinist church.

In 1739–1741 the Great Awakening swept the colonies. This evangelical movement, led in America by George Whitefield, was soon espoused by the great Jonathan Edwards of Northampton, Massachusetts.* The spirit of revival quickly permeated many of the Presbyterian congregations, especially in New Jersey and New York. Though it had an influence among the Congregationalists, the Baptists, and the Dutch Reformed, many of them were not persuaded, believing that God did not reveal himself to the individual outside the organized church. In the middle colonies, Presbyterians like Jonathan Dickinson and Aaron Burr, the Dutch Reformed Theodore Jacob Frelinghuysen, and other influential ministers aligned themselves with

---

* Whitefield has been described as an Anglican Methodist by affiliation, a Calvinist by orientation, and an apostle of rebirth through conversion.

Whitefield. Other followers of the new movement were the graduates of the "Log College," a seminary founded in 1727 by William Tennent, Sr., on Neshaminy Creek, Pennsylvania, including the founder's sons, Gilbert, John, William, and Charles. All insisted that the synod ordain candidates for the ministry even though they lacked the educational preparation which was available only in New England or Great Britain. They argued forcefully that the church must supply the expanding frontier with ministers. The "Old Lights," as the conservative party in the synod was called, proceeded to exclude Log College graduates from the ministry, and in 1741 eleven "New Light" ministers,* including the entire membership of the New Brunswick presbytery, were debarred from the synod. Admitting defeat, Dickinson, Burr, and their associates withdrew and in 1745 formed the Synod of New York, with three presbyteries and twenty-two ministers.

The Presbyterians were sharply divided in the first phase of this controversy, from 1739 to 1758. It involved, on the one hand, the preservation of localism in the church organization, a new birth of piety, and an expanding ministry; and on the other, centralism, formalism, orthodoxy, and, unwittingly, resistance to the new forces of Americanization. The newly constituted New York Synod did answer the call for ministers on the frontier, thus its influence expanded rapidly into western Pennsylvania and wherever the Scotch-Irish migrated, west and south. Simultaneously, the New Lights sought to replace the old Log College with an institution that would afford unquestionable training for candidates for the ministry. This movement resulted in the founding of the College of New Jersey (Princeton University) in 1746. Though the Philadelphia Synod, beset with difficulties in recruiting candidates for the ministry, came upon hard times, the New York Synod persevered in its efforts to effect a reconciliation. An accommodation was finally reached in 1758, for by that time many Old Light leaders were dead, animosities had softened, and the younger leaders were impressed with the contributions of the New York Synod. In the compromise, the

---

* First used by the traditionalist "Old Lights" as a term of derision.

first of several, the New York Synod succeeded in establishing qualifications for the ministry other than orthodoxy and rigid theological training. The compromise of 1758 survived until the War of Independence.

Meanwhile the Great Awakening was sweeping the colonies, and Gilbert Tennent had become its chief apostle in New Jersey. Licensed to preach in 1724 by the Philadelphia Synod, he assumed the pulpit at New Brunswick a year later. A man of great zeal, he aroused some hostility because of his impatience, which some took for arrogance. In 1739 and 1740 he proselytized with Whitefield and accompanied him on a missionary journey as far as Boston. Local ministers praised them as they "melted the congregations," and Governor Belcher, himself a Bay State Congregationalist, commended their efforts. The Anglicans, the Quakers, and the conservative element of the Dutch Reformed Church, disapproving of the emotionalism evoked by the revivalists, stood aside. In time, a number of the evangelist preachers were held up to scorn. The not entirely unprejudiced Dr. Alexander Hamilton, in his *Itinerarium* of 1744, relates that one of them "would preach for eight hours; (then) someone would take him outside until the screaming of the congregation took him back into the meeting." After half a dozen years the Great Awakening had run its course. Edwards returned to his books, and Tennent in 1745 became minister of the Second Presbyterian Church in Philadelphia.

While the Great Awakening undoubtedly revived religion among the indifferent, the Old Lights, disturbed by its excesses and its new breed of preachers, forbade ministers of one presbytery from preaching in another without sanction, and the Philadelphia Synod also forbade any presbytery from ordaining a candidate unless he held a diploma from a New England or European institution. These mandates aroused great antagonism among the New Lights. Ignoring the synod, Gilbert Tennent continued to grant licenses without the examination, a factor in the expulsion of the New Brunswick clergy "for their unwearied, unscriptural, anti-presbyterian, uncharitable, and abusive practices." * Tennent found many sympathizers within the church,

---

* In his famous Nottingham sermon, "The Danger of an Unconverted

however—men like Jonathan Dickinson, Aaron Burr, Samuel Blair, Samuel Finley, and James Davenport, the men who had founded the New York Synod in 1745 with Dickinson as moderator.

Though dubbed "apostles of ignorance," the New Jersey New Lights were determined to establish an institution of higher learning. Unable to arouse the interest of Governor Lewis Morris, in 1746 they obtained a charter from his interim successor, John Hamilton. The College of New Jersey began its existence in Elizabethtown the following year under seven trustees, among them Jonathan Dickinson of Elizabethtown and Aaron Burr of Newark. Other trustees chosen were Gilbert and William Tennent, Samuel Blair, Richard Treat, and Samuel Finley, all New Light ministers. Dickinson was elected president. The college was authorized to grant degrees, own property, choose officers and professors, establish needful regulations, and admit students of all denominations. Eight students matriculated, each paying £4. On Dickinson's death in 1748 the college moved to Newark under the presidency of Aaron Burr, the Newark minister.

The college had a warm friend in Harvard-educated Governor Belcher, who immediately obtained a stronger charter, with an enlarged board of twenty-three. Though the majority of the additional trustees were ministers, there were three laymen from New York and three from Philadelphia. Belcher suggested that the governor and several councilors be designated *pro forma* members, but since Gilbert Tennent and others were opposed, only the governor was named a trustee (as he is today).

Location and finances were pressing problems. Belcher advised the trustees to erect a building in a centrally located community, preferably one offering inducements. He favored Princeton, though there was strong support for New Brunswick. Princeton was chosen in September 1752 because it promised ten acres of

---

Ministry" (1740), Tennent demanded that the church reach out for new communicants and that ministerial candidates must include young men educated "to know God."

improved land and two hundred of woodland. When the college building was ready for occupancy in 1758, Belcher, declining to lend his name, suggested Nassau Hall in honor of William III of the house of Nassau. At the time there were seventy scholars. The governor also recommended that the college petition the assembly for permission to hold a lottery, a favorite device in the colonies for raising funds, but the assembly was lukewarm, an attitude attributed by Belcher to the Quaker members, whom he believed inimical to institutions of higher learning. Since Harvard had raised funds abroad, Belcher advised the trustees to do likewise. When several of them received encouraging letters from England and Scotland, Gilbert Tennent was prevailed upon to undertake the mission, and he was accompanied by the new president, the Reverend Samuel Davies. Nearly £20,000 was raised with the aid of ministers in England (especially London), Scotland, and Ulster; and Belcher persuaded the General Assembly of the Church of Scotland to sponsor a collection in every congregation.

President Burr, a Yale graduate and Newark minister, died just after the college was removed to Princeton, and his successor, the famous Jonathan Edwards, died after serving but a month. Tragically the institution suffered the loss of Burr, Edwards, and Governor Belcher within the span of a month. Edwards's death was a severe blow, for it had taken strenuous efforts to persuade him to move from Massachusetts. He was followed by two Yale graduates, Samuel Davies and Samuel Finley, noted New Light preachers in Virginia and Maryland respectively. Their terms, too, were short. Finally, in 1768 John Witherspoon, minister at Paisley, Scotland, was persuaded to take the post, and he served until his death in 1794.

The curriculum of the College of New Jersey, while not dissimilar to those of Harvard and Yale, and especially the latter, included more than the study of the classics and divinity; following the institution's ancient dictum to raise up men "that will be useful in the learned professions—ornaments of the state as well as the church," it was oriented toward secular studies. Witherspoon himself taught Hebrew, added the French language to the curriculum, and introduced the long-lived lecture system

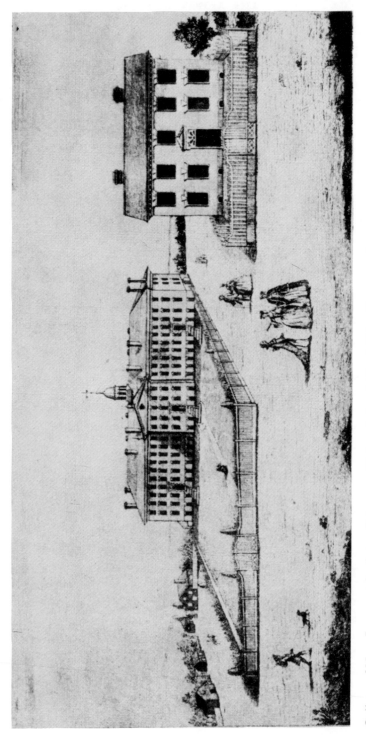

College of New Jersey, 1764 (later, Princeton University)—A North-West Prospect of Nassau-Hall with a Front View of the President's House. *From an engraving by Henry Dawkins.*

to the American college. In keeping with the Newtonian revolution in England, he emphasized natural philosophy and mathematics, and as an ardent Lockean he propounded a radical theory of moral philosophy that enabled him to embrace enthusiastically the cause of the colonists against England. Finally, as an educational leader Witherspoon receives the credit for expounding and diffusing in America the Scottish "Common Sense" philosophy—a concept of "moral sense" (conscience combined with a sense of duty) as opposed to nonrational doctrines—a rejoinder to the emotionalism of Bishop Berkeley and the skepticism of David Hume.*

By 1776 the Presbyterians were the strongest and most numerous denomination in New Jersey. Their leading congregations were in Elizabethtown, Newark, New Brunswick, and Freehold, and Essex County was their citadel. From 1738 to the Revolution, Elizabethtown had four renowned ministers: Jonathan Dickinson, Elihu Spencer, Abraham Lettletas, the Whig pamphleteer, and James Caldwell, later chaplain of the American forces in New Jersey. At Newark, Burr was minister from 1737 to 1748. The Freehold pulpit in Monmouth was occupied by the Tennent brothers, John and William, and the church itself was known as "Old Tennent Church." The East Jersey Presbyterians supported the popular cause, first in the land struggles against the proprietary faction and later against the infringement of colonial liberties by the crown. In May 1775 a committee of the synod, of which John Witherspoon was chairman, sent a strong letter to all the churches of New Jersey disavowing any intention of inflaming the people but warning that "if the British ministry shall continue to enforce their claims by violence, a lasting and bloody conflict must ensue." How prophetic!

The Dutch Reformed Church, the most ancient in New Jersey, underwent a similar period of growth and change. At the close of the seventeenth century there was a steady migration of the

---

* Witherspoon's contributions are ably summed up in Francis L. Broderick, "Pulpit, Physics, and Politics: The Curriculum of the College of New Jersey, 1746–1794," *William and Mary Quarterly*, VI (1949), 42–68.

First Presbyterian Church, Springfield. *Courtesy of The New York-Historical Society.*

Dutch from New York into Bergen and Somerset counties. Though ministers were few and overburdened, New Jersey had three remarkable Dutch clergymen: William Bertolf, the learned Theodore Jacob Frelinghuysen, and the Swiss-born John Henry Goetschius. Bertolf, the pioneer from New York City, worked in northern New Jersey organizing congregations and catechizing the children. Though disapproved of by New York's Amsterdam-trained ministers for his disregard of the liturgy and his "running around," he was until 1720 "the organizer of congregations" in New Jersey. The Raritan Valley, also pioneered by Bertolf, became "the garden of the Dutch Church."

Following Bertolf, Frelinghuysen came to the Raritan country in 1720. A learned man, he was educated at the University of Lingen in Westphalia. Suspect by the older ministers for his devotion to Pietism and evangelism, he gradually won them over. As he defended his views in several persuasive sermons, "even the hearts of his enemies were conquered." Frelinghuysen brought Jacob Schureman from New York as chorister, reader, and schoolmaster to a district where illiteracy was rife. Backed by the Consistory, the governing body of the church, he inaugurated a system of "helpers," or teachers, to whom the children would be sent for instruction. Frelinghuysen's plan of combining catechizing and schooling spread throughout the New Jersey Dutch community.

Frelinghuysen also became the leader of the Coetus or American party within the Consistory. This body, which was organized about 1737, favored greater ecclesiastical autonomy for the American churches and especially a locally trained clergy. Its members were steadily opposed by the Conferentie, the group ordained by the Amsterdam Classis. This struggle within the church lasted for years, with the liberals gradually gaining ground. Once in the majority, the Coetus undertook to examine and ordain candidates for the ministry. As the connection with the Amsterdam Classis became more tenuous, the supply of ministers dried up, and even catechisms and school texts were expensive and hard to come by. Desperately needed, the new ministers were welcomed, especially when they preached

in English. The Dutch in New Jersey were becoming American-
ized.

The catalyst in the long controversy proved to be John
Livingston, Yale graduate and erstwhile theology student at
Utrecht. Called to the Fulton Street Church in New York, he
formulated a plan of union that he took to Holland and put
before the Amsterdam Classis. Gaining approbation, he presented it to a convention of New York and New Jersey church
representatives composed of twenty-two ministers and twenty-
five elders. By now weary of the strife and believing that the
Amsterdam Classis had deserted it, the convention members in
October 1771 unanimously adopted Livingston's proposals. His
plan provided for a general governing body and five local
consistories, including those of Hackensack and New Brunswick.
Nominally subordinate to the Amsterdam Classis, the American
church was at last empowered to examine and license candidates
for the ministry and to enforce church discipline.

The third outstanding Reformed Dutch minister was John
Henry Goetschius of Hackensack and Schraalenburg, ordained
by Frelinghuysen, whose aspiration to found a collegiate seminary Goetschius adopted as his own. Beginning as a missionary
on the Pennsylvania frontier as a youth of seventeen, he settled
finally in the Hackensack Valley. Short of temper and single-
minded, he determined that the church should provide educational opportunities for ministerial candidates. In 1766, sur-
mounting all opposition, he obtained a charter for Queen's
College (Rutgers University) from the New Jersey assembly, with
authorization to give instruction in the classics and other
branches of useful knowledge. Hackensack and New Brunswick
competed for the institution, with the latter winning out. In 1769,
with the aid of Hendrick Fisher, president of the board and
long-time assemblyman, a stronger charter was granted, with the
good will of Governor Franklin. The organization of the college
was soon completed, but the war intervened, postponing the
erection of a building. Goetschius, who died in 1774, had joined
in the advocacy of the patriot cause. With the exception of a few
of the gentry in New York and a few isolated but highly
troublesome communities in East Jersey, the Dutch espoused

independence. Their ministers, fiercely American, were hunted down and their churches destroyed by the British.

The majority of the Germans in New Jersey, in contrast with those in Pennsylvania, were Lutherans. Many originated in the Rhine Palatinate, in Württemberg, in Alsace, and in the Swiss cantons. They came to America to escape the exactions and oppressions of landlords and quasi-feudal nobles, as well as for economic reasons. Those coming to New Jersey settled in the north. By 1715, Lutheran missionaries from New York were organizing small congregations on the Millstone and other branches of the Raritan in Somerset and Hunterdon. After some years of discouraging effort the settlers persuaded the Reverend Henry Melchior Muhlenberg, who had been working in Pennsylvania for eight years, to become their spiritual leader. Trained in the Pietist tradition at the University of Halle, he was their mentor for thirty years. Appalled by the widespread ignorance and illiteracy, as Berthold before him had been, he set to work finding teachers. Eventually church schools were established at New Germantown, Bedminster, and several other German villages. The first Lutheran Convention, meeting in Philadelphia in 1748 through Muhlenberg's efforts, adopted resolutions looking to the founding of parochial schools, with the Bible as the basis of education. The link with Germany was broken as a result of the Revolution, and as the German language gave way to English the children were thrown back on neighborhood schools.

The original Pietist movement of the fifteenth century spread from Moravia into Germany. Persecuted and oppressed everywhere, in 1722 a number of Pietists found refuge on the estate of Count Nicholas Ludwig Zinzendorf in Saxony. At Herrnhut, "the Lord's Watch," the Revised Church of the United Brethren was established, and many Pietist exiles succeeded in reaching this refuge. Here the high Pietist standards of religious instruction were revived, with an abiding dependence on the teachings of the Bible. Lacking a formal creed, the Moravians cultivated a warm personal piety; their sincerity commanded admiration, and in time they influenced scholars at several German universities. Halle's great German Pietist, August Hermann Francke, encouraged Count Zinzendorf to organize residential schools under Moravian sisters and brethren, with a schedule of reading, writing, catechism, and rest periods. As with the Lutherans, singing was an important activity. The older children were taught crafts and skills.

To escape war and oppression, the Moravians began to emigrate to America, particularly Pennsylvania, where they founded communities at Nazareth, Lititz, and Bethlehem. Soon their brethren were missionizing on the frontier, with a group from Bethlehem founding a settlement at Greenland (Warren County) in 1769. After 1774 the village was known as Hope. In the south, Moravian missionaries were active along the Delaware River and Bay and on the ocean front as far as Little Egg Harbor. Their position attracted some Swedes and many of the plain folk for whom the more formal creeds had lost their appeal. In the end the Pietist movement in New Jersey declined, as the Moravians simply could not muster enough missionaries to minister to the widely dispersed groups, and their stubborn adherence to the German language was a handicap. Many of their ideals and ideas were adopted by the better-organized German Lutherans.

The Swedes of Gloucester and Salem, like the Dutch in the north, were gradually absorbed by the English in spite of efforts to keep alive their native customs and institutions. For long years their patron, the bishop of Skara, sent them a succession of zealous and highly educated ministers and teachers, many of whom endured hardships and straitened circumstances. Greatest among them were Peter Kalm, sometime minister at Raccoon (Swedesboro) and famous botanist; the Reverend Israel Acrelius; and the Reverend Nicholas Collin, all of whom left valuable accounts of their experiences. In the 1750s, Pastor Acrelius recorded that though no one was able to read the ancient Swedish script, a surprising number still understood Swedish. He spoke of the small affluent class who rode to church on horseback, whose young ladies were clad in hooped skirts and other finery, and who drank tea, coffee, chocolate, and fashionable punch. The majority of the Delaware Swedes, however, were poor and lived on infertile, marginal lands. Despite all efforts, illiteracy remained widespread, especially about Penn's Neck, where the charity school was weakest.

Because of their close organization, the eighteenth-century Quakers were influential politically. Astute in gaining allies, they suffered less in New Jersey than in Pennsylvania, where the frontier Scotch-Irish hated them as the peace party. There political troubles drove them back upon themselves, and more and more they became "a peculiar people." Since many Philadelphia Quakers became men of wealth, the Yearly Meeting felt constrained to issue frequent admonitions regarding discipline. The New Jersey meetings, too, received these warnings to watch for evidence of superfluity of dress, furnishings, and houses. Young women were warned to avoid "Broidered Hair or Gold or Pearls or Costly Array," and young men "needless furniture" for their horses. Friends must also guard against "being vainly exalted or puffed up," drinking to excess, keeping unseasonable company, falling into debt, going to court to settle disputes, and selling inferior wares. Perhaps because of repetition these old Quaker tenets became lifeless. Schooling either became neglected or reverted to "guarded instruction." Whatever the cause, educational standards in New Jersey were certainly disappointing. After reviewing the problem, the important Haddonfield Monthly Meeting came to the conclusion in 1751 that Friends should make use of the neighborhood schools, as indeed most were doing, and employ the influence of the meeting to secure better-trained teachers.

Toward the end of the colonial period, new Quaker spiritual leaders emerged: John Woolman of Mount Holly and Anthony Benezet and Rebecca Jones of Philadelphia. They opposed the doctrine that Friends must withdraw from society, and they resented the charge that the Quakers were a peculiar people. Taking a more positive stance, they preached that Quakers must make known their "quiet and kindly" virtues and move from lives of contemplation to social awareness and action. Broadly, they should strive for social betterment. John Woolman was deeply concerned, as a teacher and a traveling minister, about the prevailing illiteracy and the miserable quality of the teaching of children. He and Benezet found their views widely and favorably received. Both men urged that attention be given to the education of Indians and Negroes. As early as 1755 Woolman had some success in persuading the West Jersey meetings to interest themselves in the education of Negro children, and it was he who founded the New Jersey Association for Helping the Indians. In time the efforts of Woolman and Benezet won over the Yearly Meeting, and all meetings were advised to find homes for teachers and pupils living in remote areas and to encourage Friends to enter the teaching profession. Unfortunately, the war thwarted these intentions. In New Jersey the major obstacles—the inability of the meetings to support schooling and the shortness of the term in the rural communities—were not overcome.

In 1776 the Anglican Church, despite support from the S.P.G.,* was still a minority church. Because of the rule requiring ordination by a bishop, ministerial candidates were compelled to make a trip to Great Britain, a serious obstacle. Even in Burlington and Perth Amboy the congregations were small and on occasions without a fixed minister. The church grew slowly. The S.P.G. continued to send missionaries, a mixed lot, and rarely were there a half-dozen in the colony. The royal governors, instructed to watch over the church, were indifferent. When men like Cornbury and Ingoldsby interfered in its behalf, their performances were so ludicrous that even the faithful ridiculed them. The proprietors of East Jersey, principally Anglicans, were heartily disliked because of their land monopoly, while the political antics of the St. Mary's clique in Burlington did not help the church in the south.

The Anglican minister was poorly paid. The S.P.G. missionary received £30 per annum from the society and £60 colonial money from the local congregation. The Reverend Thomas Bradbury Chandler, for example, asserted that his income was not enough to feed and clothe his family. The minister was also overworked, like his compeer in the Dutch Reformed Church. Chandler,

---

* The much-used abbreviation for the Society for the Propagation of the Gospel in Foreign Parts.

whose experience was typical, ministered to Freehold, Shrews-
bury, Middletown, and, at times, Allentown. In 1745 his parish
embraced the whole of Monmouth County. In Burlington John
Talbot, the Quaker-hater, was succeeded in 1738 by Colin
Campbell as rector. The latter served for thirty years, com-
plaining frequently that he was forced to serve the whole of south
Jersey. The next incumbent was the zealous loyalist Jonathan
Odell, who remained until the war; suspected of being inimical
to "American liberty" and paroled in Burlington, he fled to New
York and, after a sojourn in England, reappeared in New
Brunswick, Canada. William Skinner was pastor of the Perth
Amboy church from 1722 to 1757, but his immediate successors
had brief terms. At Elizabethtown, Edward Vaughan was
minister until 1747, for a term of nearly forty years. His
successor, Chandler—later forced to flee for his loyalism—was
sent to England for ordination. In 1776, there were small
Anglican congregations at Shrewsbury, Middletown, Freehold,
New Brunswick, Trenton, and Salem.

All the while, no effort was spared in the attempt to obtain an
American bishop. Ministers, vestrymen, wardens, and congregations continued their appeals unceasingly, arguing that they
could never compete with the Dissenters unless they could ordain
their own ministers. The Dissenters kept a watchful eye on these
proceedings, fearing that an Anglican bishop would be vested
with some kind of temporal authority. After the furor over the
Stamp Act had waned, Dr. Chandler wrote a number of
pamphlets in behalf of the episcopal cause, reviving a heated
controversy in the colony. In 1771 four clergymen submitted a
petition to Secretary of State Hillsborough relative to "the
distressed state of the Church through the want of bishops."
Unless a bishop was installed in America, they pleaded, "the
Dissenters will in time gain an ascendancy." The agitation for an
American episcopate failed not for want of energy or eloquence
on the part of men like Chandler but because of the indifference
of British officials at home who, ironically, feared that a separate
Anglican bishopric would lessen colonial dependence on the
mother country.

It was George Keith, the Quaker apostate turned priest, who

as the first S.P.G. missionary advocated that the Anglicans support schooling. Like the missionaries who followed him, he urged the congregations to foster parish schools and the more affluent to provide elementary education for the poorly circumstanced—the children of servants, the Indians, and the slaves. Progress was painfully slow. At Burlington, for example, Talbot did not succeed in establishing a school until 1712. Here were taught the three Rs and the catechism. Patrons were slow in forthcoming, while parents were reluctant to send their children to school during the planting and harvesting seasons. Eventually parish schools appeared at Shrewsbury, Newark, Elizabethtown, Perth Amboy, Woodbridge, and elsewhere. In the remote villages, the missionary or the lay worker did the teaching. The S.P.G. sent texts for distribution among the poor.

The S.P.G. missionary was not universally welcomed, even as a teacher. Presbyterians, Quakers, and other Dissenters feared that Anglican strength would somehow lead to the establishment of a state church. Moreover, the missionaries were instructed especially to return the Quakers to the fold, an ambition which aroused deep resentment. In 1758 Governor Bernard was instructed to forbid anyone to teach without a license, and in 1760 Governor Boone required the magistrates to examine teachers before licensing them. Though it was merely an effort to improve the quality of instruction in the neighborhood schools, popular suspicions were not allayed.

With the outbreak of the War of Independence the S.P.G. withdrew its support, and the church—regarded as an instrument of the British government—suffered a severe decline. The Anglican clergy were ordered not to use the liturgy unless prayers for the king were omitted, a change they felt, in good conscience, they could not make. A few subscribed to the patriot cause, but the majority left the colony. The churches for the most part closed, and their congregations disbanded. A number of churches suffered damage, among them St. Peter's in Perth Amboy, St. John's in Elizabethtown, and Trinity in Newark. After the war the American Episcopal Church was founded, with a national organization that conformed to conditions created by independence. The Methodist movement within the church was hardly noticeable in the colony before the war. Though its advocates were active in the colonies as early as 1760, by 1776 there were only three avowed Methodist preachers in New Jersey, with the first congregation being formed at Trenton in 1771.

Greatly strengthened by the formation of the Baptist Association in Philadelphia in 1707 and the impetus given by the Great Awakening, the Baptist denomination by 1776 was one of the largest in New Jersey. The Baptists were especially numerous in the rural villages of Monmouth, Hunterdon, Cumberland, and Cape May counties. For the most part small farmers, it was church membership rather than politics that held their interest. Unlike the Presbyterians and the Dutch Reformed, the Baptists set no high educational qualifications for their ministerial candidates. Since the individual congregations were given wide latitude in the choice of ministers, there was little difficulty in filling pulpits. Their ancient churches at Cohansey and Piscataway were augmented by strong congregations at Hightstown, Hopewell, and Cape May.

As a result of close contact with liberal Presbyterians during the Great Awakening, the younger Baptist ministers, resenting the acceptance of colleagues whom they saw as "ranters," began a long campaign in the association for an educated ministry and an educated laity. By 1747 the association was won over to the promotion of common school education, and it approved the founding of academies for the training of ministers. One of these, established at Hopewell, was conspicuously successful. From 1762 to 1773, despite the lack of support and sheer poverty, Hopewell graduated men who became influential ministers, lawyers, physicians, and teachers. There were other Baptist academies at Bordentown and Knowlton. A school for the poor and the children of slaves was founded in the village of Hope. In 1773 Hopewell Academy, its work done, was transferred to Warren, Rhode Island, as Rhode Island College; its first president, fittingly, was James Manning, a product of Hopewell. Soon Baptist youths from as far south as southern New Jersey were attending the new institution in Rhode Island (forerunner of Brown University in Providence).

Most of the New Jersey churches conscientiously attempted to supply schooling for children. Orphans and apprentices were singled out, and many were heedful of the Indian and Negro child. Despite the Great Awakening and the efforts of the several denominations, New Jersey's structure of elementary education remained loose and unintegrated, the royal government preferring to leave the responsibility to those willing to assume it. The town selectmen felt the same way, but as they were closer to the voter, from time to time they made gestures to provide teachers. The zest for public schooling nurtured by the early East Jersey settlers from New England could not flourish in an environment of so many competing sects and nationalities. The dispersal of the populace from the village to the individual farm was also an obstacle with which education-minded inhabitants seemed unable to cope. Nevertheless the gropings of churches, localities, and individuals for the education of children never ceased. Unfortunately most of the schoolteachers were not worth the fees they asked, and the itinerant teacher often turned out to be a charlatan or even a rogue. Though the war interrupted all schooling, Jerseymen were committed to the notion that primary education at least was a public responsibility. However, it was not until after 1830 that their aspirations met with success.

Higher education fared better in New Jersey. During the royal period, the need for training men for the professions (especially the ministry) was recognized, and a group of academies were founded to educate at a more advanced level. The movement gathered momentum with the establishment of the College of New Jersey and the plans for Queen's College. Beginning with the third quarter of the eighteenth century, grammar schools and academies made an appearance in a number of towns, with the best-known at Elizabethtown, Newark, New Brunswick, Princeton, Hackensack, Freehold, and Hopewell. Though most frequently sponsored by the Presbyterians, these schools served all elements of the community, imparting the rudiments of the classics, mathematics, and science.

Though many academy graduates were to attend the College of New Jersey, some chose colleges in New England, King's College in New York, or the College of Philadelphia. Only in rare instances did a New Jersey youth attend college in England or Scotland. Aside from the ministry, professional education developed slowly. Lawyers, now "a numerous breed" frequently under attack for excessive fees, generally received their training through the time-honored apprentice system. Doctors were few in number, as evidenced by the enrollment of only fourteen members when the New Jersey Medical Society, the first in the colonies, was formed in 1766; ten years later there were merely twenty-six. No more than a handful received formal training in Philadelphia or elsewhere.*

In conclusion, it should be stressed that New Jersey's educational patterns in the eighteenth century, with some exceptions, followed those of the other colonies. The household, still the major economic unit, continued to play a primary role in the education of the young. As formal schooling developed, the parents could devote more attention to the child's interests and pastimes. Hobby horses, doll houses, and Noah's arks appeared, along with children's books and games such as battledore and shuttlecock. As the child achieved recognition as an individual, parents became more patient and gave him more attention. Parental authority was upheld, but it was leavened by tenderness. Neighborhood and church schooling gradually became widespread. Few clergymen dared fail to heed the demand for instruction for the children, and the various denominations were constrained to take an interest in the founding of grammar schools, academies, and, eventually, colleges.

As pointed out above, New Jersey played a substantial role in these developments, yet the results were indifferent so far as primary education was concerned. The state of higher education, with numerous academies and two colleges, was more satisfactory. In the academies and colleges, emphasis began to shift to secular training, with less dependence on the classics and theology. New Jersey's secondary schools revealed surprising diversity and were responsive to a variety of needs, especially in the enterprising towns. As in New York City and Philadelphia, young men were able to gain instruction in the skills and crafts.

---

* For further discussion of the professions in colonial New Jersey, see Gerlach, "Revolution or Independence," 83–87.

The need for trained workers grew in the type of society that began to flourish in the communities situated along the great New York-Philadelphia highway of trade and commerce.

In the American colonies, as in England, there occurred a cultural revolution that reached its apogee during the mid-eighteenth century. Like the concurrent revolution in agriculture, its origins were in England, where it was led by John Locke and Isaac Newton. The colonies in general responded with a rising interest in science, education, and politics, and although the main impact was felt in the commercial cities and in the seats of learning, every community was influenced to some degree, many without realizing it. New Jersey, too, was affected by the intellectual ferment, but not extraordinarily so.

John Locke's proposition that nothing should be accepted that was "contrary to reason" led to a rationalization of piety. Such a tolerant and common-sense philosophy was embraced not only by intellectuals but by businessmen and churchmen of all creeds and sects. Locke and his followers held that a wholesome assent to religion could be justified on the grounds of reason, faith, and enthusiasm. Blind faith, however, should never be allowed to contradict reason. Although agreeing that piety was the end of all education, the new philosophy insisted that piety must include good works. A corollary was that the child must be treated with patience and understanding. In the colonies the views of Locke and his followers were taken up by all the progressive elements—by secular leaders, by spiritual leaders of all denominations, including many of the Pietist groups originating on the Continent, and by the leaders in higher education.

Several intellectual divines cautioned against the lurking excesses inherent in these new doctrines. They were not anti-cultural, but cautious. Cotton Mather warned against reason without faith. John Witherspoon arrived in the middle colonies fresh from Scotland, where the battle was raging, and wrote off Bishop Berkeley's enthusiasm as "a wild and ridiculous attempt to unsettle the principle of common sense by metaphysical reasoning." * It is difficult to imagine Witherspoon embracing

---

* Bishop George Berkeley, the Irish metaphysician, in 1710 published *The*

any religious movement that gave even nodding recognition to "enthusiasm." Witherspoon's doctrine of common sense spread rapidly and widely throughout the colonies, especially among the Presbyterian clergy and laity. Its conservative spokesman adhered tenaciously to the Westminster Confession, the rights of the congregation vis-à-vis the individual, the pastoral role of the clergy, and rigorous standards of education for the ministry. Witherspoon's coming to America in 1768 was a boon to the divided Presbyterian church. His authority was accepted immediately, and his doctrines were widely diffused by his disciples and students.

The cultural revolution in the colonies had many facets. As in Britain, the uses of learning were reexamined, and pedantry was universally condemned. Mid-century works such as Isaac Watts's *The Improvement of the Mind* (1754) and James Burgh's *The Dignity of Human Nature* (1761) were well known. Just emerging was the indigenous thinking of Benjamin Franklin, the leader of the utilitarian school. His views, though not original, were disseminated by means of his tracts and almanacs and were welcomed by multitudes of receptive people. As an apostle of self-education, Franklin was opposed to formal education as the panacea for all. His proposals emphasized the business of living and knowledge of the sciences in lieu of the traditional preoccupation with the classics and theology.

The eighteenth century's increasingly literate population enjoyed an astonishing outpouring of almanacs, manuals, textbooks, pamphlets, sermons, and laws. From 1725 to 1764, 60,000 almanacs were published in the colonies. The colonial printers were fortified by the Zenger decision of 1735* and responded to an eager public. New Jersey, lacking a newspaper throughout the colonial period, depended on the papers of New York and Philadelphia; nevertheless she contributed her share of almanacs and established an important magazine. Her practical people

---

Principles of Human Knowledge. His unorthodox view had disquieting effects upon a large segment of the clergy.

* Thus printer Isaac Collins could write Governor William Livingston, "My Ear is open to every Man's Instruction but to no Man's influences." During the Revolution, Collins established New Jersey's first newspaper.

demanded easy access to books, which led to the formation of library companies, town libraries, and parish libraries. Burlington responded to the need, then Trenton. The craving for knowledge was so great that several towns, again following the example set in New York and Philadelphia, offered courses in bookkeeping, surveying, and navigation for modest fees. To satisfy the more sophisticated, public forums patterned after Franklin's junto were organized.

The mid-eighteenth century revealed endless diversity and change. Contributing factors were the interaction of ethnic and religious patterns, varying economic activities, and external and internal migration. Though some communities sought to preserve their religious and ethnic solidarity, all were affected by improved communication and transportation and by the dissemination of the printed word. Due to her geographical situation, New Jersey was subjected to the continuous flow of innovation and change as it proceeded along the dynamic New York-Philadelphia highway.

Education was strongly affected at all levels, formal and informal. The newspaper and the magazine, the library and the junto manifested new levels of sophistication. Dependence on the household and the school were more than equaled by the multiplicity of choices offered by the community. Since prosperity abounded and labor was scarce, the towns supplied more than one means of entering a skill or trade, and if opportunity was not available in one place, the ambitious man could with a feeling of security move to another.

Mobility also had a significant influence in bringing the men of different colonies more closely together. There was a new interest in intercolonial relationships as leaders were brought into contact with one another. At the same time, the colleges began to emphasize education for public service rather than for the ministry alone. Printers responded to the public taste rather than the official point of view, and the able preacher was accorded a public platform.

Literature and art for the most part languished in this essentially rural colony. There were few printers in colonial New Jersey, and no regular newspaper, but James Parker of Woodbridge published the sole issue of *The Constitutional Courant* in September 1765—a violent attack upon the Stamp Act. Not until December 1777 did the *New Jersey Gazette*, published at Burlington by Isaac Collins, the provincial printer, make its appearance. Governor William Livingston, under the pen name "Hortensius," made use of the *Gazette* during the early war years in putting his views before the people. Shepherd Kollack, another patriot, published the *New Jersey Journal* at Chatham, beginning in February 1779, and it survived under various auspices until 1792. Collins and Kollack also published almanacs, valued by all country people. In 1723 William Bradford printed the New Jersey laws under a Perth Amboy imprint, but his headquarters was in New York. James Parker, who established himself in Woodbridge in 1754, published *The New American Magazine* (1758–1760), the second periodical of any sustained duration in the colonies.* It was edited by Samuel Neville of Perth Amboy, the talented justice of the Supreme Court, who used the pseudonym "Sylvanus Americanus." Most of the religious and political tracts written by Jerseymen were published in New York and Philadelphia.

The one library of mention was that of Burlington, founded in 1758 by Charles Read, secretary of the colony. Through his influence it was granted a royal charter, one of the few libraries so honored. After a year, principally through gifts, it had acquired more than 500 volumes. A few wealthy men possessed private libraries, as did the colony's lawyers, but the average family owned at most a Bible, a catechism, a hymnal, or a religious tract or two. New Jersey benefited too from the continuing efforts of the S.P.G. to supply missionary libraries.

There were several limners or portrait painters, but, as in the other colonies, most were itinerants bargaining for commissions as they journeyed from place to place. One John Watson, also a collector of paintings, established himself as a painter in Perth Amboy, while Patience Wright of Burlington won local renown through exhibiting her wax figures in London. Music was

---

* The first was the Boston *American Magazine and Historical Chronicle* (1743–1746).

confined to the churches and the local instrumentalist. Francis Hopkinson of Bordentown, a councilor in 1774 and a signer of the Declaration of Independence, composed songs and hymns for the harpsichord, and James Lyon, author of the class ode at Princeton in 1759, later wrote and published songs.

Literary efforts, too, were sparse. John Woolman's *Journal*, published posthumously in Philadelphia in 1774, is a minor classic. Samuel Smith, who was politically active, contributed his still-respected *History of the Colony of Nova-Caesaria, or New Jersey*, printed in 1765 by James Parker in Burlington and sold by David Hall, partner of Benjamin Franklin.* Philip Freneau, a Princeton contemporary of James Madison, is known as "the poet of the Revolution." His commencement poem "The Rising Glory of America," written with H. H. Brackenridge in 1771, was published in Philadelphia. Freneau's reputation as a poet, however, came with the publication of "Santa Cruz," written while he was working in the West Indies after graduation. John Witherspoon's writings, published principally in Scotland from 1756 to 1768 and consisting of tracts and sermons, won him a reputation in ecclesiastical circles. Samuel Davies, a predecessor (1759–1761) of Witherspoon as president of the College of New Jersey, produced poetry, hymns, and a notable sermon† while he was preaching earlier in Virginia.

New Jersey's public and domestic architecture is more impressive. Princeton's Nassau Hall was the colony's most admired edifice. Both in the north and south there appeared a number of tastefully built Quaker meetinghouses and Presbyterian and Anglican churches. The older octagonal Congregational meetinghouse had given way during the eighteenth century to the new-style rectangular New England–type meetinghouse. Domestic houses, with two notable exceptions, were modest indeed. The architecturally satisfying New England dwelling was not reproduced in New Jersey. The average house was little more than a

---

* See Carl E. Prince, "Samuel Smith's History of Nova-Caesaria" in Lawrence H. Leder, ed., *The Colonial Legacy*, vol. II, *Some Eighteenth-Century Commentators* (New York, 1971), 163–180.

† *The Duty of Christians* . . . , delivered in 1757.

one-story dwelling with an attic or loft. The more elaborate houses followed English tradition, and many were copied from English books on house design then circulating widely in the colonies.

New Jersey's domestic architecture did contribute the Dutch colonial and the Salem house. The Dutch house was modest in size, from thirty to forty feet wide and thirty feet deep. A story and a half high, its most noteworthy feature was its graceful gambrel roof descending in equal proportion, front and rear. The foundation walls were usually of reddish-brown sandstone, while the roofs were shingled with white cedar or pine. The upper sides, too, were of wood, generally clapboards three feet in length and an inch thick. A few of these houses may still be seen in the Paramus district. The Dutch barns were both spacious and high, with huge interior beams of hewn oak. The earliest Dutch churches were hexagonal or octagonal, as in some of the early New England meetinghouses, so that all might hear well.

The south Jersey Salem house exhibited in design the principal features of the eighteenth-century Philadelphia town house. It was two stories high, wide of front, with pent roof, handsome front doors, occasionally hooded, and interior brick end chimneys. Its unique feature was its exterior brickwork. The diamond, the zigzag, or the checkerboard pattern of purple, blue, or gray glazed brick stood out arrestingly against the red brick background. Glazed headers of Flemish bond were frequently used. The Salem bricklayer not only copied the ancient patterns of Essex County, England, but added variations of his own. Today one must search for such houses up a secluded road or beside a quiet creek, though a few are extant in Salem town itself. The Salem house compares in charm with the better-known Cape Cod or Virginia cottage.

Such was the spirit and the mind of New Jersey in 1776, a colony small in area and in population but as diverse in national origins and religious sects as any in America. The persistence of such a variety of folk—coming not only from Britain but from many Continental lands—in adjusting to one another was, in essence, the process of becoming American. Their common experience in coping with frontier conditions through many

Abel Nickolson House, Elsinboro, Salem County. *Courtesy of the Historical American Building Survey (HABS), Library of Congress.*

John and Mary Dickinson House, Woodstown, Salem County. *Courtesy of Harry Devlin, artist and photographer.*

decades and in sacrificing their native folkways, traditions, and language for something foreign drew them slowly together. Out of it emerged a spirit of self-reliance and independence. The struggle with the mother country brought this essentially middle-class people reluctantly into the vortex of stirring events not of their own choosing. Each man in the end was forced to take stock and to make a decision. Many, indeed too many, tried to steer a course of caution or of expediency, weighing each occurrence in terms of his own well-being. A number were lucky, but most were to suffer grievously for their calculated passivity.

11

INDEPENDENCE

Unlike New England and Virginia, New Jersey was slow to enter the mainstream of protest against the crown. Not until Parliament in the spring of 1774 passed the four Intolerable Acts were Jerseymen aroused. Even the Boston Massacre had attracted small notice, for the colony was preoccupied with the Skinner robbery and the crown's allowance of its latest paper money act.

When Lord North's ministry decided to retain the duty on tea as a symbol of Parliament's right to tax the colonies, Sam Adams again was given an opportunity to stir up a storm. Governor Hutchinson of Massachusetts refused to allow the tea in Boston harbor to be returned to England, as was done in New York and Philadelphia, or to be stored, as at Charleston; his stubbornness prompted the Boston Tea Party. In retaliation, Parliament had adopted the notorious Intolerable Acts that included the closing of Boston harbor and the remodeling of the Massachusetts Charter. General Thomas Gage, commander of the British forces in America, was appointed governor. In addition, the Quebec Act, intended to give Canada a more liberal frame of government, was interpreted by Americans as a subterfuge to limit their frontiers and corrupt their religion.

Events moved swiftly as Gage fortified the approaches to Boston harbor. Further abroad, when the Virginia assembly expressed its sympathy with Massachusetts, it was dissolved by her royal governor. Members gathering informally at Raleigh Tavern in Williamsburg proposed a congress composed of delegates from all the colonies. The suggestion was well received, though at the time only three assemblies were in session. In New Jersey, Speaker Cortlandt Skinner and Governor Franklin, not wishing to become involved, blocked a meeting of the legislature, on the ground that there was no pressing business. By this time the governor had cast his lot with the crown. The elder Franklin, who had fallen into disfavor in London, was soon removed as head of the colonial post office. In espousing the colonial cause, he blamed Parliament for bringing on the troubles in America. "But you," he wrote his son, "who are a thorough courtier, see everything with government eyes." Though William Franklin believed that he had been refused the Barbados post because of Lord Hillsborough's dislike of his father, he decided that his allegiance lay with the crown. He assured the English authorities that he was determined "not to give just cause of complaint." Franklin, who ranked with Hunter and Bernard as the ablest of New Jersey's royal governors, kept his head through trying times. He practiced restraint and reason, hoping until the very last that reconciliation with England could be brought about.

In June 1774, while local committees of correspondence were forming in New Jersey to demand the repeal of the Boston Port Act and to approve the call for a continental congress, Franklin confided to Colonial Secretary Lord Dartmouth that, though a congress composed of governors, councilors, and representatives might be beneficial, he feared the consequences of a body made up only of representatives and members of committees of correspondence.

The first New Jersey local committee was that of Lower Freehold, organized on June 6, 1774. The most influential was that of Essex County, formed at Newark on the 11th. The latter included Stephen Crane, Isaac Ogden, and Elias Boudinot, all in touch with the New York radicals. Delegates from the local and county committees, seventy-two in number, met as a provincial convention at New Brunswick on July 21 and elected Stephen Crane of Elizabethtown, a former assembly speaker, as presiding officer. After dutifully swearing allegiance to the king and expressing their abhorrence of independence, the delegates resolved that Parliament's acts imposing revenue laws upon them were unconstitutional and oppressive. They condemned the

Boston Port Act, appointed a committee to send provisions to Boston, approved the call for a continental congress, and pledged themselves to support its findings. They also recommended the adoption of nonimportation and nonexportation agreements and voted their thanks to those who had aided the American position in Parliament. This convention, an extralegal body, chose as its delegates to the First Continental Congress Stephen Crane; James Kinsey, son of a former assembly speaker; Richard Smith, Jr., brother of Councilor Samuel Smith of Burlington; John de Hart of Somerset; and William Livingston of Essex, all lawyers. Governor Franklin did not oppose these proceedings, believing at the time that an intercolonial body might prove to be the means of effecting an accommodation with the mother country.

At the First Continental Congress, meeting in Philadelphia in September 1774, the moderates—led by men like Joseph Galloway—proposed a union of the colonies under a written constitution. This proposal was defeated, probably because it stood small chance of acceptance by the crown. For the time, eschewing the mention of independence, the radicals, led by Massachusetts and Virginia men, pushed through a nonimportation agreement, to take effect on December 1, and a nonexportation agreement, effective the following September if no settlement had been reached by then. The nonimportation agreement would be enforced by local committees, with penalties for violations. Secondly, the congress condemned the Intolerable Acts as a bald infringement of colonial liberties. Finally it appealed to the king to redress the grievances enacted by an irresponsible Parliament. The delegates asserted that they were asking no diminution of the prerogative nor any new grant of power. Lord Dartmouth, a not unreasonable man, believed those who would sign a nonimportation agreement to be guilty of treason and took the precaution of forbidding the export of arms to America. Governor Franklin echoed the Tory view when he asserted that England must choose between suffering humiliation or compelling obedience to her laws.

Jerseymen were concerned and perplexed as pressures mounted. The majority felt that events were moving too rapidly, and many wondered whether defiance should go so far. Others, especially in the Quaker counties, desired above all a peaceable settlement. A number hesitated to disregard the advice and pleas of a governor bent upon conciliation. Chief Justice Frederick Smythe, speaking to an Essex County grand jury, belittled measures against "imaginary tyranny three thousand miles away." Nevertheless, led by members of the Essex County committee of correspondence, the Non-Importation Association was approved almost everywhere, and local committees were chosen to enforce its policies. Voters at the forthcoming elections at Elizabethtown, Newark, and elsewhere were instructed to choose a new committee with power to name delegates to a second continental congress in case the assembly was not convened. The Elizabethtown and Woodbridge committees recommended terminating trade with Staten Island because her merchants had not signed the Association. Incidents occurred: New York merchants were penalized for bringing goods secretly to Elizabethtown on the British ship *Beulah*, and in remote Greenwich, in Cumberland County, there was a miniature tea party.

But there were other viewpoints. Franklin wrote Lord Dartmouth in December that many inhabitants disapproved of the resolutions of the Continental Congress but failed to denounce them because, lacking protection, they would become objects of popular resentment. In Bergen County loyalist sympathizers were heartened by the attitude of New York City, where the Association was not being signed by everyone. Many Quakers in South Jersey, as well as some in Shrewsbury, refrained from acting because of their disapproval of violence. At their Yearly Meeting in Philadelphia, the Quakers adopted a strong protest against all illegal acts. The freeholders of Nottingham in Burlington County petitioned the assembly to make reasonable proposals lest there be a tragic civil war.

The New Jersey assembly met at Perth Amboy in January 1775. Pleading for concord, the governor deplored the resolutions of the New Brunswick convention of July and warned the representatives that it was their sworn duty to preserve their form of government. After dwelling upon the horrors of civil war, he advised them to draw up a list of grievances that he himself would present to the crown. For a brief time it seemed likely that Franklin's advice might prevail. Then William Livingston, John de Hart, and Elias Boudinot appeared in order to gain approval of the resolutions of the First Continental Congress.* They argued that the assembly's favorable vote would influence New York, whose assembly was holding back. New York, they urged, must not be allowed to stand alone as the sole dissenter among the colonies. Thus put to the test, the assembly, with only seven nays, voted to endorse the congress's acts, and a second ballot carried unanimously. The assembly also approved the Non-Importation Association and reappointed the same delegates to the Second Continental Congress, scheduled to meet in Philadelphia in May 1775. Nevertheless, its members protested their loyalty to the king and drew up a list of grievances, as the governor had recommended. Starting with those presented by the congress, the assembly added two grievances of its own: one, with Chief Justice Smythe in mind, that judges be made dependent on the lower house for their salaries instead of being on the civil list; and the other, that colonial agents be dispensed with. Franklin refused to transmit this petition to the king on the ground that, against his advice, the assembly had approved the resolves of the Continental Congress. Ignoring the governor, the assembly then sent the petition on its own responsibility.

In mid-April 1775, when General Gage sent troops into Boston to enforce the Coercive Acts, American blood was shed at Lexington and Concord. The news spread rapidly throughout the colonies, bringing the grim realization that Americans would have to fight to secure their liberties. In New Jersey, town meetings and meetings of correspondence committees were organized, and men began to drill. Governor Franklin endeavored to calm the storm and especially to scotch the rumor that British men-of-war off Sandy Hook were preparing to raid the

---

* All were members of the Elizabethtown committee of correspondence, determined advocates of a provincial congress, and members of the radical so-called Elizabethtown junto. In the house they had the support of their associate Stephen Crane and their "tool," James Kinsey. Speaker Skinner was taken unawares, and all was approved without formal dissent on the morning of January 24, the first day of the meeting.

provincial treasury at Perth Amboy. Actually the excited militia of Freehold, spurred by its committee of correspondence, marched through New Brunswick and Woodbridge to defend Perth Amboy.

Additional steps, all deemed necessary, were undertaken. On May 2, 1775, at the meeting of the New Brunswick Committee a date, May 23, was set for the meeting of the first provincial congress, to be held at Trenton. In view of the public impatience, many who had refused to do so earlier, including the townspeople of Shrewsbury, now signed the Association. Though Franklin reported that many loyalists did so through fear, men of all shades of opinion received assurances that as voters they would be represented at the provincial congress.

Franklin brought Lord North's famous "Resolution for Conciliation" before the assembly on May 15. In it North promised that colonial assemblies providing funds for imperial defense, disposable by Parliament, would be relieved of any other tax or duty except those for the regulation of trade. Unfortunately a rider restricted New England's trade to Great Britain and her West Indian islands. The New Jersey assembly bided its time, for by now all had learned of Lexington and Concord and of General Gage's being reinforced. Action was postponed until the meeting of the Second Continental Congress. Indeed several royal governors thought the times not propitious for their assemblies to consider the North proposal.

Franklin, more optimistic than some, wrote Lord Dartmouth that the assemblies might yet be won over if Lord North's "Resolution" was properly explained to them. He confided to the Cadwallader Colden faction in New York that he intended to expound the proposal fully in the New Jersey assembly in the hope that his views would be presented at the Second Continental Congress. This he did persuasively, arguing that it was only fair for the colonists to assume a just share of the defense burden. Parliament, he stated, was simply seeking a reasonable course; no definite amounts had been stipulated. The costs of defense would rise and fall with imperial necessity, and the colonial share would be no greater than that imposed in Britain. Parliament was not demanding a repudiation of the Association or any stated acknowledgment of her right to tax the colonies and, moreover, was willing to consider any reasonable counter-proposal. But should the colonies refuse to consider the North proposal for reconciliation, Franklin concluded, he would be forced to believe that this was not a dispute about colonial taxation, but that Americans "mean to throw off all Dependence upon Great Britain, and to get rid of every Controul of their Legislature." Though Franklin's masterly plea was well received by many representatives, distrust was expressed of Parliament's intention to manage the defense funds and to appoint colonial officers who would be removed from the control of the assemblies.

Prompted by Elizabethtown junto members Livingston, de Hart, and Boudinot, the New Jersey house concluded that taxation by Parliament would betray their liberties and "the just rights of the [British] Constitution." It decided to take no action before the meeting of congress, lest suspicion arise that New Jersey was flirting with the notion of abandoning the cause that united all the colonies. Though New Jersey was not to be the hoped-for spokesman for the imperial interest, Franklin was felt by Lord Dartmouth and others to have handled matters better than a number of other governors. His Lordship wrote Franklin that his speech was highly approved of in London, a compliment that the governor saw fit to keep to himself. He intended to do nothing that would antagonize the yearning of the majority for a reconciliation with the crown.

New Jersey's first provincial congress convened on May 23, 1775 in the thriving mid-province town of Trenton. There were eighty-five delegates present, with each of the thirteen counties accorded one vote. Thus Hunterdon with fifteen delegates and Essex with thirteen had no greater voice than Cape May with one. Nine assemblymen were delegates, seven from East Jersey and two from West Jersey's Hunterdon County. The Quakers were conspicuous by their absence, while the delegations from Somerset, which included Princeton's Witherspoon, were the most zealous.* Hendrick Fisher, veteran assemblyman of Somer-

---

* It was the Somerset (Princeton) radicals who had insisted that the congress be immediately convened. Half the delegates came from four "corridor counties"—Essex, Middlesex, Somerset, and Hunterdon.

set, was elected president, and Samuel Tucker, member from Hunterdon, vice president. Jonathan Dickinson Sergeant, grandson of the College of New Jersey's first president, was chosen secretary; William Paterson and Frederick Frelinghuysen, also graduates of the college, were the assistant secretaries.

After pledging allegiance to the king, the provincial congress approved the assembly's choice of delegates to the Second Continental Congress and resolved that it would henceforth appoint such delegates. It approved a declaration of obedience to all orders of the provincial congress and the Continental Congress. It resolved to maintain a correspondence with New York and Connecticut and, in sympathy with the other colonies, to lay an embargo on exports to Quebec, Newfoundland, and the Floridas. Then it resolved that companies of volunteers should be raised in every township, to be paid for by a levy over and above the regular provincial taxes. In view of the fact that New Jersey's £100,000 loan office act had finally been allowed, it was believed that, with money plentiful, it would not be difficult to raise £10,000 on a county-quota basis.* A provincial committee of correspondence was appointed (New Jersey being the last colony to do so) to act when the congress was not in session.

The Second Continental Congress, meantime, had convened on May 10, 1775. More radical than the first, it was not yet ready for independence. George Washington was appointed commander-in-chief and authorized to enlist 20,000 volunteers in New England. Until Bunker Hill was fought on June 17, the prevailing sentiment led Americans to prepare for a defensive war, while keeping open the door for reconciliation. Little attention, however, was given Lord North's proposal, which was presented in the form of a message by Richard Smith on behalf of the New Jersey assembly. On July 31, John Adams, Benjamin Franklin, Thomas Jefferson, and Richard Henry Lee of the more radical suasion brought in a report hostile to the North offer. Not

---

* Based on landed wealth, the assessments by county were: Hunterdon, £1,363; Burlington, £1,071; Monmouth, £1,069; Somerset, £904; Middlesex, £872; Gloucester, £763; Essex, £742; Morris, £723; Salem, £679; Bergen, £644; Sussex, £593; Cumberland, £385; and Cape May, £166.

only was the proposal picked to pieces, but the committee concluded that North meant what he said—that "he would never treat with America till he had brought her to her feet." The conservatives, still hopeful, carried the "olive branch" petition drafted by John Dickinson—a last appeal to the king—signed by the majority on July 8. But before it reached the king, the Privy Council, learning of Bunker Hill and of Washington's appointment, proclaimed the colonies in rebellion. The colonial emissaries were refused a hearing.

The hope of reconciliation began to diminish as a long summer of unrest and anxiety set in. Washington in August informed the New York provincial congress that British troops would certainly be sent to capture New York as the means of splitting the colonies in two, and he warned her to prepare. In New Jersey the militia of Elizabethtown was instructed to be in readiness. President Fisher, fearing British raids into East Jersey, appealed to Pennsylvania for gunpowder. A second session of the provincial congress met at Trenton on August 5, for there was much work to be done. John Dickinson Sergeant was appointed provincial treasurer, a much-needed office. Through a series of measures, the authority of the royal government gradually diminished. The congress also voted to hold annual elections, with five delegates from each county. Suffrage was granted to all men eligible to vote for members of the old colonial assembly, provided they had signed the Association. The congress was determined that in times of emergency its acts must be responsive to the will of the people. For the first time during the royal period a popularly elected body was guaranteed frequent regularly scheduled elections. The voters were also instructed to elect county committees of correspondence and inspection to exercise surveillance over disloyal persons and to constitute a link between the people and the provincial congress. In time they were to take over many functions of local government. Finally, a Committee of Safety of eleven members was established to act when the congress was not in session, replacing the provincial committee of correspondence.

Much of the second session was devoted to defense measures. All able-bodied men between sixteen and fifty were required to enlist or pay a fine of 4s. per month, and the Committee of Safety was ordered to deal with recalcitrants. Sixteen regiments, seven independent battalions, and a company of rangers were projected, with populous Hunterdon County providing four regiments and sparsely inhabited Cape May one battalion. In the recommendation of the Continental Congress, ten battalions of "minute men" were provided for. Unfortunately, the measure to raise £30,000 in taxes to bear the cost of defense was defeated. The use of collectors to seize and sell the goods and chattels of those who refused to pay their share of the previous levy of £10,000 had not been well received by the people. The loyalist element was not slow in pointing out that the tyranny of the provincial congress was greater than that of Parliament.

As the summer of 1775 wore on, the chances of reconciliation with Britain dimmed. Washington was engaged in containing the British forces in Boston while General Richard Montgomery, destined for defeat before Quebec, was slowly advancing toward Montreal. The Continental Congress was tightening its export embargo and strengthening its military preparations, although a substantial majority of that body still hoped for reconciliation. Governor Franklin wrote Lord Dartmouth that a more attractive proposal was now needed, but the latter in October replied that the king and Parliament were resolved to uphold the authority of Parliament, adding only that any colony submitting to the crown would receive a proper indulgence. On October 31 the Continental Congress learned that the king had refused to receive its "olive branch" petition and that the crown had ordered the severance of the packet line service to America, thus closing a vital line of communication. Both sides had now rejected each other's proposals. Dismayed by the course of events, two New Jersey delegates, James Kinsey and John de Hart, both moderates, resigned on November 13, 1775. (De Hart returned in March, while Kinsey never wavered in his patriotism.)

Governor Franklin meantime tried to rally the moderates and the silent loyalist following. In pointing up the dangers of the course now being pursued, he also sought to enlist the more thoughtful among the radicals. Hoping to stem the tide, he called a meeting of the assembly in Burlington on November 15. Oddly this assembly proved to be a shade more conservative, as evidenced by the fact that by a single vote a motion to hold a new election was rejected because of the majority's apprehension that radical representatives would be chosen. In his message, the governor candidly told the assembly that the king would not hesitate to "reduce his rebellious subjects to obedience." Nevertheless, he continued, it was his hope that the members would make known to the people his strong desire for the restoration of a harmonious relationship with the mother country. He minimized the grievances of Jerseymen and reminded the assembly that the crown had allowed its paper money act, thus removing a principal cause for concern. He also presented four petitions from Burlington County requesting the assembly to discourage any move toward independence and to vote the usual appropriation for the maintenance of the government. Franklin felt encouraged when several hostile measures failed to be approved, though by a narrow margin. On November 28, steps were taken to prepare a petition praying His Majesty to intercede to prevent bloodshed and expressing a desire for the restoration of peace based upon constitutional principles. The assembly then adopted several resolves pleasing to the governor: that since reports of a movement for independence had been groundless, its delegates to the Continental Congress be instructed, while urging the redress of American grievances, to seek a restoration of unity based upon constitutional principles; and that they reject all proposals for a separation from the mother country. The support bill was adopted without difficulty, leading Franklin to believe that the assembly was dedicated to the promotion of peace and order.

When the news of the assembly's actions reached Philadelphia, the Continental Congress resolved on December 4 that it would be dangerous to unity were any colony separately to petition the king or Parliament. Accordingly, John Dickinson, John Jay, and George Wythe, with New York's indecision in mind, were sent posthaste to reason with the New Jersey assembly. Their persuasive pleas stopped the sending of the petition. The governor's efforts, valiant though they were, had failed.

The full weight of a second blow fell upon the governor with the erosion of his council. Of the seven councilors sitting with the assembly, Richard Stockton, Francis Hopkinson, and John Stevens were dedicated to the popular cause; Stephen Skinner and Chief Justice Smythe were loyalists; while Daniel Coxe and John Lawrence were waverers. Of the four absentees William Alexander (the self-styled Lord Stirling) had broken with Franklin and accepted a colonial colonelcy, while James Parker, David Ogden, and Peter Kemble were uncommitted. Stockton, Hopkinson, and Stevens were Presbyterians, while Ogden, Kemble, and Lawrence were Anglicans.* The council had proved itself more radical than the house, as the governor was becoming isolated in his own establishment. Having already alluded to his personal safety in dealing with the assembly, Franklin realized following its adjournment that his days as governor were numbered. He had played for high stakes patiently, ably, and courageously, but he had lost.

Franklin had been too sanguine, for there were other forces at work. The Committee of Safety, tightening its vigilance, in January 1776 began to arrest Tory suspects, fining them £8 each and imposing bail of £50. The hunt for loyalists was led by Lord Stirling, who claimed that their numbers were increasing. He wrote John Hancock that they had enlisted 4,000 followers and were obtaining arms from a British man-of-war. Franklin, fully alarmed, wrote Lord Dartmouth asking whether he should leave the colony. His letter was intercepted, and on January 8, on Stirling's orders, he was arrested and ordered to give parole that he would not leave the colony. He was allowed to remain in Perth Amboy as a kind of governor-caretaker.

On January 31, 1776, the second provincial congress met at New Brunswick. Samuel Tucker was chosen president and Hendrick Fisher vice president. Of the forty-seven members, thirty had sat in the first provincial congress. Since it was expected that the British would attempt to take New York, military considerations dominated the proceedings. One battalion had already gone to Canada to assist the Montgomery-Arnold forces, and the Continental Congress had requested New

---

* With the coming of war only Stockton, Hopkinson, Stevens, and Alexander embraced the patriot cause. The others were quiescent loyalists.

Jersey to replace it with a third. The provincial congress, meanwhile, had run out of money. When it ordered one battalion to proceed to New York, the men could not go because they lacked arms. Consequently an emission of £30,000 in bills of credit was agreed upon. County collectors were authorized to distress the goods and chattels of delinquents and to levy fines on all refusing to accept the bills. Since the regular election of delegates was not scheduled until September, the congress voted to call a special election in May, again evidencing its determination that the delegates reflect accurately the desires of the voters. Every adult male, whether a freeholder or not, was now made eligible to vote if he had resided in New Jersey for one year. Franklin thought that a majority of the delegates were willing to declare for independence should the Continental Congress recommend it.

By February–March 1776, a large number of Jerseymen believed that a declaration would be the next step. In January, Tom Paine had published his rousing *Common Sense*, which quickly ran through 120,000 copies, and on the local scene tracts recommending separation were written by the Reverend Jacob Green* of Hanover, Morris County, future chairman of the committee that drafted the New Jersey Constitution, and by Francis Hopkinson, destined to be a "signer." Montgomery and Arnold were fighting in Canada, taking Montreal, but failing at Quebec. Opponents of independence in the Continental Congress now favored a demand for home rule under British sovereignty, an unlikely probability. In April, North Carolina's delegates were authorized to vote for independence, and several other colonies followed her lead. On May 10, the congress recommended that the several colonies adopt their own form of representative government. A number of states, including New Jersey, soon adopted constitutions. On May 15, when congress resolved that every kind of government under the crown should

---

* Green, a Harvard graduate, was the only Jerseyman to present a reasoned statement of the American position (*Observations on the Reconciliation of Great-Britain and the Colonies*, by "Friend of American Liberty," published in New York in the spring of 1776). See Gerlach, "Revolution or Independence," 684–685.

be suppressed, a declaration of independence was a foregone conclusion.

On May 28 the special election for the third provincial congress was held. Nearly half of its sixty-five members were new men.* The issue was now independence, and a majority in favor was returned. On June 10 Samuel Tucker was elected president, John Hart of Hopewell vice president, and William Paterson secretary. To block Governor Franklin's announced intention of summoning a meeting of the assembly in June, the congress voted 38 to 11 that his summons not be obeyed, and the following day, when Franklin, under duress, appeared before the congress, it resolved 48 to 11 that he was "an enemy of the liberties of this country" and should be arrested. Ordered to give parole that he reside either at Princeton, at Bordentown, or on his farm at Rancocas, he refused. Instead he transmitted a long address to the assembly defending himself and warning that its members were placing themselves "in the hands of desperate gamblers." When requested to print the address, Isaac Collins of Burlington, the province printer, returned it to the governor with the comment that he would be killed if he did so. Franklin was first imprisoned in Burlington, then on the advice of the Continental Congress he was sent to Connecticut in the custody of Governor John Trumbull. Quartered in East Windsor, he was exchanged in 1778 for President (governor) John McKinley of Delaware. He never saw his ill wife again. Franklin resided in New York City until 1782, and for a time he was president of the notorious Board of Associated Loyalists. Finally he returned to England, where he was granted compensation and a pension of £500. In 1784 he was partially reconciled to his famous father. On balance, unlike most royal governors, he was as devoted to the welfare of the colony and its people as a loyal servant of the crown could be.

Meanwhile the third provincial congress was making decisions. As Jonathan Sergeant had written John Adams, "We are passing the Rubicon and our delegates in Congress on the first of July will vote plump." On June 1, ignoring petitions from

---

* For the first time with five delegates from each county.

Middletown and Shrewsbury, the congress instructed its delegates to the Continental Congress to support all measures upholding the just rights and liberties of America and if necessary join in declaring "the united colonies" independent of Great Britain. The congress chose as delegates Richard Stockton of Princeton, a former councilor; Abraham Clark of Elizabethtown, former Essex County sheriff; John Hart, Hopewell landowner; Francis Hopkinson of Bordentown, also a former councilor; and John Witherspoon.* All were Presbyterians except Hart, a Baptist; Witherspoon was the most radical, Stockton the least. All were to sign the Declaration of Independence.

Following the advice of the Continental Congress, the provincial congress by a vote of 54 to 3 resolved to adopt a constitution.† A bona fide government was essential, it was felt, lest the acts of the provincial congress itself be challenged. Moreover, a centralized government was needed to enable New Jersey to cooperate with the Continental Congress, to maintain law and order, to care for financial needs, and to provide a defense in a situation where, as anticipated, British troops would be in New York City. On June 24, a ten-man committee, with the influential Reverend Jacob Green as chairman, was appointed to bring in a constitution. Green and Sergeant were the only men in the group known throughout the province, and Sergeant is believed to have written the first draft in advance. In any event a constitution was submitted to the provincial congress two days later, a herculean achievement under any circumstances. On July 2, the day the Continental Congress voted for independence, the proposed constitution was adopted by a vote of 26 to 9. Five West Jersey and four East Jersey votes were cast

---

* Of the delegates chosen the previous February, John Cooper never attended; John de Hart and Richard Smith resigned for personal reasons; John Sergeant had returned to New Jersey to help write the New Jersey constitution; and William Livingston became a brigadier general. John Adams suggests that Livingston was not reelected because he was reluctant to take the final step, secession. See Gerlach, "Revolution or Independence," 732n.

† A momentous vote for independence. As of this date only Maryland, New York, and New Jersey had not instructed their delegates to vote for independence.

against adoption, with two each from Cape May, Salem, and
Tory-leaning Bergen and one each from Burlington, Essex, and
Sussex. In the latter two there were strong loyalist minorities.
Astonishingly, thirty members were absent when the vote was
taken, leading Franklin to observe that the great majority of the
people disapproved of the provincial congress itself. The governor
also charged that in many counties the total vote cast for its
delegates never exceeded fifty, or a hundred at most.

The New Jersey constitution, which endured for fifty years,
was the third adopted in the colonies, those of New Hampshire
and South Carolina preceding it by a few days.* The latter had
no influence upon the authors of the New Jersey document,
whose hasty preparation precluded much in the way of innovation. Nor was there time for ratification by the people. Questions
such as the balance of power among the three branches of
government, as James Madison later noted, were never
broached. The lack of a provision for amending the instrument
proved an irritating omission. The colonial model was followed
throughout; indeed, most of the changes were made in the
endeavor to correct what the drafters considered abuses in the
royal system. It was not, then, a revolutionary document. From
the modern viewpoint the result was a practical system of
government, with increased powers for the lower house, a sharp
diminution of the executive's power, and an advance in popular
suffrage, the first in seventy years.

The constitution required a one-year residence and a property
qualification, real or personal, for voting. This represented an
effort to extend the suffrage to all adult males as well as
freeholders.† The high property qualifications were retained

---

* The Constitution of New Jersey of 1776 is included in Julian P. Boyd, ed.,
Fundamental Laws and Constitutions of New Jersey, 156–163. It contains a short
preamble and twenty-three articles.

† The clause in Article IV granting the vote to "all inhabitants . . . of full
age . . ." left the way open for women to vote in general elections, a loophole
they took advantage of from 1790–1807, a precedent in the United States.
Joseph Cooper, a West Jersey Quaker, is given credit for bestowing this boon.
See Edward R. Turner, "Women's Suffrage in New Jersey: 1790–1807," *Smith*

(£500 for membership in the lower house and £1,000 for the upper house or legislative council), thus maintaining the old axiom that ability resided in wealth or financial success. Each county was entitled to three representatives and one councilor, elected annually by the voters. The provision for annual elections satisfied an aspiration that had never been realized under the royal regime. Though removing the freehold qualification and extending the suffrage to all whose estate was worth £50 was praiseworthy, the machinery of voting left something to be desired. Usually there was but a single polling place in each county, and in many of these voting was by voice instead of by secret ballot. Election officials, apt to be partisan, were selected on the day of balloting, and in addition there were no safeguards against dishonesty at the polls.

Only three areas were beyond legislative authority: the right of trial by jury, religious freedom as then defined, and the provisions for annual elections. Otherwise, the lawmaking powers of the general assembly, as the houses jointly were called, were practically unlimited. The assembly was vested with large appointive powers, curtailing those of the governor severely. The houses, meeting jointly, chose all provincial officers, including the governor, the secretary of state, the treasurer, the supreme court justices, and even the county justices and justices of the peace. Terms of office were short, usually a year. The justices were subject to removal by impeachment proceedings or by trial for misbehavior. The council, sitting with the governor, constituted the highest court of appeals and a court of pardons.

A principal consequence was a very weak executive, itself a pent-up response to long-standing feuding with royal governors.* Elected annually, the governor had no veto, no appointive power to speak of, and few clearly defined executive functions. He presided over the council, was captain-general of the armed forces, and in his judicial capacity was chancellor, surrogate, and

---

College Studies in History, I (1916), 165–187 and Charles R. Erdman, Jr., *The New Jersey Constitution of 1776* (Princeton, 1929), 82–87.

* In addition to Erdman's *The New Jersey Constitution*, see the comments of Allan Nevins, *The American States during and after the Revolution* (New York, 1924), 44–45. Nevins emphasizes the influence of the New York radicals.

president of the court of appeals. Fortunately the first governor, William Livingston, was elected annually from 1776 until his death in 1790, commanded the respect both of the assembly and of the inhabitants, and gave the office the prestige of his personality. Except for the method of naming judges and the limitation of their terms, the judiciary followed the royal system in jurisdiction and procedures.

The constitution contained some safeguards for the individual. Those accused of crimes were guaranteed the same privileges of witnesses and counsel as their prosecutors. The estates of suicides would no longer be forfeited but would descend to the heirs. There would be no established church, and no one was compelled to support a church or to attend public worship. Protestants would enjoy full civil rights, a provision which left something to be desired for the non-Protestant minorities. No officials holding positions of profit under the government were eligible for election to the assembly.

Even at this late date, the provincial congress cast a backward look. Presumably at the behest of President Samuel Tucker, it voted that in the event of a reconciliation with the mother country, the constitution was null and void. Actually the word "colony" instead of "state" was used until July 17, when the style "State of New Jersey" was adopted.

The new general assembly met on August 27 at the College of New Jersey's Nassau Hall. The first order of business was the election of a governor. The initial ballot resulted in a tie between the well-to-do and able attorney Richard Stockton and the "retired" New York lawyer, William Livingston, now residing at "Liberty Hall," Elizabethtown.* After some maneuvering by the politically potent John Stevens and John Cleve Symmes, Livingston was elected. Member of a prominent New York family, a Yale graduate, and a distinguished member of the New York bar, though a poor speaker, Livingston was an influential writer on matters of public concern who had slowly but surely been drawn to the republican cause.† Despite his limited powers as

---

* Stockton became chief justice.

† Livingston was forty-nine in 1772 when he moved to Elizabethtown, too young to retire. John Adams regarded him as plain, not elegant; sensible and learned. When governor, Livingston was dubbed the "Don Quixote of the

William Livingston, first governor of the State of New Jersey (1776–1790). *Courtesy of the New York Public Library Picture Collection.*

Liberty Hall, "Ursino," Elizabeth. *Courtesy of The New York-Historical Society.*

governor, he served his state and the nation devotedly through-out the Revolution. He became a trusted friend of General Washington and, where humanly possible, never failed him. It was fortunate indeed for the patriot cause that these two leaders worked together patiently and purposefully through New Jersey's years of hardship and tragedy.*

On July 2, 1776 the Continental Congress approved Richard Henry Lee's resolution for independence, and on July 4 the Declaration was signed. New Jersey's delegates had played little part in these momentous proceedings; only John Witherspoon enjoyed any intercolonial reputation, and he did not arrive in Philadelphia until July 1.† Hopkinson was present on July 28, Stockton on July 1, and de Hart on July 4. By then, only New York and Delaware hung back. Jonathan Dickinson Sergeant was instrumental in securing New Jersey's affirmative action.‡

Years later, in commenting upon the unanimous adoption of the Declaration—"thirteen clocks were made to strike together" —John Adams asserted that the future historian must examine the motivation within each colony, for the mere recital of events was not sufficient to explain the miracle. Historians have vouchsafed the accuracy of Adams's statement. Each colony accepted the Declaration as an individual community, with its hopes, to a degree at least, distinct from the common aspirations that bound them all together.

Jerseys" by Rivington's Tory *Royal Gazette*. A brigadier, he boasted that the British would rather hang him for his writing than for his military valor. With a price of 2,000 guineas on his head, numerous attempts were made to capture him by the British and by the New Jersey loyalists.

* Livingston never had more than eight votes cast against him in the elections for the governorship. As late as 1781 he received the unanimous vote of the assembly.

† Witherspoon's pastoral letter supporting the American cause, sent to all congregations of the Philadelphia Synod on June 29, 1775, greatly enhanced his reputation as a patriot. See Gerlach, "Revolution or Independence," 602–603.

‡ See Edmund C. Burnett, ed., *Letters of the Members of the Continental Congress,* I (Washington, 1921), xlix–liii, for attendance of the New Jersey members.

New Jersey in some respects was not typical. Far from being a prime leader in the movement for independence, she tended to lag behind. Her procrastination arose from no organized opposition, and there were no propaganda campaigns to stir and divide the populace. New Jersey had no newspapers, her pamphleteers were few, and there were no rousing political sermons. The loyalist opposition, though present, was not publicly organized until the actual fighting began. Thomas Bradbury Chandler, the Anglican minister, was the leading Tory publicist, but as the persistent advocate of an Anglican bishopric his pleas were given small heed in this strongly Dissenter community. From the beginnings the established church was suspect and her communicants relatively few.

New Jersey was more remote from the crown and Parliament than most of the colonies. She had little direct contact with imperial policy-making in important matters such as defense. Predominantly rural, her citizens were more concerned with their farms than with politics. On the whole, New Jersey was prosperous, adding to the general contentment, and there were few class divisions. Governor Franklin, the dean of American governors, was a colonial, and through the years he had won a modicum of respect. Jerseymen believed that their governor would protect their interests vis-à-vis the crown. Franklin, too, had persevered in his dealings with the assembly, striving successfully to gain allowance for the loan office act and to resolve irritating altercations like that pertaining to the quartering of troops. Local partisan measures absorbed the attention of the assembly more than matters of empire. The governor not only held the assembly in check, but was able on occasion to assert the crown's authority by challenging privileges that the lower house thought of as its own.

New Jersey's convention of 1774, though resolving that Parliament's acts were unconstitutional, not only swore allegiance to the king but expressed its abhorrence of independence. Yet, hardly two years later, her delegates signed the Declaration of Independence. What, then, were the factors leading to such a rapid turnabout? Two considerations were paramount, one bolstering the other. Ever since the Stamp Act Congress there had been a strong desire to act in concert with the other colonies, particularly with her neighbors, Pennsylvania and New York. Thus in the New Jersey convention the delegates not only condemned the Intolerable Acts but resolved to approve the call for a continental congress and to adopt nonimportation and nonexportation agreements. Though New Jersey's responses were halting and at times qualified, at no juncture did she contemplate separating herself from the common cause. And because of the determination of Congress that New York must be drawn into the fold, New Jersey's position was important. The appearance of congressional delegates before the assembly in November 1775 was only the most dramatic evidence of Congress's desire for New Jersey's full cooperation. These same pressures were exerted on an informal basis throughout the meetings of the First and Second Continental Congresses.

The second factor in the progress toward independence lay in the personality and philosophy of her leaders—in the assembly, in the provincial congresses, and in the Continental Congress. The patriot party was not organized as such, because of the wide divergence of views represented by the individuals within it. The men who guided New Jersey toward independence were of varying origins, varying experiences in government, varying constituencies, and varying outlooks. At the start and almost to the end, a conservative (though not a Tory) element was conspicuous in the lower house of the assembly. Not only the Quaker members but others remote from the currents of the times were repelled by the prospect of violence, let alone that of separation from the mother country.

The delegates to the convention and the provincial congresses, then, were not fiery radicals plumping for separation and rebellion. All popularly elected and responsive to the wishes of their constituents, they dealt soberly with the problems of differences with the mother country. Public opinion was conditioned gradually through the efforts of local grievance committees organized as far back as the Stamp Act controversy. Since such committees were close to the people, the local communities were predisposed to enforce their mandates. By 1776 New Jersey had fashioned a network of communication through which the members of the provincial congresses could act. They, in turn, elected under a broad suffrage, could regard themselves as spokesmen of the people.

Not only was New Jersey's leadership marked by a lack of demagoguery, but through the months it changed perceptibly. In the provincial congress, where one delegate felt that in good conscience he was not prepared to take the next step, his place was quietly filled by a successor dedicated to the more advanced position.* There emerged no counter-revolutionaries. The same process took place among New Jersey's delegates to the Continental Congress; thus her signing of the Declaration of Independence was accompanied by no marked civil strife. There were neutrals and loyalists, but they were not sufficiently organized to oppose the steady trend toward independence.

New Jersey's delegates to the Continental Congress were not its leaders. The colony was small, its grievances not marked, and its delegates practically unknown. Francis Hopkinson, James Kinsey, William Livingston, Richard Stockton, and others were able men, but their reputations did not extend much beyond the middle colonies. Though relatively inactive, they played the important role of keeping New Jersey abreast of the movement toward independence.

With the Declaration there remained the fearsome necessity of upholding its boons on the field of battle. In New Jersey events moved so rapidly that the inhabitants could hardly accommodate themselves to their flow. Confronted with the impending conflict, each man had to search his soul and ascertain where his convictions lay. With many, preoccupied with their farms or with their crafts, the upheaval of 1776 came as a shock. There were elements of the population, convinced minorities, whose minds were made up, but it is questionable whether a majority had committed itself either to independence or to war. Acceptance or rejection did not depend on economic or social status—in either

---

* Only a few names carried over from 1765 to 1774. Hendrick Fisher, influential assemblyman from 1765 to the Revolution, stands out, with mention also of "Honest" John Hart, Joseph Borden, Jr., Richard Smith, Jr., Samuel Tucker, and young Richard Stockton.

"Morven," Princeton residence of Richard Stockton, now the official residence of the governor of New Jersey. *Courtesy of the New Jersey Department of Labor and Industry.*

camp one found rich and poor, landed and landless, farmers and merchants, high-ranking and lowly officials, ministers, lawyers, doctors. Some of the staunchest patriots were far from revolutionary; above all, they wished to preserve their historic rights. As more than one historian has noted, their aspirations were conservative, for they sought mainly to preserve what they had. What counted was the driving zeal of a small cadre of dedicated men convinced that the sole remedy lay in independence, no matter what the price.

The loyalists felt with Governor Franklin that the revolutionary government could not endure or satisfy "a people who have once tasted the sweets of British liberty under a British constitution." On the loyalist side were several important men, ranging from major office-holders to the sheriffs of several counties. The majority of the East Jersey Board of Proprietors was loyalist, while the neutral Quaker element of the West Jersey Council reflected the strong Quaker opposition to violence. On the whole, the New Jersey Quakers sought to withdraw from the conflict, with many refusing to contribute to the war effort. The Anglican clergy was loyalist, with one exception, and a number of them left the state. The conservative Conferentie wing of the Dutch Reformed Church, rooted in Bergen County, was loyalist; but the liberal Coetus adherents, centered in the Raritan Valley and led by Hendrick Fisher and the Reverend Jacob Hardenburgh, upheld the patriot cause.

The most deeply committed patriots were found in the Calvinist groups: the old Congregationalists, the Presbyterians, the old Scottish element, and the newer Scotch-Irish. The Presbyterians led the way. From the Elizabethtown congregation came, for example, William Livingston; Abraham Clark, a "signer"; Elias Boudinot, later president of Congress; Generals Mathias Ogden and Elias Dayton, and Captain Jonathan Dayton; and the future military chaplain, James Caldwell. Dr. John Witherspoon was the patriot leader in the central part of the state. In the summer of 1774 Witherspoon told John Adams that all his students were Sons of Liberty, and in congress in 1776 he is alleged to have stated that the colonies were not only "ripe" for the Declaration of Independence, but "in danger of becoming rotten for the want of it." To the south, from Morris to remote Cumberland counties, wherever there were enclaves of men of New England descent, one found conspicuous patriots. In addition to Stockton, Hopkinson, and Lord Stirling, the patriots counted in their ranks strong new men like William Paterson, Joseph Reed of Burlington, and Andrew Sinnickson of Salem, of Swedish descent.

A number of loyalists left the state, the largest group for New York City. The great majority could not or would not leave their homes with the outbreak of hostilities. As the machinery of government slowed to a halt when New Jersey was occupied by British troops, the inhabitants became engaged in bitter civil strife. Groups on both sides committed lawless acts, neighbor was pitted against neighbor, and law and order broke down. Though the property of departing loyalists was confiscated, as was to be expected, too often men took the law into their own hands and seized the property and goods of others. Many joined loyalist bands because they were harassed and badgered by their neighbors or simply to protect themselves from pillage. In the famous case of James Moody, the Sussex farmer, he and seventy of his neighbors went over to the British in a body. Similarly, uncommitted men who were threatened by loyalist bands joined the patriots. The British occupation provoked charges and counter-charges at an ever-increasing tempo of violence. This atmosphere of distrust pervaded community after community. Shrewsbury folk, for example, accused of trading with the enemy, incurred the wrath of Freehold men, only a few miles distant. All the while, life became more and more precarious. Here was no short presence of conflicting forces or a fleeting experience with passing armies but year upon year of wearing occupation. In the beginning, however, countless numbers abhorred the thought of war and the dislocation of their lives; while some, as always, reveled in the tumult of events.

12

WAR AND REVOLUTION

On July 29, 1776, residents along the New Jersey shore witnessed the long-anticipated arrival of the British. General Sir William Howe's troops were being transported from Boston to Staten Island, a site that controlled the entrance to the Hudson and the Raritan. Here Howe awaited the fleet and army from England under the command of his brother, Admiral Lord Richard Howe. Together their forces would number more than 32,000, the largest ever assembled by Britain on foreign soil. New Jersey faced its first real test of war. Up to now there had been only brushes—when militia were called upon to put down Tory bands; when privateers were bringing their prizes into Little Egg Harbor Bay; and when British men-of-war attempted to seize the brig *Nancy*, laden with arms and ammunition destined for Philadelphia, at Cape May.

New Jersey's battalions now joined Washington's forces in defense of New York. The appearance of British troops cheered the New Jersey Tories, a number of whom were now stationed on Staten Island. Others, whenever expedient, were arrested as traitors by order of the provincial congress and removed from the scene. Washington soon learned the bitter lessons of commanding a volunteer army manned by the "summer soldiers" whom Tom Paine assailed in his *Crisis* papers, published later in the year. At an early date, New Jersey troops clamored to return to protect their families or to harvest their crops. Thus the Flying Corps, first stationed at Perth Amboy, never achieved the high purpose expected of it. In August, the New Jersey legislature made an effort to help, dividing all men between sixteen and fifty into two contingents, with each recruit serving in the corps during alternate months. This assist, with additions from Pennsylvania, brought General Hugh Mercer's Flying Corps temporarily to 5,000. Late in the month it moved to Fort Lee on the Jersey side of the Hudson opposite Fort Washington. These two strongholds were charged with withstanding a British advance up the Hudson or into New Jersey proper. Mercer, Washington's trusted aide, experienced great difficulty merely in keeping his restless recruits from disappearing.

On August 27 General Howe, reinforced with the 20,000 British and Hessians transported by his brother, opened the campaign. Overwhelming the Americans on Long Island, he moved easily over to Manhattan, and on September 18 the Americans retreated grudgingly to Fort Washington. On November 16 Howe forced the evacuation of Fort Washington, and five days later he took Fort Lee, which, for strategic reasons, Washington ordered abandoned. Outmanned, Washington beat a hasty but, on the whole, an orderly retreat. The occupation of New Jersey had begun. Washington yielded ground slowly, refusing to be trapped. He moved through Hackensack, Newark, New Brunswick, Princeton, and Trenton, destroying bridges and fighting delaying tactics where possible. Arriving in Trenton on December 2, he commandeered enough small boats to effect a crossing into Pennsylvania. Deprived of all means of ferriage, the British could not follow. Washington returned to Trenton on December 25–26, winning a brilliant victory, which he followed with a swift sortie at Princeton and a successful withdrawal through Kingston to Somerset Court House. He then took up winter quarters at Morristown behind the defensible Watchung Mountains.

Despite her commendable cooperation during the preceding six months, New Jersey failed miserably in her first test. In truth, Jerseymen were being plunged into civil war with all its attendant horrors. On November 30, 1776, with the state all but subjugated, General Howe offered full pardon and protection of property to all who would abandon the patriot cause. He soon claimed that 2,700 families had done so, including assemblymen and officials. They were given "protection papers" which, unhappily, were little honored by the British troops. Patriots were forced to flee as the enemy advanced, and the legislature hastily adjourned from Princeton to Trenton, then to Bordentown, where it broke up. Speaker John Hart returned to Hopewell; Richard Stockton was captured in Monmouth and roughly treated;* and Witherspoon, after dismissing his students, departed Princeton for Philadelphia. Large numbers crossed the Delaware into Bucks County. The population was helpless as villages and farms were plundered, houses gutted, mills destroyed, orchards chopped down, and livestock driven off. Heinous crimes were committed. Tories, too, ranged the countryside in armed bands and joined in the pillaging, while the patriots, aided by the militia, retaliated.

The American response that followed Washington's successes at Trenton and Princeton was guerrilla warfare. Day and night, from Perth Amboy to New Brunswick, the patriots ambushed small British cantonments. Outposts and patrols were especially vulnerable. The New Jersey militia forced the abandonment of Hackensack, Newark, and Elizabethtown, confining the enemy to a long narrow thoroughfare and forcing him to transport supplies from New York. The British troops, cooped up in garrisons, suffered sickness and outbreaks of smallpox. All this aided Washington, whose situation at Morristown was becoming desperate. With enlistments running out, his forces had dwindled to 4,000. His men were ill and starving, and they lacked clothing and supplies. Congress could do nothing for him; indeed only his choice of Morristown as a base saved him from disaster. With the arrival of British reinforcements in mid-February 1777 at Perth Amboy, Washington pondered the enemy's next move. In April, General Lord Cornwallis with 4,000 men made a raid that was turned back by General Nathanael Greene at Basking Ridge, and in May another attack was halted at Bound Brook.

Meanwhile, with the appearance of some experienced foreign officers, Washington began to drill his troops. Late in May he moved his army to Bound Brook, whence he could either move

---

* Broken in health, he died in 1781 at the age of fifty-one.

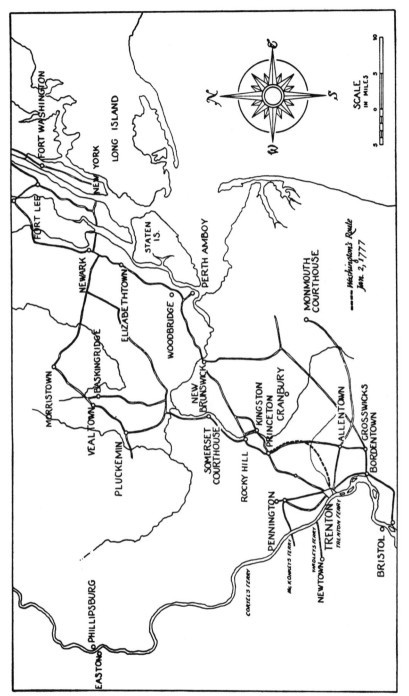

"Theater of War Operations in New Jersey." From Alfred Hoyt Bill, *The Campaign of Princeton, 1776–1777* (copyright 1948 by Princeton University Press), map on p. 8. Reprinted by permission of Princeton University Press.

readily toward Peekskill on the Hudson or cover Howe's flank should he proceed toward Philadelphia. In June 1777, after probing as far as New Brunswick, Howe returned to Staten Island, and on July 21 he embarked for the head of Chesapeake Bay. Although Washington marched overland and confronted him, Howe succeeded on September 25 in taking Philadelphia. Through the fall Washington continued to harass Howe's forces while the British, in turn, were preoccupied with clearing the Delaware River forts. By December, Forts Billingsport, Mifflin, and Mercer had fallen after staunch resistance by the Americans on both banks. Though Howe probed Washington's defenses, he was too cautious to risk a major battle. Both armies went into winter quarters, Howe in Philadelphia and Washington in bleak Valley Forge. The one satisfying American achievement was the surrender of Burgoyne's army at Saratoga on October 17, 1777.

As the principal theater of the war shifted to Pennsylvania, New Jersey was far from quiescent. General Sir Henry Clinton at Staten Island made raids on Bergen and burned Kingston in New York, and his activities prevented the New Jersey militia from aiding Washington. But the patriots retaliated: inexperienced New Jersey volunteers performed yeoman service in labor battalions in defense of the Delaware River forts, and Count Casimir Pulaski's light cavalry used American-occupied Trenton to forage for Washington at Valley Forge. Until recalled, the latter's men were useful in holding in check the bands of Tories and outlaws that preyed on south Jersey; thereafter, the Tory "West Jersey Volunteers" headed by a Gloucester tavernkeeper engaged in widespread depredations and furnished the British in Philadelphia with provisions. Commenting on conditions in south Jersey, the Swedish pastor Nicholas Collin wrote, "Everywhere distrust, fear, hatred, and abominable selfishness. . . . Parents and children, brothers and sisters, wife and husband, were enemies of one another." State and local government was practically in suspension.

In the north, too, there were widespread disorders as the militia and the patriot bands tried to break up the movement of provisions from profiteers and loyalists to the British on Staten Island, Paulus Hook, and Perth Amboy. The task was difficult, and as in south Jersey the innocent suffered with the guilty as informers and spies ranged the countryside. With a strong loyalist organization in Bergen County, provisions sifted to the British like sand through a sieve. The legislature, which met finally in the fall of 1777 at Princeton, was impotent. Although full authority by now was vested in Governor Livingston and the Committee of Safety, with little means of enforcing their mandates their task was impossible. The government and the courts were accused of corruption, the latter because of alleged favoritism in selling forfeited Tory property. Livingston was deeply disturbed because he had to turn a deaf ear to Washington's pathetic pleas for provisions and supplies.* The infant American states were treating Washington as shabbily as did the Congress.

Loyalism in New Jersey followed the pattern established in most colonies.† Until the spring of 1777, the loyalist-leaning inhabitants, with some exceptions, were content to stay out of the army. Unhappily they were overtaken by the course of events: the decision of Congress in March to disarm the disaffected, and that of June declaring that any persons aiding Great Britain were guilty of treason. When in July 1776 the local committee of safety had demanded that all men take the required oath of allegiance to the patriot cause, the most conspicuous loyalists began to leave. Included were not only former beneficiaries of the crown, but certain men of strong principle. The latter were persuaded by their admiration of the British constitution and by the orderliness of the British government and its institutions. Others were variously motivated: by the presumed invincibility of British arms, utter disbelief in an American victory, a dread of economic loss under the republic, or simply the fear of violence. The vast majority of the loyalists who remained were fragmented and poorly organized.

---

* Washington ranked Livingston as second only to Trumbull of Connecticut as a patriot among the governors for his unflagging war effort.

† See especially Wallace Brown, *The Good Americans* . . . (New York, 1969), *passim.* Paul H. Smith, *Loyalists and Redcoats* (Chapel Hill, 1964), stresses the military aspects of loyalism.

Great store was set by the New Jersey loyalists upon the occupation of New York and the conquest of New Jersey. They became discouraged, however, when the British military not only failed them but practically ignored them as a meaningful party. Nevertheless many did what they could: as individuals they served in the British forces and engaged in fifth-column activities in occupied districts. Because of the organizing ability of General Cortlandt Skinner, the New Jersey Volunteers performed as one of the three best loyalist units on the battlefield. It is believed that there were at most 5,000 active New Jersey loyalists. Besides Governor Franklin, the royalist office-holders, and the Anglican clergy (with the exception of Robert Blackwell), the most prominent loyalists were Cortlandt Skinner; lawyers David Ogden, Daniel Isaac Brown, and Daniel Coxe; the physician, Abraham Van Buskirk; the merchant, Robert Drummond; and the spy and soldier, James Moody. The Quakers, insofar as possible, remained neutral, as did hundreds of individuals who tried not to attract attention. The pressures upon the neutral became greater and greater as the war wore on. As a suspect, the neutral too was drawn into a civil war that raged throughout the province. Toward the close of the war, the active loyalist went into exile, generally by way of New York, either to Canada (especially Nova Scotia) or to England. A number returned to face hostility, discrimination, or ostracism, depending on the locality.

Among the unhappy casualties of the war were the Dutch of Bergen County, who from the summer of 1776 until the end of the fighting found themselves occupying the neutral ground between the British in New York and the Americans behind the Ramapo ranges. They were at the mercy of both, subject to the feints of opposing forces and to the never-ceasing raids in search of food, livestock, horses, and equipment. No farmer or townsman was safe.

Bergen County Dutchmen were divided among themselves, however. The Coetus party of the Reformed Church, first led by the Reverend John Henry Goetschius and after his death by the Reverend Dirck Romeyn, a College of New Jersey graduate, maintained a precarious existence in the face of great difficulties.

The Conferentie party, strengthened by the presence of the British in New York, was in the saddle as Howe swept through New Jersey, and in subsequent years it continued to be a menace. Civil war was as acrimonious in Bergen as in any part of America. Whole families were divided in their allegiance, and neighbor suspected neighbor. Each of the factions furnished not only recruits but spies and counterspies. Many of the Dutch inhabitants were tempted by the lure of British gold. Colonel Abraham Van Buskirk early raised an effective Tory force, Van Buskirk's Greencoats, from whom no inhabitant was safe. His troops and contingents of the New Jersey Volunteers ranged at will through Bergen and Essex counties.*

How the American commander-in-chief, with 8,200 sick and starving men, managed to contain Howe's army of 19,500 in Philadelphia has been amply recorded by historians. Happily, in March 1778, the experienced Baron Frederick von Steuben came to Valley Forge and set to work reorganizing the American army with a thoroughness that won Washington's unqualified praise. General Nathanael Greene became quartermaster general, with assurances of full support from Congress. By spring, with re-cruitments up, the Americans had become professional soldiers, and their esprit was high. In April came the thrilling news of the French alliance together with the intelligence that Lord North's government was making tenders of peace.

General Howe's occupation of Philadelphia was inefficient, slack, and corrupt; he was replaced by General Henry Clinton as commander-in-chief, with orders to return the British army to New York. The British dared not move by sea, for the strong

---

* Colonel Levi Pauling of the American army observed, "The good people of Bergen County lay greatly exposed to internal and external enemies, and the internal enemies have a free recourse to New York, the center and head of all British activity." Thomas Jones, a Tory judge critical of General Sir Henry Clinton, wrote of one of his Bergen County raids: "Two of the detachments made large circuitous raids . . . and, according to orders, drove in all the cattle, hogs, horses and sheep that fell in their way, whether the property of Whigs or Tories, royalists or rebels, and indiscriminately robbed the inhabitants of whatever they found in their houses." Quoted in Adrian Leiby's meticulously researched *The Revolutionary War in the Hackensack Valley* (New Brunswick, 1962), 103, 140.

French fleet that was reportedly near at hand could wreak havoc with the transport ships. Only the heaviest guns, superfluous equipment, and 3,000 Philadelphia loyalists were taken aboard. On July 17, 1778 the British army, heavily encumbered with stores and equipment, moved to the New Jersey side and made for New York by land. Washington, proceeding up the west bank of the Delaware, sent Henry Lee's cavalry, Maxwell's brigade, and Cadwalader's Pennsylvanians to harass their rear. By the time the British reached Haddonfield, the patriot guerillas were out in force, felling trees and wrecking bridges in their van and ambushing them on all sides. Stretched out along the road for eight or ten miles, the enemy was highly vulnerable. On the 26th, after ten days' exposure to both blazing sun and heavy torrents of rain, the exhausted British reached Monmouth Court House.

Meanwhile Washington had crossed the Delaware and was moving toward New Brunswick. Clinton decided to proceed through Middletown and make for Sandy Hook, where transports would meet him. Washington, with 11,000 well-trained men, turned east through Princeton until within striking distance. In council, Generals Greene, Wayne, and Lafayette urged a decisive battle, but Charles Lee, senior general, was opposed. Though Lee's supporters held the majority, Washington, on further consideration, ordered Maxwell and Morgan to harass the enemy rear, moved his army to Kingston, and dispatched Lafayette to Cranbury to block Howe from any shift to New Brunswick. Hindered by a day's downpour, Washington paused at Englishtown as Lafayette, augmented by the forces of Morgan, Maxwell, and others, 5,000 strong, began to close with the British rear. To appease the disgruntled Lee, Lafayette relinquished his command to his senior. Despite explicit orders from Washington, Lee failed to carry them out.

The Battle of Monmouth Court House was almost catastrophic for the Americans. Lee, after an unforgivable delay, attacked Cornwallis's rear. Ignoring the pleas of Lafayette and others, he issued an order to retreat. As the Americans converged on the narrow, crooked road to Englishtown, Cornwallis, bolstered with cavalry and light infantry, harassed them on all sides.

Refusing to make a stand on defensible ground, Lee found himself in a situation that was rapidly disintegrating. On reaching the battlefield, Washington quickly comprehended what was happening. Ordering Lee to the rear, he rallied the troops and began to fight. Clinton, sensing a major victory, sent up reinforcements. Before Washington could complete his defenses, darkness fell. Not until dawn did Washington learn that the British had withdrawn and were well on their way to join the main force. In truth both armies were exhausted. Fighting all day, the temperature a stifling 97 degrees, hundreds of men and horses on both sides succumbed to sunstroke. Monmouth was a severe disappointment, for an American victory might have ended the war. There were some consolations: the British army had been compelled to retreat and had lost 2,000 men on the march from Philadelphia. Lee was tried for his shabby behavior but was accorded a relatively light punishment. He retired, a disillusioned man, and died in October 1782.

The American army moved leisurely to White Plains, and New York again became the major objective. The British, receiving the news of a strong French fleet with a complement of 4,000 troops off Sandy Hook, were on the defensive. Neither Washington nor the French commander, Admiral D'Estaing, believed their combined forces were strong enough to take New York. The latter, on orders, soon set sail for the West Indies to cope with a strong expeditionary force dispatched there by Clinton. Washington set up a defensive arc from Danbury to Elizabethtown and awaited developments, eventually taking up winter quarters near Raritan Village, New Jersey. During the winter, there were only minor brushes with the enemy. In June 1779 began what Washington called "a desultory kind of war" that lasted for the remainder of the year. In December the American commander was back at Morristown, in winter quarters, having spent the whole summer trying to arrange with D'Estaing for a major attack on New York. By mid-winter the American army stood at 10,400 men, while Clinton, reinforced, could muster 28,000. The winter, if anything, was worse than that spent at Valley Forge. Blizzards closed the roads, and, lacking provisions and supplies, the Americans lived from hand to mouth. Washington was driven to relying on the local magistrates to bully farmers into supplying food, for they refused to accept the depreciated Continental currency. Without pay the soldiers were unruly, and Washington was compelled to take stern disciplinary measures. His despondency was increased by the news of British successes in Georgia and South Carolina.

Nevertheless, by 1780 there was an underlying confidence among patriots that was shared by the New Jersey populace. When the Hessian General Knyphausen advanced on Morristown, the farmers—now full-fledged guerilla fighters—compelled him to retreat. Governor Livingston, endowed with the saving grace of humor, reported, "At the middle of the night the enemy sneaked off and put their backsides to the Sound near Elizabethtown." * The chagrined General Clinton, on his return from capturing Charleston, South Carolina, made a major feint on Morristown with 5,000 men, cavalry units, and heavy guns, but his forces were repulsed by General Greene in a strong position behind Springfield. The British retreated to Staten Island, leaving the village in flames. This was the last serious military engagement in New Jersey.

In July 1780 a large French expedition arrived in Newport, Rhode Island, where it was promptly immobilized for eleven months by a superior British fleet. Washington, with headquarters at West Point, kept sufficient pressure on Clinton to discourage him from launching an attack on Newport. Nevertheless the American cause was again languishing as war weariness set in. Continental currency had reached a nadir of 1,000 to 1; Congress was impotent; and Benedict Arnold's treason was a personal blow to Washington. The army again spread out in a defensive perimeter from Connecticut to New Jersey as Washington took up winter quarters at Morristown. The winter of 1780–1781 was a repetition of the previous one. The army was in desperate straits, lacking food, clothing, and even powder; and

---

* A French officer noted, "New Jersey, which almost touches the fortifications of New York, has displayed heroic constancy. Its militia assembles of its own accord at the sight of a redcoat. Their governor is a Roman." See Nevins, *American States*, 302–305 for an assessment of New Jersey's and Livingston's role during the war.

The Wick House, Morristown. Built in the 1750s, the house served as the quarters of Major General Arthur St. Clair in the winter of 1779–1780. *Courtesy of the National Park Service, Morristown National Historical Park, Morristown, New Jersey.*

early in 1781 Washington had to deal with serious mutiny. Only a man of his indomitability could have coped with the situation, for he knew only too well that his soldiers' grievances were real.

Meanwhile the British were successfully pursuing a new objective, the conquest of the American South. In August 1780 General Horatio Gates was given a drubbing at Camden by the brilliant Cornwallis, and only the engagement at King's Mountain in October gave any solace to the patriots. The traitorous Benedict Arnold, now a British general, burned Richmond. The year 1781, however, brought heartening changes. Daniel Morgan defeated Colonel Banastre Tarleton at Cowpens, and General Greene (now in command in the American South), though defeated at Guilford Court House, forced Cornwallis to withdraw to Wilmington, North Carolina. Greene lost again at Hobkirk's Hill, but here too Cornwallis's losses were so great that he returned to Charleston. Later in the month Cornwallis advanced swiftly north to Petersburg, Virginia, effecting a junction with the British troops in Virginia. His forces now stood at 7,000. Washington began to feed troops into the southern theater. General Anthony Wayne, with reinforcements from Pennsylvania, joined up with Von Steuben and Lafayette. Cornwallis was ordered to send 3,000 men by sea to New York; he then moved to Yorktown and began to build fortifications. Rochambeau, the French general at Newport, marched his army of 7,000 to join Washington's forces on the Hudson. Although the British had every reason for believing that New York was still the major American objective, Washington did not believe that he was strong enough to combat Clinton's army of 14,000, with the British fleet in control of the waterways. At this juncture Washington conceived the brilliant plan of marching the combined American-French forces to Yorktown, meeting up with Admiral de Grasse's fleet there, and capturing Cornwallis's army. Their arrangements completed, Washington and Rochambeau left the Hudson on August 31, and by October 5 Yorktown was invested. Completely hemmed in, Cornwallis surrendered on October 19, 1781.

But the war dragged on. The British evacuated Savannah and Charleston, leaving only the main force in New York, as

Washington took up winter quarters at Newburgh on the Hudson. During the tedious winter months Washington, worn out and irritated, warned Congress that the troops must be paid, lest a dangerous situation develop. However, glorious news was in the offing, for Great Britain decided to call a halt. On April 6, 1783, Carleton informed Washington that preliminary peace articles had been signed in Paris and that the king had proclaimed a cessation of hostilities. Washington then issued a victory proclamation that was read to every regiment.

In New Jersey, as elsewhere, demobilization became the order of the day. The troops were granted indefinite furloughs, understandably permanent. Though the men were allowed to retain their arms and equipment, there was widespread disappointment when only four months' pay was given. Most left peaceably, though violence ensued when the "new recruits" marched from Lancaster, Pennsylvania, to Philadelphia to picket Congress for arrears and more liberal severance pay. Congress President Elias Boudinot of New Jersey and several other members were roughly handled. Its deliberations interrupted, Congress moved to Princeton, where for four months it convened in Nassau Hall. Washington, summoned to advise, resided in nearby Rocky Hill. On November 4, when Congress adjourned to meet again at Annapolis, Washington left for New York to take over the city from the British.

New Jersey lay divided and prostrate. Like most states outside New England, she had had to contend with a large resident Tóry element throughout the war. On the battlefields, even in the distant South, her sons had fought against one another. At home, since Tory activities had never ceased, the civil strife endured until the end. As late as the spring of 1782 there were killings and hangings. Many of the worst incidents of the later years were perpetrated by the skillfully operated Board of Associated Loyalists in New York City, under the supervision of ex-governor William Franklin. At the first intimation of peace, Carleton disbanded the organization. Soon thousands of refugees, including scores of Jerseymen, accepted exile in Nova Scotia. The lot of those remaining in the state was pitiful. Reduced to poverty because of the forfeiture of their property, disenfranchised, and marked for life, many had difficulty in reestablishing themselves as merchants, tradesmen, and shopkeepers. Governor Livingston, a magnanimous man, strove to heal these wounds, himself pardoning seventeen loyalists who had been tried and sentenced to hang. Even in the national congress, it took five years of effort to bring about the repeal of the loyalist disenfranchising act.

The State of New Jersey was left with an uneven economy as profiteering, black marketing, and the clandestine trade with the enemy disappeared. The iron industry, stimulated by the war, collapsed. Unhappily a series of bad harvests slowed the recovery of agriculture. With the currency in chaos, the farmers, unable to pay their taxes, much less their debts, faced ruin.

The state legislature, to its credit, grappled energetically with these major economic problems. It replaced the valueless Continental currency with "emission money" of its own, and though that too declined in value, it helped stem the tide of inflation. As the new money came back into the treasury in the form of tax receipts, a currency shortage developed. The economic distress pyramided, and the hard-pressed debtor demanded the emission of loan office certificates, the favorite colonial remedy. Though opposed by creditor interests, a measure was adopted on behalf of the debtor class, along with other ameliorative acts. "Revenue money" was issued as the state assumed responsibility for paying the interest on Continental obligations owed by its citizens. Steps were taken to fund the state debt of $750,000, including payments of arrears to soldiers, and the indebtedness to military suppliers. These salutary measures, though they took time, aided in the restoring of confidence and normal conditions, but not until 1787 did New Jersey recover from the war.

In other spheres normalcy came slowly indeed. Most difficult, because of the disruption of the churches, was the revival of common schooling, for which there was as yet no state and little public support. The institutions of higher learning—the College of New Jersey and Queen's College—came to life quickly, however. When President Witherspoon departed Nassau Hall, "the citadel of sedition," in 1776, he wondered "whether he should ever teach there again" or "whether he would hang as a traitor." The College of New Jersey had had an intermittent existence during the war years, while Queen's College, after a precarious status at Millstone and North Branch, resumed operations at New Brunswick in 1781. The New Jersey Medical Society also revived in 1781 and resumed its fight against quackery.*

The churches were hard hit. In countless instances their congregations had broken up, their ministers had dispersed, and their edifices had been pillaged, damaged, or destroyed. Half the Presbyterian congregations, for example, were without pastors, and the Dutch Reformed Church was little better off. The Anglican Church, a war casualty, could muster but three clergymen. All three denominations had the task of structuring national organizations that would conform to conditions created by independence. Despite the enfeebled condition of organized religion, certain humanitarian impulses revived. Most notable were the continued vitality of the high ideals of equality expounded in the Declaration of Independence and the heritage of John Woolman's influential writings, which, together with the good works of the Presbyterians, kept alive the cherished hope of ameliorating the condition of the slave.

In assessing the movement toward independence, one must guard against the assumption that the trend in New Jersey was inevitable—rooted in long-smoldering discontents in the economic and social environment. One must also resist the temptation to find the causes of revolt against the crown in the proprietary system of the seventeenth century, in the quarrels of the assembly with the royal government, or in such later controversies as the barracks-support measures or the disagreements over the tenure of supreme court justices. By 1763 even the crown had recognized implicitly certain important rights of colonial self-government. In the economic sphere, similarly, there is little ground for contention that the seeds of the War of Independence were rooted in the old quitrent system, the land struggles of the mid-eighteenth century, or even the stubborn easy-money aspirations of Jerseymen. Moreover, the formal

---

* Leonard Lundin, *Cockpit of the Revolution* (Princeton, 1940), 157, 409.

economic prohibitions of the crown hardly touched this colony.

The War of Independence was not so much inevitable as unexpected in New Jersey. Here there were few warnings of the impending conflict. Even the so-called Boston Massacre aroused little interest in a colony absorbed in the theft of provincial funds from Treasurer Skinner's house. Throughout the crucial years following the Stamp Act controversy, New Jersey's attitudes were swayed by those of her powerful neighbors, New York and Pennsylvania. The leaders of the Continental Congress saw fit from time to time to prod the New Jersey provincial congresses to take action, not only to enlist New Jersey in the cause, but to activate lagging New York. Actually New Jersey, North Carolina, Georgia, and Delaware were the least affected by events among the thirteen colonies; they had the least to gain or to lose through rebellion.

Colonial New Jersey shared with many colonies a common historical tradition and experience but was in some respects unique. Her people originated in an astonishing number of Dissenter groups stemming from the Protestant Reformation. Her earliest settlers were Congregationalists from New England and Quakers from Great Britain and Ireland. Early and late, many other strains appeared: small enclaves of Dutch Reformed, Swedish and Finnish Lutherans, French Huguenots, and Scotch Presbyterians. Among later arrivals were German Lutherans, German and Swiss Pietists, and Scotch-Irish Presbyterians. Denominations and sects of every hue flourished in this tolerant social environment. The Presbyterians were composed of several factions joined uneasily in a strong centralized organization. The Baptists, too, were numerous and even more united. The Dutch Reformed constituency was firmly rooted, but like that of the Presbyterians it included liberal and conservative wings, rendered more divisive by the war. The Quakers wielded considerable influence throughout the colonial period, despite the fact that their numbers dropped proportionately during the eighteenth century. The Anglicans never ceased to strive for status, but, suspect as the national church, their efforts failed to yield fruit. "If a plurality of religious belief and refusal to accept authority of any one church on grounds other than those dictated by the individual conscience can be described as distinctly American," writes historian Wesley Frank Craven, "New Jersey was the first of the English colonies to become American."

When he was governor of the Duke of York's great proprietorship extending from Connecticut to Maryland, Richard Nicolls pointed out perceptively that the New Jersey portion held the best promise of population growth and economic development. New York, he indicated, did not afford areas of fertile well-drained land sufficient to attract land-hungry settlers. As her later governors complained, she lacked the rich tax revenues of a numerous and growing body of freeholders and was forced to content herself with riches derived from the furs and pelts of her frontier. All the while, however, the incomparable port of New York City was developing and in the long run proved to be her greatest asset. Despite New Jersey's efforts to develop ports, New York was destined to embrace all of northern New Jersey in her hinterland, just as Philadelphia would envelop West New Jersey.

The gift of New Jersey by the duke to his friends Berkeley and Carteret was an irritant to Nicolls and to many who followed him. Governor Edmund Andros attempted in vain during his governorship to reassert the duke's suzerainty over New Jersey, and several years later Governor Dongan complained bitterly that New York, "cooped up at the very center of the King's dominions," was not strong enough to defend the colony from the French. Though his pleas to reunite the Jerseys to New York were ignored, they were never entirely forgotten. In 1688, with a French war in the offing, the crown placed New York and the Jerseys under Sir Edmund Andros as governor-general of the Dominion of New England. Hopefully, the charters of the other proprietaries such as Maryland and Pennsylvania would be terminated as well. The Revolution of 1688 intervened, and as King William became preoccupied with France and Ireland, the New Jersey proprietors were able to gain a respite.

The Board of Trade, created in 1696 with strong advisory powers, strove to bring all the colonies under the direct rule of the crown. By now convinced that proprietorships were incongruous in a developing empire, England was weary of dealing with proprietary factions in America. Though its overall efforts failed, the board in 1702 forced the surrender of the New Jersey proprietorships, its single victory. These two had become a nuisance more than the others—an anachronism that was of little service to the inhabitants and a misfit in the imperial scheme of colonial government.

The royal colony of New Jersey united the eastern and western divisions* and provided an assembly sitting alternately at Perth Amboy and Burlington, with the royal governor of New York as her chief executive, a unique situation. Thus from 1702 until 1738 New Jersey had an absentee governor and three capitals, the third being New York City. As the eighteenth century wore on, the defense of New York colony was paramount in the minds of those directing imperial policy. By the time New Jersey received her own governor in 1738 the crown was able to impose its will upon the colony, despite sporadic opposition in the assembly.

Royal government in New Jersey followed the usual pattern, with a governor appointed by the crown, a council whose members must be approved by the crown, and an elected assembly. In the adjustments to royal rule, the qualifications of voters and their representatives in the lower house came into question. But there was little opposition to a restricted franchise, since the average citizen owned a freehold or its equivalent in personal property. Though the very real privileges of self-government spelled out in the original Concessions of East and West Jersey were obscured by the bitter factionalism of the proprietary years, Jerseymen never forgot them. Time after time in their struggles with the royal governor these historic rights were reasserted. Local government was little disturbed during the royal period, and in this sphere the inhabitants continued practically without interference† to elect their officials, assess and

---

* East and West Jersey retained their separate identities politically, economically, and socially. By 1776, although these ancient divisions were blurred along the New York-Trenton corridor and to an extent along the Delaware above Trenton, this sense of division was apparent south of Burlington until well into the nineteenth century.

† With its mixed county-township form of government, the New Jersey town meeting never exerted the influence in the assembly that prevailed in early

collect local taxes, and adopt the ordinances needful to their well-being.

Since government in the eighteenth century had fewer tasks and accepted fewer responsibilities than in the twentieth, the bureaucracy of an American colony was infinitesimal. The budget of the rich colony of Massachusetts in the mid-eighteenth century, for example, with only six full-time officials, was but £25,000. In 1774, in poorly circumstanced New Jersey, the figure was about £3,000 (with £1,400 for salaries, of which the governor received £1,200). In these two, as in the others, the patronage consisted in bestowing a substantial number of part-time jobs, whose perquisites were the fees collected.

In New Jersey, county and town governments were simply structured. The county was governed by a board of supervisors consisting of the county judges and two freeholders chosen annually by each town. In the towns, two selectmen were elected annually, and these men chose three officers—assessor, collector, and clerk. Overseers of the roads and overseers of the poor rounded out the list of the principal local officers.

Government at all levels had, for the most part, a regulatory function; the main responsibilities were keeping the peace and providing the revenue to maintain the common school, where one existed, the orphanage, and a simple system of poor relief. The poor, the elderly, and the sick were cared for by relatives or neighbors, and in some instances by the local church congregation. On occasion, the local community cared for "helpless children," binding them out until they were old enough to be apprenticed. For the most part the family took care of its own; there were no legions of welfare workers or bureaucrats to distribute largess. "With its strong commitment to private property," writes historian Richard McCormick, "New Jersey was an orderly society."

The rise of patriotism in this rural colony must be attributed to a small number of leaders recruited from all segments of society. Thoughtful men, they were not themselves motivated by radical political or social doctrines. They won over their fellow country-

Massachusetts. See Michael Zuckerman, *Peaceable Kingdoms* (New York, 1970).

men less by ideological than by personal persuasion. Fortunately there had developed among the patriots a valuable chain of communication that ran from the Continental Congress, through the keystone provincial congresses, to the countless local committees. Although New Jersey's delegates to the Continental Congress played no leading role in the great deliberations leading to the Declaration of Independence, they nourished the spirit of independence among the patriot following. Persistence, awareness, and conviction carried the day in New Jersey.*

New Jersey never faltered in her dedication to the cause that by 1775 was uniting the colonies. She was determined, no matter what the price, and no matter how fleeting her interest in the issues that were stirring up her sister colonies, to cooperate with them in their opposition to the policies of the crown. This unwavering stance was far from historic, since New Jersey had evidenced little interest in the Albany Conference of 1754 and only passing concern for later intercolonial relationships. The spirit of independence, much less revolution, did not spring up spontaneously.

As early as 1909 the historian Carl Becker argued that the War of Independence prompted a second revolution that led to widespread reforms in America, such as the broadening of the franchise to include mechanics, artisans, and small farmers. In 1926 J. Franklin Jameson extended the Revolution's consequences to include reforms in the legal and social structure. Today's scholars are fairly well agreed that the American Revolution should be construed as two revolutions, more or less parallel: one the rebellion to achieve independence, and the second a reordering of American governance and society. Some historians insist that this second revolution has yet to be completed and that it has affected nations other than the United States.†

---

* The "great debate" in New Jersey was never so animated as to prevent her delegates to the Continental Congress from frequently absenting themselves for family or business reasons. They were not frowned upon for doing so.

† Milton M. Klein, "The American Revolution in the Twentieth Century," *The Historian*, XXXIV (1972), 213–229, examines these changing interpretations of the American Revolution.

The proponents of this idealistic theory adduce contemporary evidence to support it. For example, in 1776 John Adams wrote, "We are in the midst of a revolution, the most complete, unexpected, and remarkable as any in the history of nations." Benjamin Rush, another signer, in 1787 stated that though the late war was over, only the first act of the Revolution had been concluded. In 1826 Thomas Jefferson, who had once alluded to his famous preamble to the Declaration as "commonplace" and "hackneyed sentiments," thought the better of it. Tom Paine, the radical, was more explicit in his life-long conviction, repeated as late as the French Revolution of 1789, that "the independence of America, considered merely as a separation from England, would have been a matter of little importance, had it not been accompanied by a revolution in the principles and practices of government." More philosophically, he wrote, "We see with other eyes; we hear with other ears; and we think with other thoughts, than those we formerly used."

Some view this broader interpretation with skepticism. To them the colonists were on the whole prosperous and content, and their leaders were the most conservative of men. Few of them regarded the Revolution as a class war inaugurating a great social transformation. The Revolution, they contend, was uniquely an American event, and its most obvious peculiarity was that it was not a revolution at all. It was fought to preserve the kind of democracy that was already present. Charles M. Andrews, writing in 1926, viewed the Revolution as a political and constitutional movement only. "At bottom the fundamental issue was the political independence of the colonies." The late Clinton Rossiter insisted that since the colonists had by 1776 achieved a broad participation in government, it was a preserving revolution; there was certainly no pressing need to undertake a socioeconomic revolution within the colonies. In his judgment, "a first American revolution" marked by large advances in self-government had already taken place. The war with Britain was fought to secure an acknowledgment of these gains.

In applying the dual-revolution thesis to New Jersey, one must conclude that the Revolution was a conservative one. The colony's espousal of independence exhibited her determination to join with the other colonies in upholding the rights and privileges to which she believed herself entitled. Her franchise was broad, and popular sentiment was to increase rather than to limit it. There was no aristocratic cabal consciously striving to monopolize the provincial government. Admittedly there was a wealthy class—prosperous, but hardly monopolistic—just as there were enclaves of poor. Both groups were relatively inconspicuous in a society characterized by great mobility and by an abundance of opportunities for the average citizen to rise—economically, socially, and politically.

The supporters of independence came from every stratum of society. The movement created no province-wide divisiveness, induced the formation of no organized mobs of urban radicals, and brought forth no sweeping demands for economic and social justice. The loyalists suffered exile and the confiscation of property only because they opposed separation. Jerseymen were fighting essentially to preserve the existing imperial relationship. Finally, New Jersey's patriot leadership was conservative, not radical; and though it shifted from year to year, it did not change its basic character. Through ten years, from 1774 to 1783, not a single leader espoused a program of internal reform. During the war and the early postwar years, New Jersey's leaders were preoccupied first with maintaining and then reactivating the orderliness and prosperity of the past. The decisions taken were pragmatic: to promote the war effort and to stem the disintegration of the governmental process. New Jersey's constitution of 1776 was conservative, attempting only to correct what were thought to be the maladjustments of royal government. Wracked by war and disorganization, New Jersey's full participation in the "second American Revolution" would await the termination of a long recuperative period.*

---

* For a considered appraisal of this issue, see Larry R. Gerlach, "New Jersey in the Coming of the American Revolution," Papers, New Jersey History Symposium, 1970, 8–20.

APPENDIX

THE CHIEF PROPRIETORS, THE PROPRIETARY GOVERNORS, AND THE ROYAL GOVERNORS OF NEW JERSEY, 1664–1776

THE PROPRIETARY PERIOD, 1664–1702

James, Duke of York, Proprietor of the Duke's Province, *Mar. 1664–Dec. 1688*
    The Duke's governor, Colonel Richard Nicolls, governed New Jersey until arrival of the proprietors' governor, *Sept. 1664–Aug. 1665*
Proprietors of New Jersey, Lord John Berkeley and Sir George Carteret, *June 1664–July 1676*
    Deputy governor, Philip Carteret, *Aug. 1665–July 1676*

THE DUTCH RECONQUEST, AUG. 1673–NOV. 1674

East New Jersey, 1676–1702 Proprietors and Governors	West New Jersey, 1676–1702 Proprietors and Governors
Sir George Carteret, *July 1676–Jan. 1680*	John Fenwick and Edward Byllynge, *Mar. 1674–Feb. 1675*
Elizabeth, Lady Carteret, *Jan. 1680–Feb. 1682*	The Byllynge Trustees, *Feb. 1675–Sept. 1680*
	Edward Byllynge, Chief Proprietor and Governor (absentee), *Sept. 1680–Jan. 1687*
Deputy governor Philip Carteret, *Aug. 1665–Feb. 1682*	

297

The (Twelve) Twenty Four Proprietors, their heirs and assigns, *Feb. 1682–Apr. 1702*

Governor Robert Barclay (absentee), *Sept. 1682–Oct. 1690*

Deputy governors:
Thomas Rudyard, *Sept. 1682–Jan. 1684*
Gawen Lawrie, *Jan. 1684–Oct. 1686*
Lord Neil Campbell, *Oct. 1686–Mar. 1687*
Andrew Hamilton, *Mar. 1687–Aug. 1688*

(Illegal governors, Samuel Jennings and Thomas Olive, elected by West Jersey assembly, *May 1683–Oct. 1684*)

Deputy Governor John Skene, *Nov. 1685–Aug. 1688*

THE SIR EDMUND ANDROS INTERLUDE, AUG. 1688–APR. 1689

Andrew Hamilton, *Apr. 1689–Apr. 1692*

Dr. Daniel Coxe, Governor and Chief Proprietor (absentee), *Feb. 1687–Mar. 1692*

Deputy Governor John Skene, *Apr. 1689–Apr. 1692*

EAST NEW JERSEY AND WEST NEW JERSEY, 1692–1703

The English Proprietors of West New Jersey and the West Jersey Society, 1692–1702

The English Proprietors of East New Jersey, 1692–1702

Governor Andrew Hamilton, *Apr. 1692–Apr. 1698*
Governor Jeremiah Basse, *Apr. 1698–June 1689*
Governor Andrew Hamilton, *Aug. 1699–Aug. 1703*

ROYAL GOVERNORS

Lord Cornbury, *Aug. 1703–Dec. 1708*
Lord Lovelace, *Dec. 1708–May 1709*
Lt. Gov. Richard Ingoldsby, *May 1709–Apr. 1710*
Robert Hunter, *June 1710–July 1719*
William Burnet, *Oct. 1720–Apr. 1728*

John Montgomerie, *Apr. 1728–July 1730**
William Cosby, *Aug. 1732–Mar. 1736*
Lewis Morris, *Aug. 1738–May 1746*
Jonathan Belcher, *Aug. 1747–Aug. 1757*
Thomas Pownall, *Sept. 1757*
Francis Bernard, *June 1758–July 1760*
Thomas Boone, *July 1760–Oct. 1761*
Josiah Hardy, *Oct. 1761–May 1763*
William Franklin, *May 1763–July 1776*

---

* During intervals between governors the president of the provincial council was acting governor, except in August 1757, when the council as a whole acted as the chief executive. For a comprehensive list of New Jersey's civil officers during the royal period, see Donald L. Kemmerer, *Path to Freedom* (Princeton, 1940).

BIBLIOGRAPHY

The standard bibliography of New Jersey history is Nelson R. Burr, *A Narrative and Descriptive Bibliography of New Jersey*, New Jersey Historical Series (Princeton, 1964–1965), XXI. A model of its kind, it includes all printed sources from 1609 to 1964.

SECONDARY SOURCES

GENERAL WORKS

Competent contemporary histories of colonial New Jersey are few. However, Samuel Smith, a Quaker merchant and a member of the provincial council, published *The History of the Colony of Nova Caesaria, or New Jersey . . . to the Year 1721. . . .* (Burlington, 1765), a work that includes valuable source material.

Two nineteenth-century works, useful though dull reading, are Thomas F. Gordon, *The History of New Jersey* (Trenton, 1834) and Isaac S. Mulford, *Civil and Political History of New Jersey* (Camden, 1848).

The early twentieth century saw the publication of three substantial cooperative undertakings that refined the work of earlier historians and moved beyond the recital of purely political events. Sections in all of them are useful, and a number are excellent. These works are Francis B. Lee, ed., *New Jersey as a Colony and State . . .*, 4 vols. (New York, 1902); Irving S. Kull, ed., *New Jersey, A History*, 6 vols. (New York, 1930–1932); and William S. Myers, ed., *The Story of New Jersey*, 5 vols. (New York, 1945).

The colonial period is dealt with in three studies in the Princeton History of New Jersey: John E. Pomfret, *The Province of West New Jersey, 1609–1702* (Princeton, 1956) and *The Province of East New Jersey, 1609–1702* (Princeton, 1962); and Donald L. Kemmerer, *Path to Freedom, The Struggle for Self-Government in Colonial New Jersey, 1703–1777* (Princeton, 1940). Kemmerer's able narrative emphasizes political and economic factors. In the New Jersey Historical Series, published in conjunction with the New Jersey Tercentenary celebration in 27 volumes plus supplementary studies (Princeton, 1964–1965), there are two brief, attractively written volumes dealing with the colonial period: Richard P. McCormick, *New Jersey from Colony to State, 1609–1789* (Princeton, 1964) and Wesley Frank Craven, *New Jersey and the English Colonization of North America* (Princeton, 1964).

Edwin P. Tanner, *The Province of New Jersey, 1664–1738* (New York, 1908) and Edgar J. Fisher, *New Jersey as a Royal Province, 1738–1776* (New York, 1911), both studies in the Columbia University series in History, Economics, and Public Law, are meticulously researched and mark the beginning of work on New Jersey history by trained historians. As Tanner and Fisher present their findings topically, one must go elsewhere for the flow and interaction of events.

A number of general works on colonial history discuss New Jersey. By far the most important is Vol. III of Charles M. Andrews, *The Colonial Period of American History* (New Haven, 1937). Andrews is unexcelled in his treatment of early American settlements. Substantial also are the sections in Herbert L. Osgood's earlier *The American Colonies in the Seventeenth Century*, 3 vols. (New York, 1904–1907), especially II, Pt. iii, Ch. 8, and *The American Colonies in the Eighteenth Century*, 4 vols. (New York, 1924–1925), I, Pt. i, Ch. 12; II, Pt. i, Chs. 18–19; and II, Pt. iii, Ch. 5. Lawrence H. Gipson has a chapter on New Jersey (III, Ch. 6) in his multivolume *The British Empire before the American Revolution*, 15 vols. (Caldwell, Idaho, and New York, 1936–1970). Thomas J. Wertenbaker in his *The Founding of American Civilization: The Middle Colonies* (New York, 1938) discusses important cultural aspects in New Jersey history not treated elsewhere.

PRECEDING THE ENGLISH CONQUEST OF 1664

Material on the Delaware or Lenni-Lenape Indians is found in many of the works cited below. The standard anthropological references are Dorothy Cross, *The Indians of New Jersey* (Trenton, 1935) and Daniel D. Brinton, *The Lenape and Their Legends* (Philadelphia, 1885). A. C. Myers, ed., *William Penn's Own Account of the Lenni Lenape or Delaware Indians*, appears in a revised edition (Somerset, N.J., 1970) and is a valuable source.

The history of the Dutch, Swedes, Finns, and New Haven colonists on the Delaware is so inextricably mingled that most of the works cited in this section touch all of them. Likewise many works on New Netherland treat the Bergen County and Delaware River areas of New Jersey.

The outstanding study is Amandus Johnson, *Swedish Settlements on the Delaware, 1638–1655*, 2 vols. (Philadelphia, 1911). All others are in one way or another derivative. Worthy of mention is Christopher Ward, *The Dutch and Swedes on the Delaware, 1609–1664* (Philadelphia, 1930). More specialized are Evelyn Page, "The First Frontier, The Dutch and Swedes," *Pennsylvania History*, XV (1948), 276–304, an application of the Turner thesis; C. A. Weslager, *Dutch Explorers, Traders, and Settlers in the Delaware Valley, 1609–1664* (Philadelphia, 1961); and J.

H. Wuorinin, *The Finns on the Delaware, 1638–1655* (New York, 1938). Unique source materials have been compiled in A. C. Myers, ed., *Narratives of Pennsylvania, West Jersey and Delaware* (New York, 1912) and in J. Franklin Jameson, ed., *Narratives of New Netherland, 1609–1664* (New York, 1909), volumes in *Original Narratives of Early American History*. Amandus Johnson also edited *Instruction for Governor Printz* (Philadelphia, 1930), the colorful governor of New Sweden.

New Haven's abortive efforts to settle south Jersey are discussed in Isabel M. Calder, *New Haven Colony* (New Haven, 1934) and specifically in Johnson's *Swedish Settlements*. Pomfret's *West New Jersey* gives a summary account. The antics of Sir Edmund Plowden on the Delaware are described in Lee's *New Jersey*, I, Ch. 3; in Father William Keller's "Sir Edmund Plowden and the Province of New Albion," *Historical Records . . . of the U.S. Catholic Historical Society*, XLI (1953), 42–70; and in Johnson's *Swedish Settlements*.

A standard work on New Netherland is E. B. O'Callaghan, *History of New Netherlands*, 2 vols. (Philadelphia, 1846–1848). The most readable recent studies are Llewelyn Powys, *Henry Hudson* (New York, 1928); E. L. Raesly, *Portrait of New Netherland* (New York, 1945); and Henry H. Kessler and Eugene Rachlis, *Peter Stuyvesant and His New York . . .* (New York, 1959). Mrs. M. G. Van Rensselaer, *History of the City of New York in the Seventeenth Century*, 2 vols. (New York, 1909), a work of broader dimension than its title suggests, contains an account of Dutch activities on the west bank of the Hudson. Pomfret's *East New Jersey* brings together the material on this topic.

Adrian C. Leiby, *The Early Dutch and Swedish Settlers of New Jersey*, New Jersey Historical Series, X (Princeton, 1964), is the most recent comprehensive account of the Dutch in East Jersey and carries the story into the eighteenth century. Bertus W. Wabake, *Dutch Migration to North America, 1624–1860, A Short History* (New York, 1944); Richard C. Amerman, "Dutch Life in Pre-Revolutionary Bergen County," *Proceedings of the New Jersey Historical Society*, hereafter cited as *P.N.J.H.S.*, LXXVI (1958), 161–181; and Wertenbaker, *Middle Colonies* discuss New Jersey's Dutch heritage.

The most valuable material on the later Swedes on the Delaware is contained in four contemporary works: Thomas Campanius Holm, *A Short Description of the Province of New Sweden . . .* , *Memoirs* of the Historical Society of Pennsylvania, III (Philadelphia, 1934), first published in Stockholm in 1702; Joachim Reincke, "Journal of a Visit among the Swedes of West Jersey, 1745," *Pennsylvania Magazine of History and Biography*, hereafter cited as *P.M.H.&B.*, XXXIII (1909), 99–101, written by a Moravian missionary; Israel Acrelius, *A History of New Sweden . . .* , *Memoirs*, Historical Society of Pennsylvania, XI (Philadelphia, 1876), originally published in Sweden, 1759; and Amandus Johnson, ed., *The Journal and Biography of Nicholas Collin, 1746–1831* (Philadelphia, 1936).

The printed sources for the Dutch and Swedish settlements on the Delaware are in Berthold Fernow, comp., *Documents Relating to the History of the Dutch and*

Swedish Settlements on the Delaware River . . . , *1624–1682*, XII (Albany, N.Y., 1877), in *Documents Relative to the Colonial History of the State of New York*, 15 vols. (Albany, N.Y., 1856–1887). For the Dutch in New Netherland, including the west bank of the Hudson, see the earlier volumes of the New York *Documents*. William A. Whitehead, ed., *New Jersey Archives*, hereafter cited as *N.J.A.*, I (Newark, 1880) includes New Jersey source materials printed in the New York *Documents*.

THE PROPRIETARY PERIOD

The principal documentary sources are F. W. Ricord and William Nelson, eds., *N.J.A.*, I–III (Newark, 1880–1886) and Aaron Leaming and Jacob Spicer, *The Grants, Concessions, and Original Constitutions of the Province of New Jersey* (Philadelphia, 1752, reprinted Somerville, N.J., 1881). A number of the principal early documents also appear in Julian P. Boyd, ed., *Fundamental Laws and Constitutions of New Jersey, 1664–1964*, New Jersey Historical Series, XVII (Princeton, 1964), together with an excellent introduction and comments. Important also are William Nelson, ed., *Calendar of Records in the Office of the Secretary of State, N.J.A.*, XXI (Paterson, 1899), and F. W. Ricord and William Nelson, eds., *Journal of the Governor and Council, N.J.A.*, XIII–XVIII (Trenton, 1880–1893), especially XIII.

The best account of the short-lived proprietorship of James, Duke of York, is in Andrews, *Colonial Period*, III, Chs. 2 and 3. The important Duke's Laws are printed, *inter alia*, in *The Colonial Laws of New York*, 5 vols. (Albany, 1894), I, 5–100.

William A. Whitehead treats the origin and history of the West New Jersey proprietary in *East New Jersey under the Proprietary Government* (rev. ed., Newark, 1875), and Pomfret's *East New Jersey* fills the gaps in Whitehead's account. Andrews, *Colonial Period*, III, Ch. 4 has a masterly summary. For the proprietary relationships to the crown see Wesley Frank Craven, *The Colonies in Transition* (New York, 1968).

New Jersey, like the other colonies, has a full array of county, township, and local histories. They are listed in Burr, *Bibliography*, especially 78–99. Though few are outstanding, good material is found in such works as Edwin F. Hatfield, *History of Elizabeth, New Jersey* (New York, 1868); William A. Whitehead, *Contributions to the Early History of Perth Amboy* (New York, 1856); Edwin Salter, *A History of Monmouth and Ocean Counties* (Bayonne, 1890); Joel Parker, "Monmouth County During the Provincial Era," *P.N.J.H.S.*, 2d ser., III (1872), 17–39; E. M. Woodward and J. F. Hageman, *History of Burlington and Mercer Counties, New Jersey* . . . (Philadelphia, 1883); Trenton Historical Society, *A History of Trenton, 1679–1929*, 2 vols. (Princeton, 1929); Frank H. Stewart, comp. and ed., *Notes on Old Gloucester County, New Jersey* (Philadelphia, 1917), a source book; Thomas Cushing and Charles E. Sheppard, *History of . . . Gloucester, Salem, and Cumberland, New Jersey* . . . (Philadelphia, 1883); and Lucius Q. C. Elmer, *History of Early Settlement and Progress of Cumberland County* . . . (Bridgeton, N.J., 1869).

John E. Pomfret identifies the original shareholders and fractioners down to 1702 in "The Proprietors of the Province of East New Jersey," *P.M.H. & B*, LXXVIII (1953), 251-293, and presents a final list in his *East New Jersey*, appendix. His article, "The Apologia of Governor Lawrie of East Jersey, 1686," *William and Mary Quarterly*, XIV (1957), 344-357, and Richard P. McCormick's "The Revolution of 1681 in East Jersey: A Document," *P.N.J.H.S.*, LXXI (1953), 111-124 also fill gaps. McCormick has also published "The Province of East Jersey, 1609-1702," *P.N.J.H.S.*, LXX (1952), 81-96. See also an earlier article, David McGregor, "The Board of Proprietors of East Jersey," *P.N.J.H.S.*, n.s., VII (1922), 177-195.

George P. Insh, *Scottish Colonial Schemes, 1620-1686* (Glasgow, 1922) describes the Scottish migration to East Jersey, and William A. Whitehead, *East Jersey*, reprints in its entirety George Scot's *The Model of Government in East Jersey . . .* (1685), the best promotion tract on East Jersey. Robert Barclay and William Penn, two East Jersey proprietors, in their efforts to win James II to religious toleration, laid themselves open to a charge of Jacobitism. On this point see John E. Pomfret, "Robert Barclay and James II: Barclay's 'Vindication,' 1689," *Bulletin, Friends Hist. Assoc.*, XLII (1953), 33-40.

The West New Jersey proprietary, 1674-1702, is discussed in Tanner's *Province of New Jersey* and Andrew's *Colonial Period*, III, Ch. 4. In the light of new material see also Pomfret's *West New Jersey* and his "West New Jersey: A Quaker Society, 1674-1775," *Wm. and Mary Qtly.*, VIII (1951), 494-519.

William Penn's biographers have tended to neglect his important involvement in the founding of West New Jersey, thus missing the dawn of his interest in America as well as a significant aspect of New Jersey and Quaker history. The exception is Rufus M. Jones, *The Quakers in the American Colonies* (London, 1911).

A. L. Rowse, *The Cousin Jacks: The Cornish in America* (New York, 1969) contains the most recent treatment of the dissimulations of the Quaker Cornishman, Edward Byllynge (Billing), the chief proprietor. Two excellent articles on Byllynge appear in H. L. Brinton, ed., *The Children of Light* (New York, 1938): "The Problem of Edward Byllynge: His Connection with Cornwall," by L. V. Holdsworth, and "The Problem of Edward Byllynge: His Writings and the Evidence of His Influence in the First Constitution of New Jersey," by J. L. Nickalls. For evidence that Byllynge, not Penn, actually wrote the famous Concessions of West New Jersey, see John E. Pomfret, "The Problem of the West Jersey Concessions, 1667/7," *Wm. and Mary Qtly.*, V (1948), 95-105. This is not to say that Penn, as well as his lawyer, Thomas Rudyard, were not fully consulted. In addition, with the friendly support of Julian P. Boyd, then librarian of the Historical Society of Pennsylvania, the writer was able to reconstruct the list of the original shareholders and fractioners of West New Jersey—see John E. Pomfret, "Thomas Budd's 'True and Perfect Account' of Byllynge's Proprieties in West New Jersey, 1685," *P.M.H. & B.*, LXI (1937), 325-331. For a final list of shareholders to 1702, see Pomfret, *West New Jersey*, appendix.

For the role of the exasperating Major John Fenwick of Salem see Pomfret, *West New Jersey*; E. G. Johnson, "Memoir of John Fenwick, Chief Proprietor of the Salem Tenth," *P.N.J.H.S.*, IV (1849), 53–89; and Frank H. Stewart, *Major John Fenwick* (Woodbury, 1939). For the colonists' later difficulties with Edward Byllynge, important contemporary sources are: John Tatham, Thomas Revell, and Nathaniel Westland, *The Case Put and Decided . . .* (Philadelphia, 1699), and Samuel Jennings, *Truth Rescued from Forgery and Falsehood. . . .* (Philadelphia, 1699). There are important references in Norman Penney, ed., *The Short Journal and Itinerary Journal of George Fox* (Cambridge, Eng. 1925). The best account of Daniel Coxe, later chief proprietor and promoter extraordinary, is "Biographical Notice of Dr. Daniel Coxe," *P.M.H. & B.*, VII (1883), 317–337.

Unusual among the promotion tracts on West Jersey is Thomas Budd, *Good Order Established in Pennsylvania and West Jersey* (London, 1685). Though Budd supported Jennings against Byllynge, William Penn assured George Fox that Budd gave a good account of the Quaker colonies. The following articles on West Jersey settlement are useful: John Clement, "The Proprietary Towns of West Jersey," in *Early Settlements of New Jersey* (Camden, 1882); *First Settlement of Newton Township* (Camden, 1877), both pamphlets; Carlos E. Godfrey, "The True Origin of Gloucester County, N.J.," *Camden Historical Society Proc.*, I (1922), 3–8; "When Boston was New Jersey's Capital," *P.N.J.H.S.*, n.s., LI (1933), 1–8; and "Origin of the Counties of New Jersey," *N.J. Law Journal*, XLVII (1925), 235–236; John Paine, *History of the West New Jersey Society* (London, 1895); and John Clement, *West New Jersey Society* (Camden, 1880), a pamphlet. Clement and Godfrey were the most careful workers among the older local historians. A notable source for West New Jersey's early history is Henry C. Reed and George J. Miller, eds., *Burlington Court Book of West Jersey, 1680–1709* (Washington, 1944). These extensive records not only present in full the work of the principal court but, in reporting actual cases, give a rare insight into early New Jersey society.

For a reevaluation of the political history of the proprietary period, see John R. McCreary, "Ambition, Interest, and Faction: Politics in New Jersey, 1702–1738," Ph.D. dissertation, University of Nebraska, 1971.

THE ROYAL PERIOD, 1703–1776

Far less has been written on the royal period than on the proprietary period. The best accounts are found in the comprehensive works of Kemmerer, *Path to Freedom*; Tanner, *The Province of New Jersey*, latter part; and Fisher, *New Jersey as a Royal Province*. In fact Kemmerer has written the only satisfactory narrative account of these years. Since New York's governor until 1738 was also governor of New Jersey, useful material is found in the appropriate histories of New York, especially David M. Ellis, James A. Frost, Harold C. Syrett, and Harry J. Carman, *A Short History of New York State* (Ithaca, 1957, 1967) and A. C. Flick, ed., *History of the State of New York*, 10 vols. (New York, 1933–1937). Flick's cooperative work is written topically and is uneven for the earlier periods.

Useful also are Gordon B. Turner, "Colonial New Jersey," *P.N.J.H.S.*, LXX (1952), 229–245, and Edward P. Lilly, *The Colonial Agents of New York and New Jersey* (Washington, D.C., 1935).

The best travel accounts are Carl Bridenbaugh, ed., *Gentleman's Progress . . . 1744* (Williamsburg, Va., 1948), the best edition of Alexander Hamilton's *Itinerarium, The America of 1750*; Peter Kalm's *Travels in North America*, 2 vols. (New York, 1937), from the English version of 1770, edited by Adolph B. Benson; and Reverend Andrew Burnaby, *Travels through the Middle Settlements in North America, 1759–1760* (London, 1774; reprinted New York, 1904, from the 3d ed., 1798), with introduction and notes by Rufus R. Wilson. Burnaby was an intelligent Englishman whose comments on the future of the colonies are of interest. He passed through New Jersey in 1760. For other travel references see Burr, *Bibliography*, 3–27 and *passim*.

There are few biographies of New Jersey's royal governors preceding William Franklin, appointed in 1763. Many are given notice, however, in the *Dictionary of American Biography* and similar biographical works. See also Charles W. Spencer, "The Cornbury Legend," N.Y. State Historical Assoc. *Proceedings*, XIII (1914), 309–320, and Gordon B. Turner, "Governor Lewis Morris and the Colonial Conflict," *P.N.J.H.S.*, LXVII (1949), 260–304. A valuable source, used freely in John F. Burns, *Controversies between Royal Governors and Their Assemblies in the Northern American Colonies* (Boston, 1923) is . . . *The Papers of Lewis Morris . . .* , published by the New York Historical Society (New York, 1852) with a biographical memoir; and *The Papers of Lewis Morris, Governor . . . of New Jersey from 1738–1746*, N.J. Hist. Soc., *Collections*, IV (Newark, 1852). Governor Jonathan Belcher's *Papers* were published in the Massachusetts Historical Society *Collections*, ser. 6, VI–VII (Boston, 1893–1894).

Little has been written of New Jersey's participation in the colonial wars with France. The standard general work is Howard H. Peckham, *The Colonial Wars, 1689–1762* (Chicago, 1964). On New Jersey's role see Lee, *New Jersey*, I, Ch. 22, and the summary chapters contained in Tanner and Fisher. Also useful are R. Wayne Parker, "New Jersey in the Colonial Wars," *P.N.J.H.S.*, n.s., VI (1921), 193–217, and Joseph F. Folsom, "Colonel Peter Schuyler at Albany," *P.N.J.H.S.*, n.s., I (1916), 160–163. Bruce T. McCully touches on New Jersey's efforts in "Catastrophe in the Wilderness: New Light on the Canada Expedition of 1709," *Wm. and Mary Qtly.*, XI (1954), 441–456.

The outstanding treatment of the entire period 1760–1776 in New Jersey is Larry R. Gerlach, "Revolution or Independence? New Jersey 1760–1776," Ph.D. dissertation, Rutgers University, 1968. Dr. Gerlach's comprehensive account is based largely upon manuscript sources heretofore unused by New Jersey historians.

For a discussion of New Jersey's local issues preceding the Revolution, in addition to Gerlach see Arthur D. Pierce, *Smugglers' Woods: Jaunts and Journeys in Colonial and Revolutionary New Jersey* (New Brunswick, 1960); the pertinent sections in Kenneth Scott, *Counterfeiting in Colonial America* (New York, 1957);

Donald L. Kemmerer, "Judges' Good Behavior Tenure in Colonial New Jersey," *P.N.J.H.S.*, XVI (1938), 18–30; and the excellent account of Jerome J. Nadelhaft, "Politics and the Judicial Tenure Fight in Colonial New Jersey," *Wm. and Mary Qtly.*, XXVIII (1971), 46–63.

Gerlach, "Revolution or Independence," 33–49, contains the most succinct discussion of two important topics—New Jersey's close ties with New York and Pennsylvania and her relatively weak direct links with the British government.

THE REVOLUTIONARY PERIOD, 1775–1783

A great deal has been written about New Jersey during the Revolution, much of it of poor quality. See especially the many references in Burr, *Bibliography*, 64–88.

The standard works are Gerlach, "Revolution or Independence? . . ." through the year 1776; Leonard Lundin, *Cockpit of the Revolution: The War for Independence in New Jersey* (Princeton, 1940), a volume in the Princeton History of New Jersey series; Alfred Hoyt Bill, *New Jersey and the Revolutionary War,* New Jersey Historical Series, II (Princeton, 1964), balanced though brief; and David Bernstein, "New Jersey in the American Revolution," Ph.D. dissertation, Rutgers University, 1970. Douglas Freeman, *George Washington, A Biography*, IV and V (New York, 1951–1952) is indispensable for military operations in New Jersey.

Useful local studies are: James C. Connolly, "Quitrents in Colonial New Jersey as a Contributing Cause for the American Revolution," *P.N.J.H.S.*, n.s., VII (1922), 13–21, somewhat strained, and "The Stamp Act Congress and New Jersey's Opposition to It," *P.N.J.H.S.*, IX (1924), 137–150; David L. Cowen, "Revolutionary New Jersey, 1763–1787," *P.N.J.H.S.*, LXXI (1953), 1–23, a balanced statement; Joseph E. Folsom, "New Jersey's Part in the Revolution," *P.N.J.H.S.*, 3rd ser., VII (1912), 65–74; and two articles by Cornelius Vermeule, "Number of Soldiers in the Revolution," *P.N.J.H.S.*, n.s., VII (1922), 223–227 and "Service of the New Jersey Militia in the Revolutionary War," *P.N.J.H.S.*, n.s., IX (1924), 234–248.

Phases of the Revolution in New Jersey are dealt with in Adrian C. Leiby, *The Revolutionary War in the Hackensack Valley* (New Brunswick, 1962); William S. Stryker, *The Battle of Monmouth* (Princeton, 1927); and Andrew D. Mellick, *The Story of an Old Farm* (Somerville, 1889), a minor classic touching the Revolution in the Raritan Valley and republished by Hubert G. Schmidt as *Lesser Crossroads* (New Brunswick, 1948). Another specialized work is Edward A. Fuhlbrugge, *An Abstract of New Jersey Finance During the American Revolution* (New York, 1937).

Two excellent treatises on the loyalists or Tories are William Nelson, *The American Tory* (London, 1961) and Paul H. Smith, *Loyalists and Redcoats* (Chapel Hill, N.C., 1964), and Wallace Brown has written two readable general works, *The King's Friends* . . . (Providence, 1965) and *The Good Americans* . . . (New York, 1969). The New Jersey loyalists are treated in E. Alfred Jones, *The*

Loyalists of New Jersey . . ., N.J. Hist. Soc., *Collections*, X (Newark, 1927). His conclusions are challenged by Cornelius G. Vermeule, "The Active New Jersey Loyalists," *P.N.J.H.S.*, n.s., LII (1934), 87–95. Vermeule contends that there were only 1,100 active loyalists, compared with the generally accepted figures of from 3,000 to 5,000. A Van Doren Honeyman, "Concerning New Jersey Loyalists in the Revolution," *P.N.J.H.S.*, LI (1935) is a balanced view. Paul. H. Smith in "American Loyalists: Notes on their Organization and Numerical Strength," *Wm. and Mary Qtly.*, 3d ser., XXV (1968), 258–277, estimates that 2,650 men served in New Jersey loyalist units. The contemporary Tory account is James Moody, *Narrative . . . Since the Year 1776* (London, 1783; reprinted, New York, 1938).

For political changes during the critical period see Allan Nevins, *The American States During and After the Revolution* (New York, 1924), a path-finding work with material on New Jersey, and the definitive work by Richard P. McCormick, *Experiment in Independence* (New Brunswick, 1950). Standard works on the New Jersey constitution of 1776 are Charles R. Erdman, Jr., *The New Jersey Constitution of 1776* (Princeton, 1929); John F. Bebout, *The Making of the New Jersey Constitution* (Trenton, 1945); and Gladys G. Pidcock, *Constitutional Reform in New Jersey, 1776–1844* (Somerville, 1941). Gerlach, "Revolution or Independence? . . ." and Nevins, *American States* contain pertinent comments. The constitution is printed in Boyd, ed., *Fundamental Laws*, 155–163.

Biographies of Jerseymen for the Revolutionary period are William A. Whitehead, "Biographical Sketch of William Franklin, Governor of New Jersey from 1763 to 1776," *P.N.J.H.S.*, 1st ser., III (1848), 137–159; Catherine Fennelly, "William Franklin of New Jersey," *Wm. and Mary Qtly.*, VI (1949), 361–382; and William H. Mariboe's University of Pennsylvania doctoral dissertation, "William Franklin" (1962). Theodore Sedgwick, *Memoir of the Life of William Livingston* (New York, 1883) is the nearest approach to a biography; both Franklin and Livingston are deserving of new biographies. Milton M. Klein, "The American Whig: William Livingston of New York," Ph.d. dissertation, Columbia University, 1954, deals incidentally with Livingston's New Jersey career. Some of Livingston's letters appear in *Selections from the Correspondence of the Executive of New Jersey, from 1776 to 1786* (Newark, 1848). Livingston's wartime administration is ably analyzed in Margaret B. Macmillan, *The War Governors in the American Revolution* (New York, 1943).

The standard biography of Witherspoon is Varnum L. Collins, *President Witherspoon: A Biography*, 2 vols. (Princeton, 1925). See also T. J. Wertenbaker, "John Witherspoon" in Willard Thorpe, ed., *The Lives of Eighteen from Princeton* (Princeton, 1946), 68–86; Moses C. Tyler, "President Witherspoon in the American Revolution," *American Hist. Rev.* (1896), 171–679; and John Rodgers, ed., *The Works of John Witherspoon*, 4 vols. (Philadelphia, 1800–1801). Other biographical references are: Ashbel Green, *The Life of Ashbel Green* (New York, 1849); William A. Duer, *The Life of William Alexander, Earl of Stirling*, N.J. Hist. Soc., *Collections*, II (New York, 1847); George H. Danforth, "The Rebel Earl,"

Ph.D. dissertation, Columbia University, 1955; and Alan Valentine's inadequate *Lord Stirling* (New York, 1969). Additional biographical works are:Elias Boudinot, *Journal of Events in the Revolution* (Philadelphia, 1894); George A. Boyd, *Elias Boudinot, Patriot and Statesman, 1740–1821* (Princeton, 1952); Gertrude S. Wood, *William Paterson of New Jersey* (Fairlawn, N.J., 1933); and Julian P. Boyd, "William Paterson" in Thorpe, ed., *The Lives of Eighteen from Princeton* (Princeton, 1946) 1–23.

LAND AND BOUNDARIES

Because the New Jersey proprietors succeeding Berkeley and Carteret sold shares and fractions of shares of land, the land system became almost hopelessly complicated, giving rise to factionalism and lawsuits that lasted until the Revolution.

The literature is extensive, with accounts in all the standard histories already cited, especially Pomfret's *East New Jersey* and *West New Jersey* for the early period and Kemmerer's *Path to Freedom* for the years 1702–1776. The land problem is treated topically and in some detail in Tanner and Fisher. Gary S. Horowitz treats a dramatic period in "New Jersey Land Riots, 1745–1755," Ph.D. dissertation, Ohio State University, 1966.

Among the many specialized references are John R. Stevenson, "The Councils of the Proprietors of West New Jersey, Organized 1687," *P.M.H. & B.*, XVIII (1894), 496–503; Frederick R. Black, "The Last Lord Proprietors of West Jersey: The West Jersey Society, 1692–1702," Ph.D. dissertation, Rutgers University, 1966; William T. McClure, "The West New Jersey Society," *P.N.J.H.S.*, LXXIV (1956), 1–20; Keith Trace, "The West Jersey Society, 1763–1819," *P.N.J.H.S.*, LXXX (1962), 266–280, a good summary; Edgar J. Fisher, "Colonial Land Conflicts in New Jersey," Union County Hist. Soc. *Proceedings*, I (1923), 3–12; and E. S. Rankin and Benjamin Fletcher, "The East Jersey Proprietors," *P.N.J.H.S.*, LXII (1944), 146–155. Edwin F. Hatfield's *History of Elizabeth, New Jersey* (New York, 1868), though antiproprietary, is of value. In addition to the references to the land problem cited earlier, still others are found in Burr, *Bibliography*.

In addition to *N.J.A.* I–III and XXI, another primary source of value is George J. Miller's edition of the *Minutes of the Board of Proprietors of the Eastern Divison of New Jersey*, to date three volumes covering the years 1685–1764 (Perth Amboy, 1949–1960), of which Vol. I is the most important. The records of the West Jersey proprietors are in Burlington, unpublished, but for the historian they are disappointing. Significant materials on the land problem for the proprietary period in East Jersey are found in Preston W. Edsall, ed., *Journal of the Courts of Common Right and Chancery of East Jersey, 1683–1702* (Philadelphia, 1937) and H. Clay Reed and George J. Miller, eds., *The Burlington Court Book . . . 1680–1709* (Washington, D.C., 1944) for West Jersey. Both courts had final jurisdiction. Two rare contemporary imprints are *A Bill in the Chancery of New-Jersey . . .* (New York, 1747) and *An Answer to a Bill in the Chancery of*

New-Jersey (1752). These treatises, diffusely written, manifest opposing views of the land struggle during an acrimonious period in East Jersey and contain intriguing historical references to earlier aspects of the problem.

Boundary disputes between East and West Jersey and between New Jersey and New York lasted for more than a century and evoked an extensive literature. Summaries for the proprietary period are found in Pomfret, *East New Jersey*, 110–111, 269–275, and Pomfret, *West New Jersey*, 73–75, 152–156; and for the royal period in Tanner, *Province of New Jersey*, 633–641 and Fisher, *New Jersey as a Royal Province*, 236–239. Gerlach, "Revolution or Independence," 93–106, contains thorough research on the boundary problems for the years 1743–1776.

RELIGION

As with all the colonies, the literature concerning religion in early New Jersey is voluminous. Burr's *Bibliography*, 145–160, reveals its extent. Frederick L. Weis, "The Colonial Clergy of New York, New Jersey, and Pennsylvania, 1628–1776" (American Antiquarian Society reprint, Worcester, Mass., 1956) provides the background and a useful compendium. See also Weis's earlier work, *The Colonial Churches and the Colonial Clergy of the Middle and Southern Colonies, 1607–1776* (Lancaster, Mass., 1938).

There are treatments of the religious aspects of early New Jersey history in the standard works of Lee, Kull, Myers, Tanner, Fisher, and Pomfret. The single general treatment is Wallace N. Jamison, *Religion in New Jersey: A Brief History* (Princeton, 1964). An early source for proprietary East Jersey is the oft-quoted "Memorial of Col. Lewis Morris Concerning the State of Religion before 1700," *P.N.J.H.S.*, 1st ser., IV (1849), 118–121. Noteworthy reference works are Nelson Burr, "The Religious History of New Jersey before 1702," *P.N.J.H.S.*, LVI (1938), 169–190 and 245–266, which emphasizes the religious diversity; James W. Smith and E. Leland Jamison, eds., *Religion in American Life* (Princeton, 1961), Vol. IV of which, written by Burr, treats New Jersey's role; Peter H. B. Frelinghuysen, *Theodorus Jacobus Frelinghuysen* (Princeton, 1938), which discusses the Pietist movement; James Tanis, *Dutch Calvinistic Pietism in the Middle Colonies: A Study of . . . Frelinghuysen* (The Hague, 1967), which emphasizes Frelinghuysen's theology; and Thomas Brainerd, *The Life of John Brainerd . . .* (Philadelphia, 1765). Frelinghuysen's *Sermons . . .* have been edited by William Demarest (New York, 1856).

The Great Awakening in New Jersey is treated in Frederick W. Brink, "Gilbert Tennent, Dynamic Preacher," *Journal of the Presbyterian Historical Society*, XXXII (1954), 91–107; William Hanche, "New Jersey Moulders of the Presbyterian Church," *J. of Presby. Hist. Soc.*, XXIV (1946), 71–82; Thomas S. Capers, "The Great Awakening in the Middle Colonies," *J. of Presby. Hist. Soc.*, VIII (1916), 296–315; Martin E. Lodge, "The Great Awakening in the Middle Colonies," Ph.D. dissertation, University of California (Berkeley), 1965; and Charles H. Maxson, *The Great Awakening in the Middle Colonies* (Chicago, 1920).

Material on the various denominations and sects is inexhaustible. For the

Dutch Reformed Church see Edward T. Corwin, *A History of the Reformed Church*, 4th ed. (New York, 1902), and for the New Jersey congregations, *Tercentenary Studies, 1928: A Record of Beginnings, Reformed Church in America* (New York, 1928). Accounts of individual congregations are cited by Leiby, *Early Dutch . . . Settlements*, 124–125.

For the Congregational Church, see W. B. Brown, "The Early History of Congregationalism in New Jersey and the Middle Provinces," *Congregational Quarterly*, XIX (1877), 531–539; T. Aird Moffatt, "Newark Settled by a Congregational Church," *P.N.J.H.S.*, 3d ser., X (1915), 13–24; and W. S. Nicolls, "Early Newark as a Puritan Theocracy," *P.N.J.H.S.*, V (1930). Wertenbaker's *The Middle Colonies* contains an excellent treatment both of Dutch Calvinism and Congregationalism.

On the Presbyterians see the general works by Charles A. Briggs, *American Presbyterianism . . .* (New York, 1885) and Leonard J. Trinterud, *The Forming of An American Tradition: A Re-examination of Colonial Presbyterianism* (Philadelphia, 1949); and the chapters in Wertenbaker, *The Middle Colonies*. See also Charles W. Drury, "Presbyterian Beginnings in New England and the Middle Colonies," *J. of Presby. Hist. Soc.*, XXXIV (1956), 19–35 and George H. Ingrim, "History of the Presbytery of New Brunswick," *J. of Presby. Hist. Soc.*, IV (1919), No. 6.

The Baptists, like the Friends, kept careful records. Material relating to their early history is found in A. D. Gilette, ed., *Minutes of the Philadelphia Baptist Association from A.D. 1707 . . .* (Philadelphia, 1851). An important source is Morgan Edwards, *A History of the Baptists in New Jersey*, II (Philadelphia, 1792), *History of the American Baptists*. Useful also are Henry C. Vedder, *A History of the Baptists in the Middle States* (Philadelphia, 1898); Thomas S. Griffiths, *A History of Baptists in New Jersey* (Hightstown, N.J., 1904); and Norman H. Maring, *The Baptists in New Jersey* (Valley Forge, Pa., 1964).

The primary sources for the New Jersey Anglicans are the reports and records of the S.P.C.K. and the S.P.G., transcripts of which are in the Library of Congress. In this voluminous correspondence one gains the impression that the S.P.G. missionary was more prejudiced than pious. Nelson R. Burr has written *The Anglican Church in New Jersey* (Philadelphia, 1954), a definitive study characterized by thoroughgoing research and accuracy. The long-time efforts in New Jersey as elsewhere to obtain a suffragan bishop are discussed by Arthur L. Cross, *The Anglican Episcopate and the American Colonies* (Cambridge, Mass., 1902) and Carl Bridenbaugh, *Mitre and Sceptre: Transatlantic Faiths, Ideas, Personalities, and Politics, 1689–1775* (New York, 1962).

An important work for Anglican as well as Quaker history is Ethyn W. Kirby, *George Keith, 1638–1716* (New York, 1942). Keith's journal was published in London in 1706 and is reprinted in Edgar L. Pennington, ed., "The Journal of the Reverend George Keith," *Historical Magazine of the Protestant Episcopal Church*, XX (1951), 343–487. John Talbot of Burlington is discussed by the same author in *Apostle of New Jersey, John Talbot, 1645–1727* (Philadelphia, 1938), with

Talbot's letters included. For the first Methodist endeavors, consult *The Journals of the Rev. Francis Asbury . . . 1771–1815*, 3 vols., (New York, 1821).

The literature of the Quakers is extensive. Their American records are at Friends Meeting, Philadelphia, with important collections at Swarthmore and Haverford Colleges. Older works touching New Jersey Friends are James Bowden, *History of the Society of Friends in America*, 2 vols. (London, 1854); Charles Evans, *Friends in the Seventeenth Century* (Philadelphia, 1875); William C. Braithwaite, *The Second Period of Quakerism* (London, 1919), for the proprietary period; and Rufus M. Jones, *The Later Period of Quakerism*, 2 vols. (London, 1911).

The best discussion of the New Jersey Friends is in Rufus M. Jones, *The Quakers in the American Colonies* (1911, reprinted New York, 1966). Glimpses of early New Jersey Quakers are found in John L. Nickalls, ed., *The Journal of George Fox*, rev. ed. (Cambridge, Eng., 1952) and *The Short Journal and the Itinerary Journal of George Fox* (Cambridge, Eng., 1925). See also John E. Pomfret, "West New Jersey: A Quaker Society," *Wm. and Mary Qtly.*, VIII (1951), 494–519 and Ch. 12 of his *West New Jersey*, which contains some new material. The references on John Woolman are Janet P. Whitney, *John Woolman, American Quaker* (Boston, 1942), and the chapters in Jones, *The Quakers in the American Colonies*. Phillips P. Moulton, ed., *The Journal and Major Essays of John Woolman* (New York, 1971), supersedes all earlier editions of Woolman's writings. The social outlook of New Jersey's Quakers is treated in Sydney V. James, *A People Among People: Quaker Benevolence in Eighteenth-Century America* (Cambridge, Mass., 1963).

Indispensable for the New Jersey Lutherans are the *Journals of the Reverend Henry Melchior Muhlenberg*, 3 vols. (Philadelphia, 1942–1958). Harry J. Kreider, *Lutheranism in Colonial New York* (New York, 1942), a scholarly work, touches New Jersey. In addition to the references cited earlier on the Swedish Lutherans, an important source is Reverend Nicholas Collin, "A Brief Account of the Swedish Mission in Raccoon and Penn's Neck," *P.N.J.H.S.*, III (1948), 105–122. The general work on the Moravians is J. Taylor Hamilton, *A History of the Church Known as the Moravian Church . . .* (Bethlehem, Pa., 1900). In the main the New Jersey references deal with the Hope colony: "A Forgotten Moravian Settlement in New Jersey," *P.M.H. & B.*, XXXVII (1913) 248–252; Charles F. Kluge, "Sketch of the Settlement of Hope, New Jersey," *Transactions of the Moravian Hist. Soc.*, I (1856); and Henry Race, "Greenland in New Jersey, A Historical Sketch . . . 1768–1808," *P.N.J.H.S.*, 2d ser., XI (1891), 195–206.

OTHER SPECIAL TOPICS

On the land and the people, useful introductory references are: Kemble Widmer, *The Geology and Geography of New Jersey* (Princeton, 1939); R. H. Whitbeck, "Geographical Influences in the Development of New Jersey," *Journal of Geography*, VI (1908), 177–182; and John E. Brush, *The Population of New Jersey, 1620–1950* (New Brunswick, 1956).

For the early period the standard references on population are: Evarts B.

Greene and Virginia D. Harrington, *American Population Before the Federal Census of 1790* (New York, 1932) and Stella H. Sutherland, *Population Distribution in Colonial America* (New York, 1936). Both cull the printed sources for New Jersey. For an excellent comment on colonial population figures, see Wesley Frank Craven, *The Colonies in Transition*, 15–16.

Turning to national origins, the New England Puritans, the Dutch, Swedes, Finns, and Scots are treated in works mentioned above by Amandus Johnson, Leiby, Pomfret, and Wertenbaker. Additional references are: Samuel C. Worthen, "The Influence of Puritan and Other New England Elements in New Jersey," *Genealogical Magazine of New Jersey*, III (1928), 89–96; A. Van Doren Honeyman, "The Early Scotch Element of Somerset, Middlesex, and Monmouth Counties," *Somerset County Historical Quarterly*, VI (1917), 1–2; and Albert E. Koehler, *The Huguenots or Early French in New Jersey* (Bloomfield, N.J., 1955). For the eighteenth-century German migration see Albert B. Faust, *The German Element in the United States . . .* (Boston, 1909); and Theodore F. Chambers, *The Early Germans of New Jersey* (Dover, 1895). Material on the eighteenth-century Scotch-Irish migration into New Jersey is found in Charles A. Hanna, *The Scotch-Irish or the Scot in North America*, 2 vols. (New York, 1902); Henry J. Ford, *The Scotch-Irish in America* (Princeton, 1915); James C. Leyburn, *The Scotch-Irish, A Social History* (Chapel Hill, N.C., 1962); and Ian C. Graham, *Colonists from Scotland* (Ithaca, N.Y., 1956).

On the Negro and slavery, the best introduction is Winthrop D. Jordan, *White Over Black: American Attitudes Toward the Negro, 1550–1812* (Chapel Hill, 1968). Two excellent recently published books that discuss the nature of African slavery and its importation into the West Indies are Carl and Roberta Bridenbaugh, *No Peace Beyond the Line, . . . 1624–1690* (New York, 1972) and Richard S. Dunn, *Sugar and Slaves: The Rise of the Planter Class in the English West Indies, 1624–1713* (Chapel Hill, 1972). The mores of slavery in the West Indies reached all the mainland colonies. A small number of Barbadians came to New Jersey as planters in the late 1670s. Arthur Zilversmit, *The First Emancipation: The Abolition of Slavery in the North* (Chicago, 1967) is the major study of northern abolition sentiment.

For slavery in New Jersey, see the treatments in Lee, *New Jersey*, IV, Chs. 1 and 2 and in Kull, *New Jersey*, II, Ch. 21. Additional references are Henry S. Cooley, *A Study of Slavery in New Jersey* (Baltimore, 1896); A. C. Keasby, "Slavery in New Jersey," *P.N.J.H.S.*, 3d ser., IV (1907), 147–154 and V (1908), 12–20 and 79–86; James C. Connelly, "Slavery in Colonial New Jersey," *P.N.J.H.S.*, n.s., XIV (1929), 181–202; Simon F. Moss, "The Persistence of Slavery . . . in a Free State," *Journal of Negro History*, XXXV (1950), 289–314; Francis D. Pingeon, "Slavery on the Eve of the Revolution," New Jersey History Symposium *Papers* (Trenton, 1970), 41–53; and two pamphlets published by the Camden Historical Society with notes by Charles S. Boyer, *Slavery and Servitude in West Jersey*, Bulletin No. 10 (1948) and *The Attitude of the Society of Friends Toward Slavery*, Camden History, I, No. 6.

On political and constitutional phases, see Lucius Q. C. Elmer, *The Constitution and Government of the Province and State of New Jersey*, N.J. Hist. Soc., *Collections*, VII (Newark, 1872) and John Whitehead, *The Judicial and Civil History of New Jersey* (Boston, 1897). For voting and suffrage, see Richard P. McCormick, *The History of Voting in New Jersey: A Study of the Development of Election Machinery, 1664–1911* (New Brunswick, 1953), a standard work. See also Donald L. Kemmerer, "The Suffrage Franchise in Colonial New Jersey," *P.N.J.H.S.*, LII (1943), 166–173; Robert H. Rich, "Election Machinery in New Jersey," *P.N.J.H.S.*, LXVII (1949), 198–211; and J. R. Pole, "Suffrage Reform and the American Revolution in New Jersey," *P.N.J.H.S.*, LXXIV (1956), 173–196. Julian P. Boyd, ed., *Fundamental Laws . . .*, prints in full "The Constitution of the State of New Jersey, July 2, 1776," as well as earlier constitutional documents.

For the law and the courts the principal references are Richard S. Field, *The Provincial Courts of New Jersey*, N.J. Hist. Soc., *Collections*, III (New York, 1849) and Edward C. Keasby, "Jersey Justice," N.J. Bar Association *Year Book* (1919–1920), 39–61. See also Harry B. Weiss and Grace M. Weiss, *An Introduction to Crime and Punishment in Colonial New Jersey* (Trenton, 1960). The important sources for the earlier period are Reed Miller, *The Burlington Court Book . . .* and Edsall, *Journal of the Courts of Common Right and Chancery. . . .*

On New Jersey's finances and paper money emissions, see Donald L. Kemmerer, "The Colonial Loan-Office System in New Jersey," *Journal of Political Economy*, XLVII (1939), 867–874 and his "A History of Paper Money in Colonial New Jersey, 1668–1775," *P.N.J.H.S.*, LXXIV (1956), 107–144; E. Peter Ellerteen, "Prosperity and Paper Money: The Loan Office Act of 1723," *New Jersey History*, LXXXV (1967), 47–57; and Richard T. Hoober, "Finances of Colonial New Jersey," *The Numismatist*, LXIII (1950), 72–86, 152–158, 206–216, and 336–347. There are also substantial treatments of the money question in Tanner, Fisher, and Kemmerer; and for the later period in Gerlach, "Revolution or Independence."

Writings on economic history are fragmentary and scattered. Jeanette P. Nichols, "Colonial Industries of New Jersey, 1618–1815," *Americana*, XXIV (1930), 299–342 is basic. More specialized are Charles S. Boyer, *Early Forges and Furnaces in New Jersey* (Philadelphia, 1931); George H. Danforth, "Lord Stirling's Hibernia Furnace, *P.N.J.H.S.*, LXXI (1953), 174–186; James M. Ransom, *Vanishing Ironworks of the Ramapos . . .* (New Brunswick, 1966); Arthur D. Pierce, *Iron in the Pines . . .* (New Brunswick, 1957); and Collamer W. Abbott, "Colonial Copper Mines," *Wm. and Mary Qtly.*, XXVII (1970), 293–309, which touches upon the importance of New Jersey copper.

Carl R. Woodward has written two books on agriculture: *The Development of Agriculture in New Jersey, 1640–1880* (New Brunswick, 1927), a summary, and *Ploughs and Politicks: Charles Read of New Jersey . . . 1715–1774*, an indispensable work. See also his "Agricultural Legislation in Colonial New Jersey," *Agricultural History*, III (1929), 15–28. Little has been written on labor, but Richard B.

Morris, *Government and Labor in Early America* (New York, 1946) contains references to New Jersey. The standard work on transportation is Wheaton J. Lane, *From Indian Trail to Iron Horse: Travel and Transportation in New Jersey, 1620–1860* (Princeton, 1959), a volume in the Princeton History of New Jersey. See also Richard P. Powell, "Transportation and Travel in Colonial New Jersey," *P.N.J.H.S.*, XVI (1931), 284–310. Gerlach, "Revolution or Independence," Ch. 1 is the best summary of New Jersey's economy for the period 1760–1776.

The definitive work on education is Nelson R. Burr, *Education in New Jersey, 1630–1871* (Princeton, 1942), aslo a volume in the Princeton History of New Jersey series. See also Ira T. Chapman, "Education in New Jersey," in Myers's *New Jersey*, I, Ch. 23. Thomas Woody, *Quaker Education in the Colony and State of New Jersey . . .* (Philadelphia, 1923) is important. On New Jersey's colonial colleges, see John Maclean, *History of the College of New Jersey . . . to . . . 1854*, 2 vols. (Philadelphia, 1877), and Thomas J. Wertenbaker, *Princeton, 1746–1896* (Princeton, 1946), scholarly and readable. On special phases of higher education, see Donald R. Come, "The Influence of Princeton on Higher Education in the South before 1825," *Wm. and Mary Qtly.*, II (1945), 359–396, and Francis L. Broderick, "Pulpit, Physics, and Politics: The Curriculum of the College of New Jersey, 1746–1794," *Wm. and Mary Qtly.*, VI (1949), 42–68; George P. Schmidt, *Princeton and Rutgers: The Two Colonial Colleges of New Jersey* (Princeton, 1964); Richard P. McCormick, *Rutgers: A Bicentennial History* (New Brunswick, 1966); and William H. S. Demarest, *A History of Rutgers College, 1766–1924* (New Brunswick, 1924). Lawrence A. Cremin's *American Education: The Colonial Experience, 1607–1783* (New York, 1970) discusses higher education in New Jersey against the broad colonial background.

In the fields of the arts and the crafts little has been written, since New Jersey's achievements were modest. Burr's *Bibliography* contains a number of references on topics such as glass-making, ceramics, silver-making, and furniture-making. New Jersey's colonial architecture is touched upon in Thomas J. Waterman, *The Dwellings of Colonial America* (Chapel Hill, N.C., 1950). Wertenbaker gives special attention to New Jersey architecture in *The Middle Colonies, passim*. See also William S. Turner's lecture, "New Jersey Architecture," *P.N.J.H.S.*, LV (1937), 289–296 and A. Lawrence Kocher, "Gambrel Slopes of Northern New Jersey," *Architecture*, LV (1927), 35–40, reprinted in *Bergen County History Annual* (1970), 35–40, with photographs in the original article identified.

For the professions see David L. Cowen, *Medicine and Health in New Jersey: A History* (Princeton, 1964); Stephen Wickes, *History of Medicine in New Jersey . . . from A.D. 1800* (Newark, 1879); Fred B. Rogers and A. R. Sayre, *The Healing Art: A History of the Medical Society of New Jersey* (Trenton, 1966); and New Jersey Medical Society, *The Rise, Minutes, and Proceedings of the New Jersey Medical Society, 1766–1858* (Newark, 1875). For the legal profession see Anton Hermann-Chroust, "The Lawyers and the Revolution in New Jersey," *American Journal of*

Legal History, VI (1962), 286–297 and Frank B. Ward, "The American Revolution and the Legal Profession in New Jersey, 1740–1799," senior thesis, Princeton University, 1966. Henry N. MacCracken has written *The Trials of James Alexander, 1715–1756* (New York, 1964).

The best checklist of New Jersey printing is Constance Humphrey, "Checklist of New Jersey Imprints to the End of the American Revolution," *Papers of the Bibliographical Society of America*, XXIV (1931). See also William Nelson, *Some New Jersey Printers and Printing in the Eighteenth Century* (Worcester, Mass., 1911), 43–149. From 1723 to 1783 there were 306 New Jersey imprints, beginning with the laws printed by William Bradford at Perth Amboy. See also William H. Benedict, "James Parker, the Printer of Woodbridge," *P.N.J.H.S.*, VIII (1923), 133–138. Parker was New Jersey's first printer. Richard F. Hixson, *Isaac Collins . . .* (New Brunswick, 1968), is a biography of the printer of the *New Jersey Gazette*, the state's first newspaper. The earliest newspapers are touched upon by Kenneth C. Jennings in Myers, ed., *New Jersey*, II, Ch. 3. Jennings also discusses New Jersey's first magazine, *The New American Magazine*, published at Woodbridge, 1758–1760. See also "The New American Magazine," *Rutgers University Library Journal*, XIII (1939), 29–51, and the discussion in Lyon N. Richardson, *History of Early American Magazines* (New York, 1931). References to New Jersey's sparse colonial literature appear in Burr, *Bibliography*, 238–242 and in Moses C. Tyler's standard surveys: *A History of American Literature, 1607–1765* (New York, 1878; reprinted, Ithaca, N.Y., 1949) and *The Literary History of the American Revolution*, 2 vols. (London and New York, 1897; reprinted, New York, 1941). The newspapers of the Revolution are treated in Warren E. Stickle, "State and Press in New Jersey during the Revolution," *New Jersey History*, LXXXVI (1968), 158–170, 236–250.

A number of biographical studies have already been noted above, and the three cooperative histories—Lee, Kull, and Myers—have many biographical notations. For important persons, consult *The Dictionary of American Biography* and *The National Cyclopedia of American Biography*. English colonial governors and other important British officials are given notice in the Dictionary of National Biography and in many county histories.

OFFICIAL SOURCES

For the colonial period an essential source, though there are many gaps, is William A. Whitehead, William Nelson, and F. W. Ricord, eds., *Documents Relating to the Colonial History of the State of New Jersey* (*New Jersey Archives*), especially I–IV (Newark, 1880–1886). Here are assembled documents from the British Public Record Office and other British depositories, those in the New York and Pennsylvania Archives relating to New Jersey, and the indigenous New Jersey documents.

The laws of proprietary New Jersey together with the proceedings of the proprietary assemblies are in Aaron Leaming and Jacob Spicer, *Grants, Concessions, and Original Constitutions . . . to Queen Anne* (Philadelphia, 1752), and the laws for the royal period are in Samuel Allison, ed., *Acts of the General Assembly of the Province of New Jersey, 1702–1775* (Burlington, 1776); Samuel Neville, *The Acts of the General Assembly . . . from 1753 . . . to . . . 1761*, 2 vols. (Woodbridge, 1761); and William Paterson, ed., *Laws of the State of New Jersey, 1703–1798* (New Brunswick, 1800). Available also are *Votes and Proceedings of the General Assembly of the Province of New Jersey, 1702–1776*, printed after each session.

F. W. Ricord and William Nelson, eds., *The Journal of the Governor and Council, 1682–1775*, *N.J.A.*, XIII–XVIII (Trenton, 1890–1893) is indispensable. See also the *Journal of the Procedure of the Governor and Council of the Province of East Jersey . . . from 1682* (Newark, 1848) and *Journal and Votes of the House of Representatives of the Province . . . of New Jersey* (Jersey City, 1872). Those of the later period are in manuscript in the State Library, Trenton. Of use also are John Hood, ed., *Index of the Laws of New Jersey between . . . 1663 and 1903* (Camden, New Jersey, 1905) and William Nelson, comp., *Bibliography of the Printed Proceedings of the Provincial Assembly of New Jersey, 1717–1776 . . .* (Somerville, 1899).

For the Revolutionary period see *Minutes of the Provincial Congress and the Council of Safety of the State of New Jersey, 1774–1776* (Trenton, 1879); *Acts of the Council and General Assembly of the State of New Jersey (1776–1783)*, comp. Peter Wilson (Trenton, 1784); *Journal of the Votes and Proceedings of the Convention of the State of New Jersey* (Burlington, 1776); *Votes and Proceedings of the General Assembly of the State of New Jersey* (Newark, 1848); *Selections from the Correspondence of the Executive of New Jersey from 1776 to 1786* (Newark, 1848); and *Minutes of the Council of the State of New Jersey* (Jersey City, 1872).

The principal printed British sources for New Jersey colonial history are W. L. Grant and James Munro, eds., *Acts of the Privy Council of England, Colonial Series*, 6 vols. (London, 1908–1912); *Journal of the Lords of Trade and Plantations . . . 1704 . . . 1782*, 14 vols. (London, 1920–1938); and *The Statutes at Large*, 10 vols. (London, 1786; ed. T. E. Tomlins and J. Raithby, London, 1811).

MANUSCRIPTS

William Nelson, ed., *The Calendar of Records in the Office of the Secretary of State, 1664–1703*, *N.J.A.*, XXI is a guide to thousands of manuscript items, including abstracts of the proprietary and land records. The most important manuscript sources are in the New Jersey State Library and the Office of the Secretary of State, both in Trenton, and in the British Public Record Office, London. The state-held manuscripts include such important materials as the minutes of the supreme court, provincial commissions, and land records. See also the *Calendar of the State Library Manuscript Collection* (Newark, 1939). For the period 1760–1776, see Larry R. Gerlach's "Revolution or Independence," 772–782. This modern study lists much heretofore uncited manuscript material.

The New Jersey Historical Society, Newark; the Princeton and Rutgers University Libraries; the Historical Society of Pennsylvania, Philadelphia; and the New York Historical Society, New York City, all have extensive manuscript collections relating to colonial New Jersey. The religious records of the various denominations, many of which have been preserved, are of great historical value.

The papers of Lewis Morris, Robert Hunter Morris, James Alexander, and Ferdinand John Paris are at the New Jersey Historical Society, and there are also Paris papers at the Historical Society of Pennsylvania. A collection of Alexander and Morris papers is contained in the Rutherfurd Collection, New York Historical Society. Stanley N. Katz has published "A New York Mission to England: The London Letters of Lewis Morris to James Alexander, 1735-1736," *Wm. and Mary Qtly.*, XXVIII (1971), 438-484. Governor Belcher's papers, as well as the bulk of William Livingston's, are at the Massachusetts Historical Society, Boston. The George Washington Papers, Library of Congress, Washington; the Papers of the Continental Congress, National Archives, Washington; and the Lloyd W. Smith Collection, Morrisville National Historic Park, are invaluable for the historian of Revolutionary New Jersey.

The records of the East Jersey proprietors are in the Proprietors Office, Perth Amboy, and those of the West Jersey proprietors in the Proprietors Office in Burlington. Their boards still exist, membership being valued principally for sentimental reasons. The East Jersey Board, because adverse public opinion superseded legal right, collected no quitrents with the advent of the Revolution. Yet unclaimed land discovered today can be obtained only from the proprietary boards. The town of Bergen, interestingly, in tidying up its affairs, in 1809 purchased from the East Jersey Board for $1,500 a release from its ancient quitrent obligation of £15 per annum on its town lands.

The West New Jersey Council has long since ceased making original surveys; since 1922 only a half-dozen have been made. A recent surveyor-general, Benjamin Sleeper, commented that he had little utility except "to hold the key to the office and answer questions of genealogists." The West Jersey proprietors are the proud possessors of the American copy of the Concessions and Agreements of 1676-1677.

The Directors of the West Jersey Society in 1876 distributed the society's remaining funds, $50,000, then "relinquished for all time" their ancient custom of meeting annually, electing officers, and "enjoying a good English dinner." The voluminous records of the society are in the Public Record Office, London. Industrious researchers and historians have by now made use of the manuscripts of all three in their studies of New Jersey's colonial period.

BIBLIOGRAPHICAL

In addition to Burr's *Bibliography*, see William A. Whitehead, "Catalogue of Books, Pamphlets, and Other Publications Referring to . . . Colonial Period

Exclusive of the Public Documents of the State," N.J. Hist. Soc., *Collections*, V (Newark, 1858), Appendix B, 477–493.

Countless well-documented articles in addition to those already cited have appeared in the *New Jersey Historical Society Proceedings*, 1847 to date (*New Jersey History* since 1967) and in the *Pennsylvania Magazine of History and Biography*, 1877 to date. Most useful in connection with the latter is Eugene E. Doll's *Index*, vols. 1–75 (Philadelphia, 1954).

INDEX